W9-DFW-737

WHY WE LEFT

WHY WE LEFT

Untold Stories and Songs of America's First Immigrants

JOANNA BROOKS

University of Minnesota Press
Minneapolis
London

The epigraph on page v was originally published in Simon J. Ortiz, *from Sand Creek* (New York: Thunder's Mouth Press, 1981). Reprinted with author's permission.

Recordings of ballads and music discussed in this book are featured on the page for this book on the website of the University of Minnesota Press, http://www.upress.umn.edu.

Published by the University of Minnesota Press
111 Third Avenue South, Suite 290
Minneapolis, MN 55401–2520
http://www.upress.umn.edu

Library of Congress Cataloging-in-Publication Data
Brooks, Joanna.
Why we left : untold stories and songs of America's first immigrants / Joanna Brooks.
Includes bibliographical references and index.
ISBN 978-0-8166-8125-9 (hc : alk. paper)
ISBN 978-0-8166-8126-6 (pb : alk. paper)
1. United States—Emigration and immigration—History—17th century. 2. United States—Emigration and immigration—History—18th century. 3. Great Britain—Emigration and immigration—History—17th century. 4. Great Britain—Emigration and immigration—History—18th century. 5. British Americans—History—17th century. 6. British Americans—History—18th century. 7. Immigrants—United States—History—17th century. 8. Immigrants—United States—History—18th century. 9. Folk music—United States—History. 10. Folk music—Great Britain—History. I. Title.
JV6451.B76 2013
305.9'06912097309032—dc23

2012049538

Printed in the United States of America on acid-free paper

20 19 18 17 16 15 14 13 10 9 8 7 6 5 4 3 2 1

They crossed country
that would lay beyond memory.
Their cells
would no longer bother
to remember.
Memory
was not to be trusted.
Aimlessly,
they crossed memory.

—SIMON ORTIZ (Acoma), *from Sand Creek*

Contents

Acknowledgments

This book was completed at the School of American Research in Santa Fe, New Mexico, with the support of an SAR Ethel Jane Bunting-Westfeldt Fellowship. I thank James Brooks and the entire staff of the School of American Research for their inspiring hospitality and generosity. Thanks as well to Paula Gunn Allen, Dana Nelson, Melissah Pawlikowski, Lisa Moore, and Peter Herman, intellectual fellow travelers, and as always to David Kamper.

This book is for my father, James Clayton Brooks (1944–2012), who gave me my life, my name, my history, and my courage. He was in flesh and blood, in sheer toughness and determination, a Brooks man through and through, but of his own spirit he made something finer and much more powerful.

INTRODUCTION

Brave Men Run

Years ago, I had the tremendous fortune of studying with Paula Gunn Allen, a foundational scholar of American Indian literature and a member of the Laguna Pueblo tribe. Paula had a vast, searching imagination and a terrific sense of humor. From her, I learned to appreciate the longevity, complexity, depth, and cosmological value of the oral traditions of Native peoples and their role in fostering a sense of community and identity. Paula urged her students to grasp the profound differences between traditional American Indian and Euro-American thought worlds. She wanted us to adopt the habit of at least trying to set aside the ways of thinking we were most accustomed to and to revision the world through indigenous perspectives. Some would say hers was a quixotic approach, but it led to wonderful moments of storytelling and insight. The world looked different through Paula's eyes. "Europe is full of indigenous people!" she would say, and then laugh her trademark raspy laugh. And then there were the times she recounted what the arrival of Anglo-Americans in Virginia must have looked like to the native Powhatan. "You see," she would say, perched at the head of the seminar table, her eyes twinkling with mischief, "the Powhatan, and the neighboring peoples, they would bathe every day in the rivers. So clean. So healthful. But the English never bathed. *Never.* So can you imagine how they looked and smelled when they came off those ships—hairy, toothless, starved, ill-prepared, feverish, and *stinky*?" Paula was not the only American Indian scholar I read who turned a critical new view on colonists lionized and celebrated in traditional histories. The "weeds of mankind" was what the great Vine Deloria Jr. once called the early Anglo-American immigrant masses.[1]

As a scholar of early American literature, I have come to appreciate the world-shifting intellectual consequences of viewing the colonization of the Americas from an indigenous perspective. As the descendent of some of the earliest English migrants to arrive in North America—a significant number of my ancestors were here before 1650, and the vast majority before 1800—that perspective has personal significance as well. With a very few notable exceptions, my ancestors were not the elite class of emigrants. We were poor people, and my Brooks family line especially continued to live as poor people for four centuries after our arrival in North America. Who are we? Who were we? Have we always been the "weeds of mankind"? Did we once belong *somewhere* on the face of this earth? If I were able to trace my ancestors back across the ocean to their specific English home places—and I generally cannot—what would I discover?

In recent years, literary, cultural, and social historians have done a wonderful job reconstructing the lives and thought worlds of African American and Native American communities in the era of colonization. I think of books like historian Stephanie Smallwood's *Saltwater Slavery* that reach deeply and compassionately into archival sources to bring striking new detail to the experience of the earliest African American slaves. I think too of books like Saidiya Hartman's *Lose Your Mother* and Jacqui Alexander's *Pedagogies of Crossing* that have fully explored the difficulties of working across violent ruptures in history such as the slave trade and colonial conquest. These scholars show that it is no simple matter to recover knowledge and reconstitute such profoundly fragmented historical relationships. Yet by fully inhabiting and acknowledging that history of fragmentation, they bring striking new insights to the question of what it means to live in the modern world: the world made by globalization.

It is not customary for scholars of early Anglo-America to assume a personal relationship to the remote historical periods we study, except in the most celebratory of ways. But as a descendent of early Anglo-American migrants and as someone who has spent much of the last fifteen years studying how common people used literature and culture to reconcile with the great human catastrophes of the colonial era, I find myself much like Hartman and Alexander hungry to understand how laboring-class English people understood their moment in history and their role in the world-shifting and often deeply destructive process of colonization. Social historians like Alison Games, Allan Kulikoff, and James Horn have done valuable work reconstructing the everyday lives of early peasant migrants to Virginia. It is a different challenge to approach this part of early American experience as a literary and cultural historian, as someone focused on ascertaining the worlds of thought and feeling my ancestors inhabited. Given that very few early English laboring-class migrants wrote about their experiences, what archives might I consult? What texts of early Anglo-American peasant consciousness could I locate? That problem is the reason for this book.

NOT FAR FROM WHERE I LIVE, there is an art museum poised on a cliff over the Pacific Ocean. A mural on its oceanfront facade features a darkened silhouette of a clipper ship lurching dangerously forward against black seas and violet skies. Spanning the top of the mural are the words "BRAVE MEN RUN IN MY FAMILY."

I've always seen that ship as a colonial transport vessel crossing the Atlantic, and I've read its darkly comical caption as a send-up of the way popular culture still depicts that emigration as a bright and heroic journey. But the words "brave men run" remind me that for most early English migrants—the large majority of whom came unfree and to the American South—colonial emigration was less about running *to* a bright and stable future than it was about running *away from* something that had become truly uninhabitable. That founding act of running away, the violent breaks it entailed, the abandonment of home places and kinspeople, how have these impacted not only the lives of early Anglo-American immigrants? Have their impacts been passed down through the generations?

My uncle Norm is the guardian of Brooks family memory. Before a series of disabling strokes, Norm stood six feet five, raven-haired, beak-nosed, a Johnny Cash sort of handsome, with Cash-like menacing swagger and Cash-like bloodlines. Uncle Norm heard it from his grandfather, my great-grandfather, John Houston Brooks that the Brooks came on debtors' boats bound for the Carolinas, but mutinied and insisted the ships sail on to Alabama.

Paper genealogy tells a different story. The first Brooks on record, my great-great-great-great-grandfather William Malone Brooks, was born in upcountry South Carolina in 1804 and was (the best I can figure) the descendent of unnamed and unidentified seventeenth-century English emigrants who bound themselves over as servants, then moved west and south to find a place of their own.

The Brooks never held on to one place for very long. By 1823, nineteen-year-old William Malone Brooks Sr. and his wife—whose name does not survive—had moved about three hundred miles west from upcountry South Carolina to rural Franklin County, Alabama. That's where my great-great-great-grandfather William Malone Brooks Jr. was born, the first of six children. In 1841, eighteen-year-old William Malone Brooks Jr. and his wife had their first child, my great-great-grandfather Robert Levi Brooks. In 1847 or 1848, both William Malone Brooks Sr. and William Malone Brooks Jr., father and son, their wives, and six or seven children apiece moved about four hundred miles west to Ouachita County, Arkansas. The 1850 census finds them there, with William Malone working as a "laborer" and a "farmer." By 1851, the entire Brooks family moved yet another three hundred miles west from Arkansas to Birdville, Texas. The 1860 census finds the Brooks yet another two hundred miles south in Bastrop.

My great-great-grandfather Robert Levi Brooks managed to get a third-grade education before leaving school to work as a day laborer. At age twenty, in 1861, he enlisted with the Confederate army. He married Catherine Ann Houston and moved south to Uvalde, Texas, in 1864, where he moved from town to town making a living as a carpenter and mechanic, before becoming completely disabled by rheumatism. The family had ten children. When Robert Levi Brooks filed for his Confederate pension, application number 11013, in 1904, he owned no real estate, only two horses, one wagon, and one harness, altogether worth no more than $100.

My great-grandfather John Houston Brooks was born in 1886 in Uvalde, Texas, the eighth of Robert Levi and Catherine Ann Houston Brookses' ten children. He married Ora Evelyn McGovern in a rocky, dusty Texas border town named Bracketville. After my grandfather Martin Levi Brooks was born in 1910, the Brooks family moved six hundred miles west across the desert to the mining town of Hayden, Arizona, where John Houston Brooks worked in the copper smelters for a decade. Eventually, he made enough money to buy a little house for his family near the cotton fields of Gilbert, Arizona.

John Houston Brooks then left his home and followed Works Progress Administration jobs north to Nevada and Oregon. Both my great-grandfather John Houston Brooks and my grandfather Martin Levi Brooks worked on the Boulder and Bonneville Dams, while my grandmother Dorothy Beatrice Davis Brooks lived in the worker camps, swatting scorpions and rattlesnakes away from her babies' cradles. John Houston Brooks lost a few fingers along the way in blasting operations, loved a good Western dime novel, and swore like a trooper. My grandfather Martin Levi Brooks broke his back working on a train trestle in Hayden, Arizona, in 1937, then learned to keep books in the construction business. He settled his family in Bell Gardens, an Okie suburb of Los Angeles, and died in 1948.

That's the Brooks story. Laborers. Almost entirely landless. For three hundred years, we followed work further and further west, moving hundreds of miles at a time, each new place having fewer trees than the last, until we found ourselves in a nine-hundred-square-foot wood-frame house at the other edge of the North American continent. Try and trace us back—California–Arizona–Texas–Arkansas–Alabama–Carolina–Virginia—and then everything breaks up in the seventeenth century in an oceanic fog of loss, forgetting, ideology, and anonymity. There is no star on the map, no cherished ancestral English village, no known home to return to. Only *Brooks,* an utterly common English surname. And ancient. From the Old English *bróc,* meaning marsh or bog or stream. *Brooks.* We took our name from the land we lived on, wherever that was.

But no one really remembers why the Brooks left. We don't remember whether we left from seventeenth-century London or Bristol, and certainly not how we came to that last stop, what highways we had stumbled along to reach the teeming, pestilent city, whether we came with our backs whip-scarred, our thumbs branded, or ears clipped or bored—the marks of felons—or whether we left with mass-printed indenture papers tucked into the breasts of our company-issued canvas suits. And where memory has failed, ideology has supplied a substitute. In 1885, steel magnate Andrew Carnegie wrote that America was "destined" for its historic rise to greatness by "the ethnic character" of its Anglo-American colonists and their descendents, my ancestors and me:

> America was indeed fortunate in the seed planted upon her soil. With the exception of a few Dutch and French it was wholly British; and the American of today remains true to this noble strain and is four-fifths British. The special aptitude of this race for colonization, its vigor and enterprise, and its capacity for governing, although brilliantly manifested in all parts of the world, have never been shown to such advantage as in America. . . . These masses of the lower ranks of Britons, called upon to found a new state, have proved themselves possessors of a positive genius for political administration.[2]

Special aptitude for colonization. Vigor. Enterprise. A positive genius for political administration. When Andrew Carnegie spoke these words in 1885, my great-great-grandfather Robert Levi Brooks, a landless laborer with a third-grade education, and his seven children were scraping by somewhere in the rocks between Menardville and Bracketville, Texas. No, we were not, as Carnegie would have liked us to believe, the exceptional ones with enough foresight, pluck, and fortitude to get out from under the grips of the feudal upper class. We were and until quite recently have been peasants living in the maw of necessity and failure, just like any other poor people on the face of the earth. And I suspect that, just like any other poor people on the face of the earth, ours is an ordinary history, animated as much by ignorance, accident, circumstance, cruelty, and abandonment as by genius, enterprise, aptitude, and vigor.

In addition to the legend of Anglo-American peasant exceptionalism, another bit of ideology that we have clung to in place of memory is the idea that we early on (and thanks in part perhaps to our *genius, enterprise, aptitude,* or *vigor*) understood America to be a land of opportunity. *Opportunity.* Is this the word my Brooks ancestors bantered about, or bit down hard on when we signed our indentures? Was the word "opportunity" in its modern sense—that suggesting an individual assessing, negotiating, and choosing from an open landscape of options—even linguistically available to the Brooks who left England in the seventeenth century? The word "opportunity" enters the English language with the Norman Conquest, deriving from the Anglo-Norman *oportunité* and the Middle French *opportunité,* meaning "an occasion for doing something." Chaucer is the first to use the word in writing, in his translation of Boethius's *Consolation of Philosophy* (1380), where he uses it simply to signify the idea of good fortune. For the gentry who take to the word, opportunity marks a shift from the older Anglo-Germanic notion of fate to a sense that an individual might encounter a chance to improve his or her own situation, even if at the expense of others. This is the sense in which "opportunity" is used in medieval and early modern English: in Wycliffe's 1425 translation of the Bible, Matthew 26:16, "He soute oportunyte to bitryae him," or even in a 1659 edition of the Bible, Proverbs 84:1, "Opportunity makes a Thief." For my ancestors and all those who left England in the seventeenth century, the word "opportunity"—had they used it—would not have carried its most familiar modern sense, with its connotations of clear judgment, rational decision-making, and foreseeable outcomes, but rather would have meant something more like an unlikely chance to get over, an opening in a generally random and turbulent universe.

Land of opportunity. Is this how we would have described the British colonies of North America? The phrase "land of opportunity" appears nowhere in the printed literature of the British North American colonies or early United States before 1800—not in pamphlets or newspapers or even broadsides. In fact, it is not until the late nineteenth century when the phrase creeps into American vernacular usage, in an 1889 newspaper obituary honoring Pennsylvania attorney general Lewis Cassidy as an Irish immigrant to this "land of opportunity," or an 1891 newspaper article describing the attractions of North Dakota for young Canadians seeking work. But the phrase "land of opportunity" was not used to refer to the United States alone. A journalist writing for the *San Antonio Express* in 1899 declared Mexico a "land of opportunity," and in 1904 then secretary of war William Taft made headlines by recommending that Yale graduates look to the U.S.-occupied Philippines, a country still reeling from the tremendous casualties inflicted by the Philippine-American War (1899–1902) as a "land of opportunity." Usage of the phrase "land of opportunity" in American newspapers skyrocketed after August 30, 1907, when steel magnate Charles Schwab gave a speech titled "America: The Land of Opportunity" to a businessmen's convention at the Pier Restaurant in Dreamland, Coney Island, New York, making front-page headlines in newspapers across the country, from New York to Idaho. At

Dreamland, Schwab foresaw endless American horizons for industrial expansion: "In 1880 it was said by those who were supposed to know that the steel business had reached its zenith. At that time the output of the steel foundries of this country was 1,000,000 tons a year. Today, it is 25,000,000. In fifty years the transportation facilities of the country will be unable to take care of the steel business alone," Schwab predicted. "There can be no financial depression of long or serious duration. Whenever there is a serious crisis someone always steps into the breach and relieves the situation."[3]

Wrong as his economic prognostications may have been, Schwab in popularizing the notion of America as a land of opportunity profoundly shaped American popular memory and self-understanding. The phrase "land of opportunity" continues to dominate our national imagination of immigration from the seventeenth century down through the present day, so much so that professional historians continue to wrestle with its influence and meaning. Witness historian Aaron Fogleman in a groundbreaking 1998 study of Anglo-American indentured servants: "The literary and historical image of America as the land of unlimited opportunity or as a 'best poor man's country' hardly resonates with the realities of servitude for most of the strangers who completed the journey in the colonial period," he wrote. Still, in striving for a more nuanced account of colonial indentured servants, Fogleman could seemingly not escape the anachronistic language of opportunity. Characterizing "the majority of unfree arrivals" as "voluntary migrants who *chose* America to seek economic improvement and could not afford the costs," he concluded that the indenture system "provided *opportunities* for improvement to many who voluntarily chose to make a go of it in the New World."[4] A few years later, in a book-length study of early English emigration to Virginia, historian James Horn returned to the word "opportunity" and its problems. "How much did the poor know about *opportunities* in the colonies?" he asked. "Should we interpret indentured servitude as mass emigration of the poor and ignorant, or did servants have sufficient knowledge of conditions in America to make informed choices about where they wished to settle and for how long?" Horn concluded:

> To argue that generally servants considered emigration in terms of perceived "life expectancies, wage rates, job opportunities, access to land and credit, the costs of starting a farm or entering a trade,

> and the like" is misleading. Most poor did not have the luxury of considering their future in such a detached manner, and it is highly unlikely that they had sufficient information to weigh their options in such a calculated way. If they had, it is improbable that so many would have left England: the risk of early death was too great.[5]

So, no, it was not the magnetic attraction of the land of opportunity that pulled my ancestors from their homes. These are just the anachronistic fables Andrew Carnegie and Charles Schwab invented about my ancestors. They bear no resemblance to my ancestors themselves. I need a story as gloriously common as we Brooks have always been—a story that sounds like family, with swagger and a little bit of menace. A story with a broken back and missing fingers: no apologies, no nostalgia.

Literature is an important repository of stories that help us understand not just what happened in history but how people thought and felt about it. Sometimes literature even catches at corners of historical memory that escape documentary sources. As literary critic Jacqueline Goldsby has written, "Literature is particularly responsive to historical developments we cannot bear to admit shape the course of our lives. How does literature imagine for us the histories we cannot admit we need to know?"[6] But the challenge of relying on literature to reconstruct the story of why we left is that so very little survives that documents the Atlantic crossing from an Anglo-American peasant point of view. For though five to seven times as many English migrated to the Chesapeake as to New England, it is New England Puritans who crafted most surviving English-language literature from seventeenth-century North America. When I stand before a lecture hall and teach the beginnings of American culture, there is virtually nothing I can share with my students to evoke the perspectives and feelings of the largest part of this continent's early English migration. Just a few scraps of paper floating on an ocean of ideology and forgetting.

Follow the scraps back. The first marks early Anglo-American peasant emigrants left were in the emigration registers sporadically kept at points of embarkation like Bristol and London. In the city archives of Bristol, there are two leather-bound volumes of "Servants Sent to Foreign Plantations" containing records for more than ten thousand emigrants between 1654 and 1686: tailors, laborers, spinsters, and husbandmen, bound for Antigua, Barbados, Jamaica, the Leewards, Montserrat, Nevis, the West Indies, Maryland, New England, New

York, Newfoundland, Pennsylvania, and Virginia. In the Bristol registers, I find these entries:

> John Brooks, yeoman, from Droitwich, Worcestershire, indentured on February 27, 1658 to Richard Veale for three years. Destination: none given.
>
> William Brooks, no occupation, from Ausly, Shropshire, indentured on October 29, 1657 to John Emmett for three years. Destination: none given.
>
> Anne Brooks, no occupation, no place of origin, indentured on August 10, 1663 to William Jelfe for five years. Destination: Virginia.
>
> Edward Brooks, mercer, from Newbury, Berkshire, indentured on April 23, 1658 to Samuell Bevice, mariner. Destination: unknown.
>
> John Brooks, occupation unknown, indentured on November 8, 1666 to Stephen Procter, for four years. Destination: Virginia.

Similar indenture records were also compiled from 1682 to 1685 at the Guildhall in Middlesex, England, containing the names of English men and women bound for Antigua, Barbados, Jamaica, Nevis, Maryland, Carolina, New Jersey, New York, Pennsylvania, and Virginia: "spinsters" and "widows," "cordwainers," "ploughmen," and "groomes." In these, we find the fragments of lives and stories: Thomas Walker, "a fatherless youth" of seventeen, from "Yorke," was indentured to the merchant Edward Talbott on August 12, 1684, for seven years, and destined for Maryland or Virginia; Mary Hewit, indentured on August 9, 1684, to Richard Cook, mariner, and who "upon oath saith her father & mother are dead, aged 18," her destination unknown; Thomas Linggood, a "coachman," twenty-seven years old, son of Christopher Linggood from High Easttowne, Essex, indentured to John Jones, a London merchant, on May 25, 1684, bound for Barbados on the ship *Friendshipp,* captain Wiliam Bedding. In Middlesex, I find only one potential Brooks ancestor:

> John Brooks, 24, blacksmith, originally of Woodingston, Worcester, bound to London merchant Thomas Arnall, on August 21, 1684, for five years, headed for Virginia on the *Jefferies.* His indentures signed with a mark.

The Port of London also kept records on thousands of indentured servants who embarked there from 1682 to 1692 and 1718 to 1759. In the *Lord Mayor's Waiting Books*, held at the Guildhall in London, we find more spinsters, carpenters, soldiers, gardeners, and shoemakers. Robert Tomlin, no age given, son of John Tomlin, hatter of Southwark, deceased, indentured to John Baxter on September 3, 1685, for seven years, and bound for Maryland; Elizabeth Oakes, his mother, served as the witness to his indenture. John Savage, son of Canterbury's Abraham Savage, deceased, no age, no occupation, bound for five years to Thomas Taylor on October 7, 1684, and headed for Virginia. In these I find the following:

> George Brooks, "a poor lad," fifteen years old, originally from Wisbitch, Isle of Ely, Cambridgeshire, indentured to John Williams, tobacconist of Lambeth, Surrey, on April 6, 1720, for seven years, and headed for Virginia. His indentures signed with a mark.
>
> Samuel Brooks, a cordwainer from Manchester, twenty-three years old, indentured to Neale Mackneale, chapman, London, on December 19, 1729. Destination: Virginia.
>
> John Brooks, "schollmaster," of Aveley, no age given; indentured on July 31, 1754 to John Smith, chapman of London. Destination: Jamaica.[7]

A few more scraps of story survive in a handful of letters written by indentured servants in early Virginia, like Richard Frethorne, who was transported to Martin's Hundred, Virginia, in 1623. In the first of three surviving letters, Frethorne wrote that the indentured English cried out "day and night—Oh! That they were in England without their limbs and would not care to lose any limb to be in England again, yea, though they beg from door to door."[8] His contemporary John Baldwin reported to friends in England in 1623 that the people in Virginia were "base all over for yf a man be sicke, putt them into a new house and there lett lie downe & starve, for noebody will come at him." The dead, Baldwin wrote, "rott above ground."[9] Baldwin's account presents a Virginia where basic norms of society—such as the proper interment of the dead—have been all but abandoned. More than a century later, in 1756, another indentured English servant in nearby Maryland voiced a virtually identical sentiment. Wrote Elizabeth Sprigs to her father John Sprigs in London:

> What we unfortunate English People suffer here is beyond the probability of you in England to Conceive, let it suffice that I one of the unhappy Number, am toiling almost Day and Night, and very often in the Horses drudgery, with only this comfort that you Bitch you do not halfe enough, and then tied up and whipp'd to that Degree that you'd not serve an Animal, scarce any thing but Indian Corn and Salt to eat and that even begrudged.[10]

There are also scraps of the story woven into the fabric of other authors' imaginings and accounts of Anglo-American colonization. In these, we find the common colonial sort repeatedly characterized as criminals. Philosopher Francis Bacon (1561–1626), a proponent of the English colonization of Ireland, lamented the peopling of the Virginia colony: "It is a Shamefull and Unblessed Thing," he wrote in 1625, "to take the Scumme of People, and Wicked Condemned Men, to be the People with whom you Plant: And not only so, but it spoileth the Plantation; For they will ever live like Rogues."[11] Decades later, in 1689, the opening pages of Aphra Behn's play *The Widow Ranter* presents a new Virginia gentry composed of "transported criminals" who "had rather starve abroad than live Pitty'd and despis'd at home."[12] The Widow Ranter herself accosts a "Boy" on the street, accusing him immediately of being a transported pickpocket:

> RANTER: Why you Son of a Baboone don't you know me?
> BOY: No Madam, I came over but in the last Ship.
> RANTER: What from Newgate or Bridewell? from shoving the Tumbler, Sirrah, Lifting or filing the Cly?
> BOY: I don't understand this Country-Language forsooth, yet.
> RANTER: You Rogue, 'tis what we transport from England first—[13]

A few pages on, in act 2, scene 2, three colonial officials talk darkly about the world they left behind.

> TIMOROUS: Well, Gad zoors 'tis a fine thing to be a good Stateman.
> FRIENDLY: Ay Cornet, which you had never been had you staid in old England.
> DULLMAN: Why Sir we were somebody in England.
> FRIENDLY: So I heard Major.[14]

Even prejudicial secondhand depictions of the early Anglo-American colonial underclass allow us to eavesdrop a bit on how people like my

Brooks ancestors might have understood their chances in the colonies. In his 1610 account of the shipwreck of a Virginia Company boat at Bermuda, William Strachey (1572–1621) records the speech of "discontents" who aimed to stir up the "common sort" by warning them that "in Virginia, nothing but wretchedness and labor must be expected, with many wants, and a churlish entreaty, there being neither that Fish, Flesh, nor Fowl, which here . . . at ease, and pleasure might be enjoyed."[15] We hear echoes of that unhappiness in Robert Beverley's *History* of the 1676 populist anti-Indian revolt now known as Bacon's Rebellion. According to Beverley, for the common people (whose minds were "already full of discontent" and "resentment") "there was nothing to be got by tobacco; neither could they turn any other Manufacture to Advantage; so that most of the poorer Sort were willing to quit their unprofitable employments, and go Voluntiers against the Indians." Nathaniel Bacon (1640s–1676), the leader of the rebellion, in his 1676 *Manifesto* blamed colonial miseries on the newly landed classes: "unworthy Favourites and juggling Parasites whose tottering Fortunes have bin repaired and supported at the Publique chardge."[16] Bitterness. Discontent. Betrayal. Suspicion. *Brave men run.*

I DON'T REMEMBER WHY WE LEFT ENGLAND. In fact, I don't even remember how it is I came to be standing in the basement of the college library in San Diego, holding in my hands the two-record set.

> THE LIBRARY OF CONGRESS
> Music Division—Recording Laboratory
> FOLK MUSIC OF THE UNITED STATES
> Issued from the Collections of the Archive of Folk Song
> Long-Playing Record L58
> CHILD BALLADS TRADITIONAL IN THE UNITED STATES
> Edited by
> Bertrand H. Bronson

Two vinyl LPs and a typewritten booklet of lyrics. A few dozen ballads drawn from the hundreds collected from the English and Scottish countryside by the nineteenth-century American ethnographer Francis James Child, re-collected in American Appalachia by English folklorist Cecil Sharp, then recorded by master American folklorist Alan Lomax during his twentieth-century travels of rural America. In small places with names like the names of small places I've seen in my own family history—Viper, Kentucky; Galax, Virginia; Mena, Arkansas—Lomax found that sixteenth- and seventeenth-century ballads first printed as black-letter broadsides in London had crossed the Atlantic Ocean and survived in popular memory.

I leave the library. The palms make a fracas overhead and flocks of escaped domesticated parrots clatter across the skies over campus. I hurry home, and when I place the vinyl records on a turntable that once belonged to my grandmother, I hear voices in these ballads that chill me with their darkness and bitterness: tale after tale of betrayal, loss, revenge, child abandonment, and murder. To my surprise, some of them explicitly reference the ocean crossing from England to America or incorporate elements of the culture of colonization. A brother murders his brother for cutting down a young tree, then flees across the ocean to cope with the shame of his crime. A young man brings a girl a gold ring and a beaver hat—the fashion that drove the North American fur trade—incurring the jealousy of her older sister, who then pushes the younger girl into a stream and drowns her. A captain on a colonial venture ship crossing the Atlantic commands a young sailor to swim over to sink a rival craft using nothing but a carpenter's augur and promising gold, land, and marriage as his reward; the cabin boy does so, but when he returns to the ship, the captain refuses to let him back on board and leaves him to drown in the open ocean. The wife of a house carpenter in England is seduced by a sailor who promises her great riches in America; she abandons her husband and young children and boards the ship, which then sinks on the high seas.

From San Diego, I follow the ballads deeper into the archive of memory, to the American Folklife Center at the Library of Congress, in Washington, D.C., where I sit six months later, holding in my hands fragile onion-skin letters on Library of Congress letterhead exchanged between Alan Lomax and singers in the rural South, from North Carolina to Texas. On my head I wear big wraparound headphones plugged into a reel-to-reel recorder, listening through hours of the more than ten thousand recordings made by Lomax and his collaborators. I can hear women singing the songs their mothers sang while standing over a washtub or plucking feathers from a chicken, songs that travel back across the generations, back over the rolling hills and Appalachian mountains, back across the ocean, back in memory to seventeenth-century England. It is November, and the air in the library has a chill. The leaves on the elm in the courtyard are turning gold and beginning to fall. I listen for cues as to how people who lived in the era of English outmigration understood their place in history and remembered it to their children. I hear the old voices, the same accent that colors the edges of my Uncle Norm's speech. I listen to hundreds of versions of the ballads, transcribing and noting with remarkable consistency their shared sense of ruefulness, desolation, and betrayal.

From expert scholars of the ballad form I learn that the genre is characteristically driven not by the exploits of a hero but by the tension of an impossible or catastrophic situation. Over time, from place to place, details may be added or sloughed away, refrains may be swapped, but the situation remains.[17] What the great Americo Paredes once observed of the Mexican-American *corrido* might also be observed of the English and Anglo-American ballad: these were popular literary forms that documented and thrived on conflict. In fact, most of the Anglo-American ballads I hear can be traced directly back to their first print appearances on black-letter broadsides in late sixteenth- and early seventeenth-century England, a time of catastrophic economic transformation and upheaval. They came into being in England's rural villages, mining towns, mill towns, and newly burgeoning cities as commentaries on their times.[18] Ballad experts also suggest that the genre thrived not only on conflict but on what Patricia Fumerton has characterized as an emerging sixteenth- and seventeenth-century "lower-order culture of placelesnness or vagrancy."[19] Displaced workers and subsistence migrants carried them along the hedgerows and highways, trafficked in the songs and their stories at alehouses and other stopping places, and delivered them to urban printers. In print, as black-letter folio-sheet broadsides illustrated with graphic woodcuts, the ballads continued to move, as they were sung, sold, and pasted up by vagrant peddlers on roads and at markets. Fumerton writes:

> Ballads traveled freely and were posted just about anywhere: on street posts, in log books, in trunks, on the milkhouse wall—sites where they might stay for a short moment before being white-washed or pasted over with a "new" issue. Their method of composition was similarly vagrant or "masterless": passed from a usually

> anonymous author, to printer, to ballad-monger, to audience (each of whom had a say in how they were "voiced") and then often back again to author / printer to be reissued in a different key.[20]

Even the topical range of the ballad and its literary form, which often unfolds a conflicted situation through the perspectives of multiple participants, manifests a "nomadic journey of provisional subjectivities" that Fumerton links to the dislocation of its times.[21]

Adapted as they were to the dislocations of their times, ballads traveled with hundreds of thousands of working poor from England to North America.[22] Some offered potent commentary on the colonial situation: "Anti-colonial ballads satirized colonial conditions," writes historian Allan Kulikoff, while colony promoters "resorted to printing pamphlets and publishing ballads that extolled the colonial virtues or played down the colonial problems."[23] Ballads served as tools of colonial promotion and recruitment, as well as anticolonial knowledge. And as they were adapted in the mouths of peasant-class colonists to survive in their new and ever-changing American environs, ballads increasingly served as a repository of narrative and an archive of story about what leaving England had meant. As Sean Wilentz and Greil Marcus wrote, "Ballads became a major form—musically, perhaps, the major form—through which Americans told each other about themselves and the country they inhabited."[24] The ballads our ancestors brought with them from England to America (and continued to sing down through the centuries that followed) may in fact be the strongest surviving archive of stories about why we left.

That this archive of recorded ballads exists in an institutionalized form owes to the work of academic folklorists like Francis Child, George Lyman Kittredge, and Francis Barton Gummere, as well as to government-paid ethnographers like John Lomax and his son Alan Lomax, and the resources of large institutions like the Smithsonian and the Library of Congress. Just as Frank Cushing and other salvage ethnographers of American Indian communities had in the late nineteenth century, many ethnographers of Anglo-American folk music and culture in the early twentieth century approached their subjects with a sense of belatedness and impending doom. Many shared in a romantic and nostalgic belief that an authentic Anglo-American folk culture with direct ties to English folk culture had survived and thrived in rural and mountain isolation, and they feared that large-scale economic changes and industrial modernization threatened its purity and continuation. As Regina Bendix has observed, professional folklorists developed a quasi-scientific methodology for identifying and collecting specimens of "authentic" folk culture, and they connected their efforts to a larger "essentializing search for national or individual character."[25] The early decades of the twentieth century also saw the founding of folk schools and folk music festivals, each of them publicly dedicated to the preservation and promotion of folk culture.[26] In truth, these projects were animated by a variety of personal, professional, social, economic, religious, and political ambitions—progressive to conservative. Rather than simply preserving Anglo-American popular culture, each constituted a "systematic cultural intervention," as David Whisnant has explained.[27] Some school and festival sponsors turned to southern traditional music as a repository of Anglo-American culture in the service of political nativism, despite robust evidence that traditional music forms were deeply infused with African American influences—think, for example, of the banjo, a traditional African and African American instrument—as American southern culture had been more generally since the eighteenth century.[28] Some folk festival and folk school founders and teachers even reintroduced English folk culture archaisms back into popular Anglo-American repertoires in an effort to bolster and improve their "authenticity." The competing professional, cultural, social, and political agendas at work in these projects often fostered disagreement and suspicion among organizers and participants. (Bascom Lamar Lunsford—a ballad singer featured in this book—routinely accused folk music collectors of being "Communists.")[29] Fictions of folk authenticity also screened out the complex lives of actual people who inhabited the rural and mountain regions, lives that were fully embedded in and adjusting to processes of change and industrialization. Despite what salvage ethnographers believed, such processes were not always the enemies of popular culture. Old-time music and bluegrass artists participated in the popular recording industry in ways that allowed them to negotiate with and even benefit from commercialization.[30] Commercial music served as a venue for the continued articulation and adaptation of popular music traditions. Indeed, as Ronald Cohen has emphasized, the commercial, traditional, and political intertwined to create the "folk revival" of the 1940s–1960s, fostering habits of improvisation, exchange, politicization, and particularization that had enriched folk forms all along. Consequently, given the circumstances of its creation, the archive of recorded ballads at the heart of this book should not be understood as a preserve of timeless authenticity, but rather as the product of a contested, mediated, politicized, and ongoing process of cultural production.

Has memory in the transatlantic world ever been otherwise? Joseph Roach has characterized the reproduction of cultural memory in the circumatlantic world—a world forged out of massive and intersecting displacements—as a process of "surrogation": "Into the cavities created by loss through death or other forms of departure . . . survivors attempt to fit satisfactory alternates." No fit is ever perfect, Roach point outs, and the process of trying to reconstitute memory itself can generate and contribute to "discontinuities, misalliances, and ruptures" as communities "continuously audition stand-ins" that can project a desirable relation to the past.[31] While the eighteenth and nineteenth centuries conducted these processes of audition and surrogation through the medium of performance, mass media like the commercial music and film industries emerged in the twentieth century as powerful producers of cultural memory. "Such memories," writes Allison Landberg, "bridge the temporal chasms that separate individuals from the meaningful and potentially interpellative events of the past. It has become possible to have an intimate relationship to memories of events through which one did not live: these are the memories I call prosthetic." She continues:

> "Prosthetic memories" are indeed "personal" memories, as they derive from engaged and experientially-oriented encounters with the mass media's various technologies of memory. But because prosthetic memories are not natural, not the possession of a single individual, let alone a particular family or ethnic group, they conjure up a more public past, a past that is not at all privatized. . . . In contrast to collective memories, which tend to be geographically specific and which serve to reinforce and naturalise a group's identity, prosthetic memories are not the property of a single group. Rather, they open up the possibility for collective horizons of experience and pave the way for unexpected political alliances.[32]

The idea of "prosthetic," for Landberg, underscores how something not authentic can fit, produce personal sensuous experience, and be useful.

Commercial media thus contribute not only to continued dislocations of the world shaped by historic transatlantic displacements but also to the surrogations through which historic displacements have been remembered.

I think it is worth noting the persistence of terms suggesting dislocation, interruption, substitution, artifice, and instrumentalization in contemporary theorists' characterizations of processes of historical memory. That the making of history and memory is an elective process shot through with considerations of power is an idea deeply familiar to us now, through Nietzsche and, after him, Foucault. But that it should also entail a form of artifice is, I sense, an idea still tinged with shame. For professional historians, that artifice is shielded behind and absolved through fastidious methodological observances that mandate personal silence. As Michel-Rolph Trouillot observes, silences enter the process of history as "conceptual tools, second-level abstractions" when facts are "creat[ed]," "assembl[ed]," "retriev[ed]," and assigned their significance.[33] But what for those of us who abandon silence to admit that we are hungry for memory we never had and that we can never come by honestly?

I think back on the missing fingers and broken backs of my Brooks ancestors, their bodies shaped by the dislocations of hard luck and hard work. If hard luck and hard work shaped their bodies of memories the same way, what shame is there now in latching onto a prosthesis? That is how I regard the archives of ballads I refer to in this book: not as a pure or authentic body of countermemory, but as perhaps the most useful literary archive of experiential-historical perspective on the transatlantic migrations of peasant-class Anglo-Americans. Stranded across centuries in dislocations of print and tape as they may be, the ballads offer points of access to a feeling experience of dislocation, and in their lyrics they consciously anchor that feeling experience to the historical fact of transatlantic migration. This book is an effort to follow the words of the ballads to a new understanding of the impossible or catastrophic situations that made England uninhabitable to my ancestors and thousands upon thousands of other English laboring-class migrants who colonized America. As I listen and learn, I begin to see the outlines of the bigger story of why we left: stories that suggest that England colonized its own lands and dislocated its own indigenous peoples before colonizing abroad. For centuries, the Brooks and so many hundreds of thousands like us maintained subsistence living on the land; then over the course of the great economic transformations of the newly modernizing mercantile capitalist world, we became disposable. We were enclosed and improved out of our own homelands, and then we crossed the ocean to try and make some gain by doing unto others as had been done unto us. *Brave men run.*

Chapter 1 will lay the groundwork for this exploration by drawing the broadest outlines of the story of early Anglo-American peasant migrants from contemporary historiography. Chapters 2 through 5 focus on particular ballads from the Anglo-American folk tradition that reveal the lived, felt, and thought dimensions of that history in particularly provocative ways. Each takes one traditional American folk ballad as a living artifact of early Anglo-American migrant consciousness and as a pathway into understanding the historical contexts of their migration, tracing the song back to its seventeenth-century origins and the cultural and historical contexts they document. In chapter 2, the ballad is "Edward," and the story it tells is how massive deforestation in England uprooted the traditional lifeways of peasant communities and propelled them toward migration. Chapter 3 focuses on the ballad "The Two Sisters," which recounts one sister murdering another out of jealousy over the gift of a beaver hat. Beaver hats and the beaver fur trade did, in fact, lead to massive changes in the Atlantic world in the seventeenth century, permanently reorganizing the lives of indigenous peoples in the Americas and standing as a symbol in England of the growing gap between the ascendant middle class and the laboring poor. "The Golden Vanity" tells a harrowing tale of a ship commanded by Walter Raleigh and his cruel betrayal of a heroic cabin boy during an Atlantic crossing. This ballad, the subject of chapter 4, reveals the critical outlook common English men and women shared on the celebrated architects of English colonialism, as well as their own disposable role in the imperial project. Finally, chapter 5 focuses on "The House Carpenter," which tells the story of a woman lured to America by a sailor who promises her great riches. She abandons her husband and children and embarks on the ocean voyage, but within a few days, the ship sinks, drowning the woman and her lover. This ballad offers a pathway into understanding how English laboring-class women viewed the colonial enterprise and their role in it. As experienced by women, colonization and all the economic changes that propelled it entailed the catastrophic abandonment or destabilization of families. This chapter also reveals how some ballads contemporary with "The House Carpenter" carried warnings from English migrants to Virginia back to the home country, comparing colonial propaganda to seduction. Given the scarcity of documented women's perspectives on Anglo-American peasant migration, this chapter makes a significant contribution to our understanding of the world of laboring women in early America and the colonial Atlantic world.

Throughout the book, I will be referring at times to my own family history. This is a gesture outside the norms of scholarly discourse, so I'd like to make my objects in doing so clear. My goal is not to call attention to my own family as having a special purchase on American experience, nor is it to suggest that people like me—the descendents of English laboring-class immigrants—should claim historical trauma as the basis for a newly privileged political identity. Quite the opposite: by telling this story I hope to underscore that the experiences of dislocation and disposability that have characterized modernity for so many people are very broadly distributed, and that modern globalization has entailed substantial losses even for those who believe or have been led to believe that they have benefitted from it. Second, in connecting this body of history to my own family, I would like to join the body of scholars who treat their own communities' histories as inhabited bodies of knowledge. Even the histories that by scholarly custom we tell in the third person belong to someone. In this book, I happen to be telling a story that belongs to my ancestors, and I hope my approach will encourage my readers to think about their own place in history. There is often a wide gulf between the particular histories we inherit from our families and the representations of history we encounter in popular culture. Thinking critically about how American history and culture are made and what responsibility we bear for shaping them is, for me, one of the most important objects of American studies. The reward for this kind of work is the expansive human solidarity that comes from knowing that our story is not so different from any other people's on the face of the earth.

CHAPTER ONE

No Land of Opportunity

Folk Ballads and the Story of Why We Left

THE STORY OF WHY WE LEFT begins in England, for if the Brooks ever belonged anywhere—and I have my doubts that we did—it was to the fens and marshes of England. If we were peasants in the fifteenth century, we may have lived on ten to thirty acres of land by copyhold agreement, paying rents to a feudal lord, enjoying land tenure rights and the ability to convey land to our children, and nominally protected against unjust or arbitrary dispossession by the force of custom. But by the late fifteenth and early sixteenth centuries that old feudal order was changing, the gentry now less interested in the old forms of political and military tribute and more interested in the commercial advantages of capital, a profound economic transformation that created new economic world systems and remade England into a modern nation-state.[1]

In the sixteenth and seventeenth centuries, the English gentry called this transformation "improvement." The Crown in order to raise revenues allowed manorial lords to convert forest demesne into leased land for enclosure and improvement through industrial farming, mining, and wood pasturage.[2] With the proceeds of their leases, they financed commercial, industrial, and colonial ventures. Land was no longer viewed as an anchoring relationship embedded in a set of use rights, but as a fungible commodity.[3] Peasants who once enjoyed copyhold land tenure were transitioned into new leaseholding agreements and charged rents as tenants at will on the land. Customary relationships between people and places were annulled or denied, and the peasantry destined for emerging wage-labor markets. "Disafforestation and enclosure could thus be regarded as a national duty," historian Christopher Hill once explained, "a kindness in disguise to the idle poor, as well as of more immediate benefit to the rich encloser."[4] Thus, peasants too, like the land itself, were believed to have been improved by their removal from heritage lands and assimilation into a modernizing economy. Historians viewing this process in retrospect have described improvement as a process of *internal colonization:* before they colonized the Americas, England and other European countries transformed their own lands, economies, and societies through a process of internal colonization that entailed the privatization of lands, the transformation of subsistence economies into market and export economies, the termination of traditional peasant lifeways tied closely to subsistence on the land, and the structural exclusion of newly landless poor from modern nation-states.[5]

Improvement entailed significant changes to the land itself. Fens, marshes, reed beds, bogs, and wetlands were drained, impacting the quality, availability, and seasonal flows of water and diminishing, destroying, or displacing populations of fish, ducks, geese, egrets, plovers, owls, frogs, otters, voles, and predatory foxes. Forests of oak, ash, beech, and hazel long governed by customary laws establishing sustainable rates of wood usage—including prosecution of greenwood cutters and protections for the ancient right of *housebote,* the right to take timber for home repairs—were systematically felled to increase pastureland for profit and to provide timber for increased military and commercial venture shipbuilding.[6] Destruction of forest and woodland also impacted populations of mammals and birds including deer, foxes, badgers, hedgehogs, rabbits, owls, hawks, woodpeckers, robins, and nightingales. As wood supplies diminished, coal-mining industries expanded. Coal production increased from 200,000 to 1.5 million tons from 1530 to 1630. Open-pit coal mines and tramways transformed the face of the land, while coal operations fouled water sources.[7]

Sixteenth- and seventeenth-century processes of enclosure attempted to rationalize the land into a commodity by marking boundaries on its surface. During the sixteenth century, only about 4 percent of open fields land was enclosed; by the seventeenth century, that grew to about 50 percent.[8] Open fields, forestlands, and wastes were fenced by hedges; sheep replaced men on new pasturelands designed to produce wool for market. Enclosure and disafforestation agreements negotiated between the Crown, lords, and tenants, even when modulated by government restrictions on depopulation, produced many peasant cottagers who received less than one acre of land—not enough to maintain a family on—and saw their rights to the commons limited, disrupted, or extinguished. The wastes, forests, and commons had played a vital role in peasant lifeways and subsistence. The ability to graze a cow or goats or sheep on nearby wastes gave peasant families fertilizer for their gardens and milk, butter, and cheese for their own use as well as for exchange or sale in local markets and thus the ability to purchase clothing; forests also provided pannage for pigs who grazed on acorns. From the forests came not only firewood and peat for fuel and *housebote* wood, thatch, and clay for home and fence repairs but also ferns as litter for domestic animals and important elements of the human food supply including berries, fruit, acorns, nuts, roots, herbs (including medicinal herbs), fish, game birds, and mammals like squirrels and rabbits, and even the occasional poached deer. People living on the land understood that common rights such as pasturage, pannage, fern, *turbary* (the right to cut turf or peat), and *estovers* (the right to take wood for household uses) were crucial to their economic independence.[9] Many reacted strongly against enclosure, fen drainage, and disafforestation. Peasants rioted, pulling down hedges, forcibly plowing converted pasturelands, and putting their beasts to pasture on former commons; these riots sometimes assumed the spirit of traditional festivals, taking place on traditional English holidays like May Day, Shrove Tuesday, or Lammas Day, and concluding with raucous bonfires.[10] In 1607, peasants from the Midlands region recorded their protest against the enclosure of almost one-fifth of the region's open lands in the form of a petition: "Wee . . . doe feele the smart of these incroaching Tirants which would grind our flesh upon the whetstone of poverty . . . [who have] depuplated and overthrown whole Townes and made thereof sheep pastures nothing profitable for our commonewealth. For the common Field being layd open would yield as much commodity, besides the increase of corne, on which stands our life."[11] Even the clergy weighed in, as one Midlands preacher observed that the "excessive covetousnesse of some" had "caused extreme want to other, and that want, not well digested, hath rioted to the hazard of all."[12]

New pressures, too, came from unprecedented growth in the English population, which doubled over the course of one century, from an estimated 2.5 million in 1520 to 5 million in 1680, growing 40 percent between 1580 and 1640 alone. Population growth meant a greater demand for food than the land had ever borne, as well as more bodies available to work it, and so growth fed England's economic transformation from feudal economy into modern commercial nation-state. Strong food demand created economic incentives for owning classes to transform even more land from customarily tenant-farmed family plots to food production for market and profit. An increased labor pool also incentivized the abandonment of customary tenant and live-in servant relationships for more casual wage-labor arrangements. As the population grew, prices rose, wages declined, diets deteriorated, and family sizes shrunk.[13]

Internal colonization changed not only the land and the people's relationship to the land but the nature of peasant existence. If most had existed in a fragile and carefully negotiated balance of subsistence on local forests, wastes, and water sources, labor in their own fields and gardens, seasonal agricultural day labor, servitude in gentry households, and other customary and obligatory economic relationships, wage labor came to assume a greater and greater role in common survival. In 1560, about 25 percent of households were headed by wage laborers, and 40 percent were headed by smallholding husbandmen; by 1620, the proportion of smallholders dropped to about 30 percent, while the proportion of wage laborers grew to about 40 percent.[14] Former small landholders and their wives and children went to work in greater and greater proportions in the wool, cloth, and coal industries, exposing their households to cyclical market depressions without the benefits of customary protections, social relationships, and obligations. Wage labor was popularly understood as the gateway to economic dependence. The arrival of cloth industries often compounded poverty, as the anonymous author of *Reasons for a Limited Export of Wool* (1677) wrote: "Though it sets the poor on work where it finds them, yet it draws still more to the place; and their masters allow wages so mean that they are only preserved from starving whilst they can work; when age, sickness or death comes, themselves their wives or their children are most commonly left upon the parish; which is the reason why those towns (as in the Weald of Kent) whence the clothing is departed, have fewer poor than they had before."[15] Households entirely dependent on wage labor, wrote historian Christopher Hill, were "so badly off in the sixteenth and seventeenth centuries that neither contemporary nor modern economists can explain how they lived."[16] Theirs was what some economic historians have described as an "economy of makeshifts," a precarious balancing of residual subsistence practices, wage labor, market activity, charity, and other practices of the economic margins such as pawning clothes and household items.[17]

Historians cite this moment as the emergence in England of a new "permanent proletariat" of landless laborers.[18] It is estimated that the proportion of landless laborers grew from between 10 and 20 percent of the English population in the sixteenth century to between 50 and 70 percent of the English population in the seventeenth century, and over that same time period workers holding less than an acre of land rose fourfold.[19] Loss of traditional land bases also created a new class of economic migrants within England. During the sixteenth century, teenagers often left their homes to seek work within a local orbit of communities, but by the seventeenth century, the employments that had once motivated young people to leave home—craft apprenticeships or living-in servant arrangements—were drying up and giving way to more casual forms of day and wage labor.[20] Between 1520 and 1700, living-in workers fell from 20 percent of the population to 10 percent.[21] In place of the traditional young betterment migrants, a new class of landless subsistence migrants emerged composed of slightly older workers in their twenties and thirties moving longer distances to search for work in more industrial and urban areas.[22] Whereas betterment migrants had stopped and stayed with kin, subsistence migrants more often stayed in barns and victualing houses or alehouses because they found their kin networks dissolving all around them.[23] In many English villages, 30 to 60 percent of the population migrated each decade.[24] Town studies yield remarkable findings: half of the surnames of a Norfolk village disappeared between 1607 and 1650; 60 percent of the population of a Nottinghamshire village disappeared between 1676 and 1688.[25] Towns in regions like Kent complained that they were being overrun by subsistence migrants, as did the leading citizens of the town of Maidstone in 1608: "Many of the poorer sort, either of their own desire or being for their idle and disordered life driven out of other places to come to inhabit and settle themselves in this town."[26] Historian Peter Clark offers the most vivid characterization of the subsistence migrant:

> The most common time for the poorer migrant to tramp was from June until October. Propelled by the dying days of the last harvest year, the hope of harvest work somewhere on the way, and the comparative usability of the roads, he would keep going until the hiring fair and its fag-end, the mop fair, failed to find him work and the autumn turned sour. Then the only recourse would be to scrape a meager living from the woodlands where if all else failed the squatter could dig for roots or eat nuts and berries. Otherwise he could stare out the winter clinging to the shackland excrescences of urban society.[27]

While most migrants were men, during dearth times entire families either separated to seek work independently or took to the road in groups. A multifamily group of twelve, comprised almost entirely of children and headed by two women, Katherine Constable and Mary Washington, was on the move in Kent during the 1630s. Washington gave birth on the road to an infant daughter named Elizabeth; when Elizabeth was six months old, the family was forced by authorities back to their home town of Malvern.[28]

Many landless laborers established makeshift cottage communities by reclaiming land in surviving forests and on wastes, fens, and commons. These cottage communities served as the homes for workers in the coal-mining, woodcraft, iron, glass, and cloth industries, as well as bases of production for the cloth industry, which "put out" much of its work to men, women, and children who spun or wove at home.[29] By the mid-sixteenth century, one in six men and one in three women and children made their living from the cottage cloth industry.[30] A 1597 law had forbidden the building of cottages on less than four acres of land, so the cottage communities erected hastily by landless laborers were viewed as illegal by local officials and targeted for destruction.[31] Long-term local residents also complained about the growth in cottage communities, as this new class of rural industrial workers, barely surviving on wage labor, vulnerable to economic downturns, added additional strain to already depleted resources of the forests, fens, marshes, and waterways. The forests where landless laborers took refuge came to be viewed as zones of disorder and lawlessness, especially when forest residents rioted against the appropriation of forest resources by industrialists or the gentry.[32] One contemporary observer described forest zones as a "nursery for the county gaols."[33] Another wrote in 1610 that the forests and woods were "the verye nurseryes of Idlenes Atheisme Beggerie perfidiousness and mere disobedience to goes and the lawes of the kingdom. . . . For poverties sake, havinge noe other meanes, [forest residents] thruste themselves into theis obscure places (as they thincke) out of the view of god or men whoe become *Rudes et Refractorij*, Lyving most baselie, prophanlie and by thefte, A peste in a Comonwealth."[34]

Other landless laborers migrated to England's cities, which experienced phenomenal rates of growth during the late sixteenth and early seventeenth centuries. London grew from fifty thousand in the 1520s to two hundred thousand in 1600 and then doubled in size to four hundred thousand by 1650.[35] By the seventeenth century, only about one in five residents of East London had been born in the city.[36] Life in London was characterized by high mortality rates, transitory and insecure personal relationships, as well as an absolute detachment from subsistence resources—social, economic, and natural—that had once sustained common English people.[37] Urbanization only compounded the commercialization of the English rural economy, as owning classes scrambled to convert their landholdings to produce food for market to keep up with skyrocketing urban demand.[38]

Increased demand due to population growth, migration, and urbanization led to incredible increases in the prices of necessities over the course of the sixteenth and seventeenth centuries. The price of food tripled from 1500 to 1570, then grew sixfold from 1570 to the early seventeenth century.[39] Rents increased eightfold between 1530 and 1640; in some areas, rents tripled between the 1570s and the 1640s.[40] During the same time period, the price of firewood, a vital resource once gleaned from forest commons, increased fifteenfold.[41] Compounding these price hikes were sharp drops in wages caused also by population growth, migration, and urbanization. Real wages fell by 50 percent from the early sixteenth to the early seventeenth century.[42] Both laborers and husbandmen made just marginally more than either the cost of subsistence or the weekly parish relief payments to the poor.[43] The commercialization of the English economy produced, according to economic historian Alan G. R. Smith, "an increasing economic polarization between those at the bottom of the rural pyramid—agricultural labourers whose wages were approximately halved in real terms during the period 1500–1650—and those who were able to produce for the market."[44]

Food became a major focal point of this polarization, as landowners converted customarily peasant-held lands to the production of food for market and wool for trade, while the people who had once subsisted on the land were required to spend wages on the purchase of food. Wage laborers in the cloth industry were especially vulnerable to market fluctuations; for them, cyclical economic depressions and harvest failures often led to dearth.[45] One contemporary observer described with alarm the survival tactics to which impoverished cloth workers resorted:

> Infinite numbers of Spynners, Carders, Pickers of Woll are turned to begging with no smale store of pore children, who driven with necessitie (that hath no lawe) both come idelie abowt to begg to the oppression of the poore husbandmen, and robbe their hedges of lynnen, stele pig, goose, and capon, and leave not a drie hedge within dyvers myles compass of the towenes where they dwell to the great destruction of all manor of grayen sowen and to the spoile of mens meadows and pastures, and spole all springs, steale fruit and corne in the harvest tyme, and robb barnes in the winter tyme. . . . Besides many other mischeifes falling owt the Weavers, Walkers, Tukkers, Shermen, Dyers and such being tall lusty men and streame pore stryght being forced by povertie stele fish, conies, dere and such like.[46]

Other impoverished workers responded to dearth with food riots. Between 1586 and 1631, rural England witnessed more than thirty food riots during which mobs of unemployed artisans (including women), complaining that they had been reduced to subsisting on "oattes dogges and rootes of nettles" (dog grass and nettle roots), seized cartloads of cheese and grain and barges of barley and malt as they made their way toward London and coastal ports.[47] Historians of the riots point out that the riots had a specific and rather articulate logic: protesters were defending customary rights of subsistence by protesting the carrying away of surplus from the lands and their people for commercial sale and profit.[48]

The emergence of a new structural class of permanently landless laboring poor created new pressures and developments in English treatment of poverty. Until the middle of the sixteenth century, the poor were conceived of in two classes: the virtuous poor—widows, orphans, the disabled—and the vicious poor—rogues, criminals, counterfeits, and vagabonds. Relief for the virtuous poor was delivered either through monasteries and religious charities or through a customary ethic of charity and hospitality that assumed responsibility for the traveling, the aged, and the infirm.[49] The unworthy poor were, on the other hand, criminalized by early sixteenth-century statutes: ordered to be stripped naked, tied to carts, whipped through town, and returned to the places of their last residences, or prosecuted as felons for vagrancy, or bound as slaves for two years to willing masters, or put in stocks, or even branded.[50] The rise of a new class of landless laboring poor in a newly commercialized English economy led to the creation with the Act of Relief for the Poor (1598) of a bureaucratic apparatus of poor relief administered through local Anglican church parishes. The act made parishes responsible for taxing their inhabitants, providing poor relief, employment, and apprenticeship opportunities for able adults and poor children, while maintaining older legal customs prescribing the whipping and return to birthplaces of vagrants and banishment or branding of confirmed rogues. Such mandates in turn gave parishes and their inhabitants incentives to keep the poor rolls thin.[51] Consequently, relief reached only a fraction of the actual poor. Historian Steven Hindle estimates that the "conjunctural poor"—those who were unable to meet their own needs by their labor—constituted on average 20 percent of the English population, while only 5 percent of the population received parish poor relief.[52] New bureaucratic relief mechanisms also did little to promote a new understanding of this new class of landless laborers, who were, in popular discourse, characterized in terms similar to those of the old vicious poor. Genteel commentators and bureaucrats alike blamed the lewdness and drunkenness of the poor for gaps and lacks in English productivity.[53] Begging children were characterized in one English town as "the Caterpillars, Frogs, Grasshoppers and Lice of Egipt . . . the plagues of this our common welth."[54]

The seventeenth century saw three new developments in English policy on the poor. First, there was a new tendency to criminalize marginal subsistence behaviors once reserved to the poor by tradition and custom such as the gathering of kindling, the pocketing of a bit of grain by threshers, or pulling wool from sheep's backs.[55] Even the ancient right to glean, practiced chiefly by women and children, was constricted and then, in some places, criminalized by the seventeenth century.[56] Women who took grain during food riots were apprehended and whipped through the streets.[57] Courts sometimes hung men for being without a means of making a living, and in London the heads of men hung for crimes as slim as coin-clipping were boiled in bay-salt and cumin seeds and put on pikes for public display.[58] Some even began to characterize subsistence activities as criminal and morally suspect, as did this contemporary commentator:

> The pretence of some small privilege, as of gathering of dead wood in a forest and the like, are only cloakes for the greates villaineies in destroyeing the wood and the game. The children are brought up in this manner & instead of being inured to labour are accustomed to laziness which must intail povety upon their posterity and charge upon an estate.[59]

In view of these powerful shifts in the public perception of the long-standing "economy of makeshifts," historian Steven Hindle describes the seventeenth century as "'stinted times' during which the poor were not only *hedged* out of the local community by enclosure but stinted out of the customary economy by the increasingly aggressive regulation of rights."[60] The right to subsist on the land as one's ancestors had done was not among those protected by the new commercial economy.

A second significant seventeenth-century development in the treatment of the poor was the emergence of the perception that the masses of landless laboring poor tramping the hedgerows and highways as subsistence migrants seeking work or access to natural resources constituted a social threat or problem. Elizabethan law had been especially punitive in its dispositions toward vagrants and vagabonds. Statute 39 c 4 was especially vivid in its characterization of the vagrant class:

> All persons calling themselves Schollers going about begging, all Seafaring men pretending losses of their Shippes or goods on the sea going about the Country begging, all idel persons going about in any Cuntry eyther begging or using any subtile Crafte or unlawful Games or ployes, or fayning themselves to have knowledge in Phisiognome Palmestry or other like craty Scyence, or pretending that they can tell Destenyes Fortunes or such other like fantasticall Imagynacons; all persons that be or utter themselves to be Proctors Procueres Patent Gatherers or Collectors for Gaoles Prisons or Hospitalls; all Fencers Bearewards common Players of Enterludes and Minstrells wandring abroade (other then Players of

> Enterludes belonging to any Baron of this Realme . . .) all Juglers Tynkers Pedlers and Petty Chapmen wandring abroade; all wandring persons and common Labourers being persons able in bodye using loitering and refusing to worcke for such reasonable wages as is taxed or commonly given in such Parts where such persons do or shall happen to dwell or abide, not having lyving otherwayse to maynteyne themselves; all persons delivered out of Gaoles that begg for their Fees, or otherwise do travale begging; all such persons as shall wander abroade begging pretending loss by Fyre or otherwise; and all such persons not being Fellons wandering and pretending themselves to be Egipcyans, or wanderin gin the Habite Forme or Attyre of counterfayte Egipcians.[61]

The statute prescribed that all of these be whipped and returned to their last known home places, while the most incorrigible and unfixable be branded with the letter "V." The Poor Act of 1598, by devolving upon parishes responsibility for caring for their resident poor, reconstructed migratory workers not only as a social threat but also as an economic liability. Thus, the 1662 Settlement Act established a system of "settlement certificates" indicating the parishes in which migrant laborers and their families belonged—either by birth, by residence of three years, or by employment of one year and one day—and authorized parish officials to remove parish newcomers who might be "chargeable" to a district. Although unevenly enforced, the law created new incentives for landlords' eviction of tenants, destruction of poor tenant housing, and the casualization of labor as employers started employing workers for less than a year in order to spare their local parishes increased poor-relief taxes. It also increased the vulnerability of migrant laboring families, especially families unable to establish a lasting home and with children born in different towns. Such families were subject to separation.[62]

The seventeenth century also saw the emergence of public and private projects to rehabilitate and employ the structural poor. Many of these projects incorporated the contemporary idea of improvement—that, like the land, the poor themselves might be improved through assimilation as workers into the emerging mercantile economy—with the Protestant emphasis on the improving spiritual value of work. In some quarters, the poor came to be seen, according to historian Paul Slack, as less a "threat" than an "opportunity": "a resource which only needed proper handling to be profitable."[63] Public projects for the improvement of the poor included the construction of hospitals and workhouses. Private proposals for dispatching the poor on the seas and in overseas commercial ventures also gained popularity. The first to propose such a scheme was Buckinghamshire gentleman Robert Hitchcock, whose *A Politic Plat for the Honour of the Pince, the Great Profit of the Public State, Relief of the Poor, Preservation of the Rich, Reformation of Rogues and Idle Persons, and the Wealth of Thousands That Know Not How to Live* (1580) envisioned the creation of a fleet of hundreds of herring boats for the containment and employment of ten thousand men.[64] In the 1580s, having begun his career establishing plantations in occupied Ireland, Walter Raleigh's half brother Sir Humphrey Gilbert (1539–83) launched a new project to colonize the land of Norumbega, or Newfoundland, proposing that "a great number of men which do now live idly at home, are burdenous, chargeable, and unprofitable to this realm, shall hereby be set on work."[65] Gilbert claimed Newfoundland for Elizabeth on August 5, 1783, an act memorialized as the founding of the British overseas empire. During the 1580s and 1590s, Richard Hakluyt also promoted the English colonization of the Americas as an opportunity for "valiant youths, rustinge and hurtfull by lacke of employment" and for the "unburdenynge of the realme with many that nowe lyve chardgeable to the state at home."[66] Wrote Hakluyt:

> Many men of excellent wittes and of divers singuler giftes, overthrowen by suertishippe [suretyship], by sea, or by some folly of youthe, that are not able to live in England, may there be raised againe, and doe their contrie goodd service; and many nedefull uses there may (to greate purpose) require the saving of greate nombers, that for trifles may otherwise be devoured by the gallowes. . . . The frye of the wandringe beggars of England, that growe upp ydly, and hurtefull and burdenous to this realme, may there be unladen, better bredd upp, and may people waste contries to the home and forreine benefite, and to their owne more happy state.[67]

Promoters of Virginia plantations were especially influential in their arguments for using colonization as a solution for the new class of landless poor. Edward Williams in his treatise *Virginia: More Especially the South Part Thereof, Richly and Truly Valued* (1650) cited disposal of surplus population (including the indigent, debtors, prisoners, parish charges, highwaymen, orphans) among the primary objectives of American colonization. He wrote:

> The republic in its present constitution abounding with so dangerous a number of male contents, who commonly like Shrubs under high and spreading Cedars, imagine the spacious height of others to be the cause of their owne lowness, may by this means be honourably secured, and such men removing their discontents with their persons, will have a brave and ample theater to make their merits and abilities emergent, and a large field to sow and reap the fruit of all their honest industrious and public intentions.[68]

Eventually, Parliament adopted such logic as its own and officially sanctioned state solutions for dispatching large numbers of landless poor. The 1662 Settlement Act encouraged deportation of migrant subsistence workers, reiterating the state's mistrust of those who "are not restrained from going from one Parish to another and therefore doe endeavor to settle themselves in those Parishes where there is the best Stocke the largest Commons or Wastes to build Cottages and the most Woods for them to burn and destroy and when they have consumed it then to another Parish and att last become Rogues and Vagabonds to the great discouragem[en]t of Parishes to provide Stocks where it is lyable to be devoured by Strangers."[69] Such individuals were to be returned to their home parishes, assigned to workhouses, or designated for transportation to the English plantations and "disposed in the usual way of Servants."

Is this who we were: "shrubs under high and spreading cedars"? Witnessing the dissolution of customary ties and obligations among English people and between the people and their land. Then, displacement. Deforestation. Fouling of water. Fencing of lands. Migration. Dearth. Exposure. Vulnerability. Rootlessness. Assimilation, or criminalization. Is this how we came finally to the port cities and signed ourselves into bonded servitude?

WE WERE NOT EXCEPTIONAL when we boarded those English merchant ships, two hundred of us at a time, indenture agreements (if we were lucky) tucked inside the breasts of our canvas coats. It was no stroke of personal genius. It was not foresight. It was not luck. It was the massive impersonal forces of history, the violent dislocations of economic modernization and war, that made millions of common people aliens in our own European and African homelands and pushed us across the water from the eastern rim of the Atlantic to the west. Nearly three-quarters of us who came to British North America during its first two centuries came in some state of unfreedom: whether as slaves, indentured servants, convicts, or redemptioners.[70] About five hundred thousand English men and women—a population twice the size of London in 1600—left England during the seventeenth century. Four hundred thousand migrated to the British North American colonies:[71] 210,000 to the Caribbean, 130,000 to the Chesapeake, 24,000 to the Middle Colonies, 21,000 to New England. Contemporary historians emphasize the tremendous scale of the outmigration from England. "By premodern standards," writes James Horn, "emigration was massive. . . . The huge flow of people who moved to America in this period can be explained only in terms of the transferal of a massive labor force."[72] Nicholas Canny writes that its enormous scale "suggests that the seventeenth-century migration was one of desperation."[73] Emigration rates averaged twenty thousand a decade in the 1630s and 1640s and peaked at twenty-five thousand a decade between 1650 and 1690 before dropping to just ten thousand a decade in the 1690s and 1700s.[74] In 1635, described by historian Allison Games as the largest recorded "embarkation from one port for any single year in the colonial period," more than 7,500 people left London—about 2 percent of the city's population.[75] A few seventeenth-century commentators noted the population loss. In 1674, economist Carew Reynell (1636–90) mourned the population decline due to war, plague, and outmigration: "Our people were consumed mightily in these late years, some three hundred thousand were killed in these last Civil Wars; and about two hundred thousand more have been wasted in repeopling Ireland; and two hundred thousand lost in the great sickness, and as many more gone to plantations."[76]

Bound laborers constituted about 60 percent of seventeenth-century English migration to mainland British North America and 70–85 percent of seventeenth-century English migrants to the Chesapeake.[77] Those who left in the seventeenth century—my ancestors and those who traveled with them—were typically young laboring men from disrupted rural areas and exhausted small industrial towns. They had traveled between ten and forty miles to port cities like London and Bristol and worked there for a few years before embarking for the Chesapeake. Those who emigrated before 1660 tended to describe themselves as farm laborers, while those who emigrated in the 1680s and later claimed some artisanal or industrial work experience.[78] Historian Allan Kulikoff offers a vivid description of their social state of alienation:

> They received neither subsistence nor succor from their families. Youths who shipped out as servants had left home years before to find work in farming or industry. Most had lived in depressed cloth villages where their families scraped by on the wasteland. As youths they had moved to London, Bristol, or Liverpool. Usually illiterate, they maintained sporadic contact with their families. Many were orphans, tenuously tied to siblings and other kin. Those without indentures were so young that they may have been abandoned by their families. Without families, they could expect no inheritance; without an inheritance, they could not marry.[79]

In England's transition from subsistence to modern export economy, these were the young men (and women) whose lives were deemed disposable.

Others left under even worse circumstances. From 1607, when the first runaway apprentice was "sent to Virginia" for stealing his master's goods, thousands of convicted felons—poor people convicted of theft and other poor people's crimes—were sentenced to "transportation" before the colonies forbade the practice in 1670.[80] Impoverished and orphaned children too were transported to Virginia, the first documented shipments being in 1618 and 1619, when the city of London raised funds to transport hundreds; in 1627, one correspondent wrote that "there are many ships now going to Virginia, and with them some 1400 or 1500 children, which they have gathered up in diverse places."[81] The term "kidnapping" has its origins in this historical moment, in the practice of seizing unwitting poor people and putting them on ships for the Americas. So too were the poor the objects of being "spirited away," a term used to describe the practice of luring bondservants on board Virginia-bound ships with food, drink, tobacco, and false promises.[82] Virginia promoter William Bullock wrote that agents known as "spirits" "take up all the idle, lazie, simple people they can intice, such as have professed idlenesse, and will rather beg than work; who are perswaded by these Spirits, they shall goe into a place where food shall drop into their mouthes: and being thus deluded, they take courage, and are transported."[83] The scene of the "cook's house," where spirited souls and others awaiting transportation were held until purchase, was described by author William Head (1637–86) in his protonovel *The English Rogue* (1666):

> He brought me into a Room where half a score were all taking Tobacco: the place was so narrow wherein they were, that they had no more space left, than what was for the standing of a small table. Methought their mouths together resembled a stack of Chimneys, being in a manner totally obscured by the smoak that came from them; for there was little discernable but smoak, and the glowing coals of their pipes. . . . Alas poor Sheep, they ne're considered where they were going, it was enough for them to be freed from a seven years Apprenticeship, under the Tyranny of a rigid master . . . and not weighing the slavery they must undergo for five years, amongst Brutes in foreign parts, little inferior to that which they suffer who are Gally-slaves. There was little discourse amongst them, but of the pleasantness of the soyl of that Continent we were designed for (out of a design to make us swallow their gilded Pills of Ruine).[84]

So grew the common perception in London and other port towns that recruiters operated primarily through a combination of deceit and entrapment.[85] In response to public outcry, Parliament soon took nominal measures to police and regulate the Virginia trade. In 1645, Parliament ordered law officers to more vigilantly pursue spirits, kidnappers, and child traffickers. Ships sailing down the Thames bearing large human cargoes were often stopped for inspection at Gravesend. From the mid-1640s, customs houses were also ordered to keep records on transportees. A Bristol city ordinance of 1654 declared

> Whereas many complaints have beene oftentimes made to the Maior and Alderman of the Inveigling, purloining, carrying and Stealing away Boyes Maides and other persons and transporting them beyond Seas and there selling or otherwise disposeing them for private gaine and proffitt and it being a crime of much villany to have children and others in such a Barbarous and wicked manner to be soe carried away Stollen and Sold without any knowledge or notice of the parents or others that have the care and oversight of them for the better preventing of such mischeifes for time to come: It is this day agreed ordained and enacted by the Maior Aldermaen

> and Comon Councell in Comon Councell assembled that all Boyes Maides and other persons which for the future shall be transported beyond the Seas as servants, Shall before their going a-Ship board have their Covenants or Indentures of service and apprentiship inrolled in their Tolzey booke as other Indentures of apprentiship are and have used to bee, and that noe Master or other officer wtsoever of any Ship or vessel shall (before such inrolmet be made) receive into his or their Ship or vessel or therein permit to be transported beyond the Seas such Boyes Maides or other persons as aforesaid.[86]

In response to the public outcry and new pressures from Parliament and local governments, transport agents developed standard, mass-printed contracts setting forth in general terms the length of indenture and freedom dues promised according to the "custom of the country." In England, indentures customarily lasted one year; in Virginia, seven. In exchange for seven years of life, the Virginia Company, for its part, pledged to place servants "as tenants upon the public land with best conditions, including a house, stock of corn and cattle, and half the profits."[87] Neither the forms nor the customs of the country provided opportunity for individual negotiation.

What was migration like for my English ancestors? Passage cost about five to ten pounds: at least half of what a laborer might earn in a year's time, while the agents who paid the price of passage could turn around and sell indentured servants at a profit ranging from two to twenty pounds.[88] Those who financed their passage by indenture might receive a basic outfit from one of the plantation companies of cloth and canvas suits, shoes, shirts, bed, bolster, rug, and blankets.[89] And before leaving English shores, indentured servants had to take an oath of supremacy acknowledging Charles I as head of the Church of England and an oath of allegiance to the king.[90] Ships newly emptied of their cargoes of American tobacco and sugar received as many as two hundred servants at a time for the ten-week return trip to North America. Indentured servants were organized into mess groups of six and allowed freedom of movement, while transported felons were kept below deck and in chains, sometimes collared and padlocked.[91] Storms, seasickness, and sickness, lice, sores, vomit, and stench compounded the misery of the voyage. Wrote one contemporary observer of the scene below decks: "There was some sleeping, some spewing, some daming, some Blasting their leggs and thighs, some their liver, lungs, lights and eyes, And for to make the scene the odder, some curs'd Father, Mother, Sister, and Brother."[92]

In the few firsthand accounts of Virginia life left by indentured servants (most of whom, historians believe, were functionally illiterate) we find that young men and women had no reason to stop cursing and complaining to their English relatives after they arrived. Richard Frethorne wrote to his parents in 1623 bewailing the dearth that defined his servant existence: no food but "peas," "loblollie (that is, water gruel)," and "a mouthful of bread"; nowhere to sleep or take refuge but on the boat itself. Frethorne's superiors marveled that his family had willingly sold him away under indentures. "People cry out day and night—Oh! That they were in England without their limbs and would not care to lose any limb to be in England again, yea, though they beg from door to door," Frethorne wrote. "And I have nothing to comfort me, nor is there nothing to be gotten here but sickness and death."[93] One-quarter to one-half of new arrivals to the Chesapeake died in one year due to the rigors of their "seasoning" or to diseases like dysentery, typhoid, and malaria.[94] Those who survived, even those who were not servants, encountered, according to historian James Horn, a "substantially lower standard of living" in Virginia: "During the second half of the century," Horn writes, "most planters after years of hard work had a standard of living little different from the lowest levels of society in England."[95] Although the variety of foods available to servants in Virginia eventually improved to include corn, wildlands fruits, and wild game, the fifty-acre plots, clothing, and tools promised indentured labor rarely materialized. About 7 percent of freed servants were able to claim the fifty acres often promised them.[96] Even those who received nominal title to lands did not have the capital necessary to survey, patent, clear, plant, or build on it. Instead, Horn continues, they "tended either to lease land or to take up laboring until they had sufficient money to buy a small holding."[97] Some maintained themselves as they once had in England in small cottages with garden plots on the margins of lands where they labored.[98] Some packed up and moved westward and southward in search of land, flowing into the upcountry Carolinas, as my Brooks ancestors did. Even those who made their way to tracts of public land newly expropriated from the indigenous peoples of Virginia and the Carolinas, reported one contemporary observer, were "neither able to sustain themselves nor to discharge their moiety, and so dejected with their scarce provisions . . . most give themselves over and die of melancholy."[99] Dramatic though this account of fatal melancholy seems, colonial records show that even those who survived their first brutal years of seasoning might expect to live only into their early forties: life expectancy in Virginia was lower than anywhere in England excepting London itself.[100] "For every ex-servant who made it into the ranks of the middling or upper classes," historian James Horn writes, "tens of others, who left barely a trace in the records, died in poverty and obscurity."[101]

As difficult as the rigors of their original seasons in Virginia may have been, more significant to the story of why we left is the way migration from England—considered in its proper context and scale—impacted how my ancestors thought of themselves and others in this newly modernizing world. Perhaps it is not too frivolous to imagine that they had their reasons for being melancholic—reasons beyond indentured servitude, false economic promises, and high fatality rates. Certainly there was the brutality of Anglo-indigenous conflicts incurred by the English expropriation of indigenous lands. "We live in fear of the enemy every hour," wrote Richard Frethorne to his parents. "We lie even in their teeth."[102] Perhaps they were shocked and unsettled by unfamiliar landscapes, the dense and unbounded forests of eastern North America, trees far taller than England's oaks, terrain unbounded by hedgerow or enclosure.[103] And what did these young displaced workers know about the plantation labor they were bound to undertake in North America; what did they know of tobacco, indigo, cotton, or corn?[104] Plantation labor culture too was radically different in many respects from the lives they had known in England. With ancient customary relationships between gentry and commoner dissolved, kin networks dispersed, working in geographically disparate and small plantation settlements, laboring under longer terms of indenture, in an unfamiliar and difficult place, my ancestors experienced the atomizing anonymity of the modern world. Historians have emphasized the impacts of this anonymity and a newly brutal colonial culture on the emerging social order of Virginia. "Distance from the constraints of a densely settled parish, a community where a servant had kin, and distance from the normal context in which agricultural servants labored under one-year contracts, not long-term indentures that could be bought or sold, together contributed to new world excesses," explains

Alison Games. "Masters disciplined servants with little regard for traditional modes of control, which, though physically violent, were kept in check by mitigating forces."[105] These conditions were not simply outlived by servants who survived, or outgrown by the few who successfully attained landowning status; they utterly shaped the American culture that would follow. As T. H. Breen and Stephen Innes write, Virginia's small planters

> were persons who learned about proper forms of behavior, about acceptable patterns of human relations, about exploitation and competition, about "careless resolute Blowes"; and embittering frustration while they were servants. The culture of these people was not an English culture neatly transferred to America and sustained there through a period of dependence and vulnerability. Rather, their culture was a peculiar hybrid, part English, part Virginian, the unique creation of indenture servitude and a raw plantation economy. One would not expect that young people schooled in this environment developed a deep sense of compassion for other men and women. They learned as adolescents to survive as best they could.[106]

Survive the best you can. Adjust to the dizzying anonymity, the head-aching strangeness, the back-scarring violence of this new world. And learn well the rules of the emerging world-economic order. Opportunity: divide, bind, bound, fence, strip, extract surplus, dispose, move on, forget. Do unto others as has been done unto you. Get over if you can. And there may be land for you yet. Over the next ridge. Or the next. Somewhere down the line.

IN ALL OF THIS, we were not exceptional: none of us, and not the continent to which we emigrated. The circumstances that made us leave were bigger than our understandings, bigger than the day-to-day survival tactics we like to remember as insightful and enterprising choices, bigger than whatever words we bantered about or bit down on as we boarded our ships or abandoned our plantation cottages to look for that lost piece of land somewhere over the next set of hills. *Opportunity:* this word, a thin and preciously simple handle on our circumstances. We were, after all, just peasants caught up in great waves of global-economic modernization that would decisively remake the world, waves that began with the internal colonization of Europe and expanded outward through the colonization of the rest of the globe. My Brooks ancestors lived through what Eric Hobsbawm called a "general crisis," "the last phase of the general transition from a feudal to a capitalistic economy."[107] British historian A. L. Beier has characterized theirs as a time of "profound social dislocations—a huge and growing poverty problem, disastrous economic and demographic shifts and massive migration."[108] Immanuel Wallerstein described it as the rise of a "capitalist world economy" that created economic zones of "core" and "periphery" that would redefine the global map.[109] Karl Polanyi characterized parallel shifts as a "great transformation": "The fabric of society was being disrupted; desolate villages and the ruins of human dwellings testified to the fierceness with which the revolution raged, endangering the defenses of the country, wasting its towns, decimating its population, turning its overburdened soil into dust, harassing its people, and turning them from decent husbandmen into a mob of beggars and thieves."[110] The economic modernization of the world began with the alienation of land from people and people from land. Customary protections and relationships to the land—the source of subsistence—dissolved under the feet of the English peasantry. Surplused and disposable English men and women like my Brooks ancestors were effectively removed from our homelands in the core and redistributed to the imperial periphery to construct through our labor the modern identity of England as a bureaucratic merchant-imperial nation-state. We were among the first peoples of the world to experience the alienating and anonymizing consequences of modernity, captured by Thomas Hobbes in *Leviathan* (1651): "The liberty of the Commonwealth... is the same with that which every man then should have, if there were no civil laws nor Commonwealth at all. And the effects of it also be the same. For as amongst masterless men, there is perpetual war of every man against his neighbour; no inheritance to transmit to the son, nor to expect from the father; no propriety of goods or lands; no security; but a full and absolute liberty in every particular man."[111] We were the first, but we would not be the last.

To read some of the most popular histories of Anglo-American colonial migration, one might not believe that my ancestors moved in a world free of such profoundly transformative and jarring forces. For example, David Hackett Fischer's *Albion's Seed* (1989) offers a neat account of the transference of British "folkways" onto American regional cultures in the colonial period that stresses above all else the continuity of the Anglo-American colonial experience. Other historians have challenged and rejected Fischer's account as nostalgic. "No identifiable English provincial culture established itself in, or exerted extensive influence on, Virginia and Maryland society," writes James Horn, instead characterizing colonial Anglo-American culture as one defined by "disjunction," "improvisation," and "accommodation."[112] Alison Games also argues that a profound "element of disjunction" characterized colonial Anglo-American experience and contributed mightily to the shaping of the Atlantic world.[113] The disjunctions and dislocations of the emerging modern Atlantic world in turn contributed to the shaping, as Patricia Fumerton has written, of newly "unsettled" modes of being: "a new notion of 'low' subjectivity that was truly spacious, that is, in every sense mobile. In essence, this unfixed, or what might be better termed 'unsettled,' subject was at all times an apprentice or journeyman. Shifting from place to place, relationship to relationship, and job to job, such a subject apprenticed in a range of different identities, or 'role speculations,' without ever attaining the 'freedom' of a whole and stable identity."[114]

How did my ancestors and other early Anglo-American peasant colonists understand themselves and their historic moment? What grasp did they have on their place in these massive locations? What narratives did they tell themselves about their place in these times? Ascertaining peasant consciousness presents us with some problems now familiar to anyone who works in colonial historiography: the problems of tracking the lives and thoughts of those who did not write through the archives of a society that privileges writing. Most of the written records that do survive tell us more about the ways the gentry viewed and tried to manage English and Anglo-American peasantry than they do about the peasantry themselves.

During times of dearth in late sixteenth- and early seventeenth-century England, moralists in the government and in the church generated their own narratives blaming laziness, godlessness, or alcohol consumption by the poor. As Christopher Hill wrote, "That 'the greatest multitude' was 'for the most part always wicked' was accepted by all parties in the church."[115] From their pulpits, Anglican leaders instructed the worthy poor to face dearth with long-suffering quietude and pressed for stronger social controls. In 1596, Anglican pastors in the dioceses of Canterbury and York were charged with preaching so that "the people would be also taught to indure this scarcity with patience, and to beware how they give care to any perswaycons or practysis of the discontented and ydle braynes to move them to repyne or swerve from the humble dutyes of good subjectes."[116] Seventeenth-century Puritan nonconformists (most of them middle class) developed a discourse that stressed the dignity of work.[117] Secular voices, meanwhile, characterized the English peasantry in almost ethnographic terms. Coal miners, cloth workers, and forest dwellers were described as "lewd," "scums and dregs," "rude," "uncouth," "barbarous," and "lawless."[118] Bureaucratic documents depicted the English peasant-proletariat as a liability to England. In his census of 1688, Gregory King estimated that of 5,500,520 residents of the kingdom, 2,795,000 "common seamen," "labouring people and out servants," "cottagers and paupers," "common soldiers," and "vagrants" were making less than they expended and were therefore "decreasing the wealth of the kingdom."[119]

Those who emigrated for the Americas were characterized as a species of the vicious poor. In Bristol, one of the largest points of embarkation for North America, the mayor attributed the family-rending dislocations of the new economic order to the moral failures of poor subsistence migrants and emigrants:

> Among those who repair to Bristol from all parts to be transported for servants to His Majesty's plantations beyond seas, some are husbands that have forsaken their wives, others wives who have abandoned their husbands; some are children and apprentices run away from their parents and masters; oftentimes unwary and credulous persons have been tempted on board by man-stealers, and many that have been pursued by hue-and-cry for robberies, burglaries or breaking prison, do thereby escape the prosecution of laws and justice.[120]

The Commission for Foreign Plantations alerted London port officials in 1634 that many of the emigrants were people of "idle and refractory humours, whose only end is to live as much as they can without the reach of authority."[121] In his colonial promotional tract *Virginia Impartially Examined* (1649), William Bullock described them as "idle, lazie, simple people . . . such as have professed idlenesses, and will rather beg then work," while Josiah Child's *A New Discourse of Trade* (1698) characterized early English emigrants to Virginia and Barbados as "a sort of loose vagrant People, vicious and destitute of means to live at home, (being either unfit for labour, or such as could find none to employ themselves about, or had so mis-behaved themselves by Whoreing, Thieving, or other Debauchery, that none would set them to work)." Their only alternatives to emigration, Child continued, were to "be hanged or starved, or dyed untimely of some of those miserable diseases, that proceed from want and Vice, or else have sold themselves for Soldiers."[122]

Whereas moralistic narratives pinned poverty on the failings of the poor, popular narratives registered economic restructuring as a process with broad and destructive consequences. Especially when set against the backdrop of the Thirty Years War on the European continent, the public trial and beheading of the king, and massive loss of life during the English Civil War, popular language of the time reflected a consciousness of widespread "troubles" that could be captured only in religious language or in the language of elemental disturbances—tumults, earthquakes, torrents, disasters, and shipwrecks.[123] Economic want or dearth was understood as symptomatic of growing tensions within and unravelings of the customary social order. As historians John Walter and Keith Wrightson explain: "The primacy of local need over individual profit, the obligations of neighbourliness and the traditional interpretation of customary rights were being increasingly denied by a significant element in local society. To deny such obligations in conditions of dearth . . . was to risk making manifest the hostilities latent within a situation of accelerating social and economic differentiation."[124] As consciousness of ongoing dearth as a product of economic restructuring grew, the poor increasingly rejected narratives that naturalized poverty and began to generate ways of understanding and reacting to their circumstances that focused on the wrongdoing of men who profited from the impoverishment of others.[125]

Antienclosure and food riots offered a powerful counternarrative to state- and church-sanctioned messages about the nature of want and the responsibility of the poor to be good subjects. In their tactics, participants in food riots, for example, articulated a clear view of dearth as the result of merchants opportunistically redirecting food away from local communities toward markets. In March 1629, 140 women led by a butcher's wife named Anne Carter forcibly boarded grain barges taking grain away to Flemish merchants and filled their aprons and caps with grain. One of the rioters, Dorothy Berry, said that she was propelled to action by "The Crie of the Country and hir owne want."[126] That "crie" sometimes found literary form in the custom of writing seditious rhymes known as "libels." One libel discovered in November 1630 at Wye read:

> The corn is so dear,
> I doubt many will starve this year;
> If you see not to this,
> Some of you will speed amiss;
> Our souls they are dear
> For our bodies have some care
> Before we arise
> Less will suffice.
> Note. The poor there is more
> Than goes from door to door
> You that are set in place
> See that your profession you do not disgrace;
> Will you know my name?
> You must be wise in the same
> A.+C.B.E.D.G.F.I.H.L.K.N.M.[127]

Even more articulate cries came from organized political movements like the Diggers, led by Gerrard Winstanley (1609–76). Winstanley, who at twenty-one years old moved from the rural parish of Lancashire to London, worked first as a tailor, then lost his business and returned to work as a cowherd, led the True Levellers in 1649 as they stormed St. George's Hill in Surrey, to plow, manure, and sow corn there, pledging to "eat our bread together by the sweat of our brows." It was, according to Christopher Hill, the first chapter in what "was intended to be the first stage in a sort of general strike against wage-labour."[128] Fabricating a biblical creation narrative of the capitalist transformation, Winstanley writing in *The True Levellers Standard Advanced* (1649) depicted the destruction of commons and land tenure and the advantage taking of owning classes over peasantry and proletariat as the betrayal of flesh against spirit, the fall from paradise, the murder of Abel by Cain, the dominion of Esau over Jacob. He wrote:

> So long as we, or any other, doth own the Earth to be the peculiar Interest of Lords and Landlords, and not common to others as well

> as them, we own the Curse, and holds the Creation under bondage; and so long as we or any other doth own Landlords and Tennants, for one to call the Land his, or another to hire it of him, or for one to give hire, and for another to work for hire; this is to dishonour the work of Creation; as if the righteous Creator should have respect to persons, and therefore made the Earth for some, and not for all: And so long as we, or any other maintain this Civil Propriety, we consent still to hold the Creation down under that bondage it groans under, and so we should hinder the work of Restoration, and sin against Light that is given into us, and so through fear of the flesh man, lose our peace. And that this Civil Propriety is the Curse, is manifest thus, Those that Buy and Sell Land, and are landlords, have got it either by Oppression, or Murther, or Theft; and all landlords lives in the breach of the Seventh and Eighth Commandments, Thou shalt not steal, nor kill.[129]

Winstanley was speaking a centuries-old, radically egalitarian strain of thought that viewed the emergence of owning classes as a betrayal, a view held by the fourteenth-century Lollards that also fueled the antinobility and antigentry popular violence that fed off the first English Civil War. The notion that an ancient Anglo-Saxon freedom had been lost with the establishment of nobility and gentry after the Norman Conquest and continued with the transition from feudalism to mercantile capitalism was articulate among those of the laboring classes who rose against the Crown, despite the fact that Cromwell categorically excluded these classes from the franchise.[130]

Populist narratives articulated in riots, libels, and political tracts suggest a consciousness among the peasant-proletariat of larger economic tensions and dislocations as well as the dissolution of customary relationships that had held the people to the land and to one another through customary obligations. The transition from subsistence to mercantile economy was viewed by the peasant-proletariat as a betrayal by the gentry on the order of Cain and Abel. Is it possible that a simple ten-week ocean crossing would have cleansed my Brooks ancestors (as if by saltwater baptism) of this sense of betrayal or bitterness? Or did something of that sense travel on in time, sharpened perhaps by dislocations and displacements further on down the road?

CHAPTER TWO

Murder the Brother Who Killed the Tree

Fratricide and the Story of Deforestation

In 1937, Library of Congress folklorist Alan Lomax brought his *School of the Air* radio program to the town of Galax in the Blue Ridge Mountains of southwestern Virginia. Galax, named after an evergreen Appalachian plant used by traditional Anglo-American and Cherokee doctors as a tonic and poultice, was already famous as a stronghold for traditional string or "old-time" music. Among the greatest expositors of that old-time tradition was the Crockett Ward family.

Born in 1873 in Grayson County, Virginia, Crockett Ward—who later styled himself Davy Crockett Ward, in honor of the American folk hero—descended from an Anglo-American family with Cherokee relations and ancestral roots in seventeenth-century Virginia.[1] The son of Enoch and Rosy (or Rosamond) Carrico Ward, Crockett grew up on Grayson County's Buck Mountain, surrounded by Ward family relatives who taught him to play fiddle. He married Lina Ward; the couple had five children. In 1921, seeking a more reliable source of livelihood, the Wards moved down from the mountain thirty miles to Ballard Creek, Virginia, near Galax, where some family members took work in the textile factories and mills. There, together with his brother Wade Ward of nearby Peachbottom Creek (banjo), neighbor Eck (or Alec) Dunford (fiddle), son Curren Ward (autoharp), son Sampson Ward (banjo), son Fields Ward (guitar and vocal), and Ernest Stoneman (guitar and harmonica), Davy Crockett Ward formed what would become a revered outfit in old-time music. His Buck Mountain Band made a record for the Okeh Phonograph Company in Winston-Salem in

1927.[2] In the 1930s, the band changed its name to The Bogtrotters, on suggestion from the family doctor W. P. Davis (himself an autoharp player), after the muddy road to the family home where so many cars bogged down.

When Alan Lomax came to Galax, Davy Crockett Ward and his Bogtrotters, wearing their customary dark blue dungarees, recorded a number of songs to contribute to Lomax's radio program and his archive of American folksong. And when her husband and sons finished singing, Mrs. Lina Crockett Ward—wearing a velvet-collared black Sunday dress, a string of pearls, and round spectacles, her gray hair pulled back in a bun—took her turn at the microphone. No fiddle or banjo or autoharp backed her. It was just Lina's lone, quavering voice against the mountain air:

How come that blood all over your coat?
My son come tell unto me.
It is the blood of my galligary hound
That hunt the deer with me.
That galligary hound blood was never so red
My son come tell unto me.
It is the blood of my galligary hawk
That flies across the field.
That galligary hawk's blood was never so red
My son come tell unto me.
It is the blood of that galligary mare
I used to ride so gay.
That galligary mare's blood was never so red
My son come tell unto me.
It is the blood of my younger brother
That used to go with me.
What'd you and him fall out about?
My son come tell unto me.
Bout cutting down yon hazelnut tree
What caused it for to be.
What will you do when your daddy comes home?
My son come tell unto me.
I'll set my foot in yonder ship
I'll sail across the sea.
What'll you do with your pretty little wife?
My son come tell unto me.

She'll set her foot in yonder ship
And sail across the sea.
    What'll you do with your children three?
My son come tell unto me.
I'll leave them here along with you
To bear your company.
    When you coming back?
My son come tell unto me.
When the sun and the moon set in the North Hills
I'm sure that will never be.[3]

The song Lina Ward sang for Alan Lomax is "Edward," one of the most venerated ballads in the Anglo-American tradition. With its roots in ancient sagas and sources in English and Scottish folk tradition, "Edward" voices a dialogue between a mother and her oldest son that leads finally to a grisly revelation: the son has killed his younger brother and flees across the ocean, abandoning his own children for a self-imposed exile of shame. What precipitated this fratricide? What initiated this sequence of murder, flight, and abandonment? The younger brother's destruction of a young tree. As I listen to the recording, I am struck by Ward's bright, almost warbling soprano, and the upbeat tone and driving rhythms of her tune. Together, voice and tune push against and drive through the dark matter of the lyrics. No hauntedness, no sentimentality. What I hear is a matter-of-factness that indulges no emotional excess.

The basic narrative pattern that persists across hundreds of variants of the ballad "Edward" documented in America is this: a mother, two brothers, a murder, and a tree. In some versions, as in the one sung by Lina Ward and also by Ora Keene Kowerman, of Russell Fork, Virginia in 1932, the tree is identified as a hazelnut. In others, for example, as sung by Meg Shook in Clyde, North Carolina, in 1917, it is a "holly bush." But it is always a young tree—even a "bush / that might have made a tree," as T. Hurke of Silsbee, Texas, put it in 1950.[4] Other versions of the ballad add dimension to the Anglo-peasant world "Edward" depicts. When famed Anglo-American ballad singer Maud Long, who learned the song from her mother, Jane Gentry of Hot Springs, North Carolina, was brought by Lomax to record in Washington, D.C., in 1947, she had Edward describing his murdered brother as one who "hoed the corn for me."[5] More detail emerges in the version sung by

Emma Hays Dusenbury of Mena, Arkansas, a former cottonpicker and small farmer, who recorded "Edward" for Alan Lomax during a marathon two-day ballad-recording session on July 28, 1936.[6] Dusenbury, who according to Lomax knew more traditional ballads than any other singer he had encountered, tells of the "old gray horse . . . that plowed my corn for me" and the "old gray hound . . . that run the deer for me" and the "old gray sow . . . that eat the corn for me." Her fine version of Edward depicts a peasant household once firmly pinioned in the subsistence economies and ecologies of British life but then totally upended by a sequence of events tracing back to an arboricide and a fratricide.

Tales of fratricide are staples of the ballad tradition. They underscore the sanctity of loyal fraternal relationships and their importance to the stability of traditional societies. Still, no matter how familiar its basic plotline, scholars have puzzled over "Edward," striving especially to understand how the cutting of a tree could motivate one brother to murder another. This has led to metaphorical readings of the tree, including the inference that "Edward" is really a narrative about incest.

But what if sometimes a tree really is a tree? For centuries, it has been customary to think that the work of interpretation requires that we look through the surface features of a text and strive to unveil its hidden meanings. It is an approach as old as the idea of allegory and an idea articulated as a literary-critical practice since Dante at least. But it has gained power and political currency in recent decades as contemporary literary scholars have pursued interpretation as a way to disclose political ideas embedded in culture. This tradition of "symptomatic reading," as it is sometimes called, has its roots in the psychoanalysis of Sigmund Freud, the Marxist poststructuralism of Louis Althusser, and, most importantly, the work of literary critic Fredric Jameson. But we are now beginning to reexamine both the methodological dominance of symptomatic reading and the potential virtues of surface reading: reading practices that interrogate the inherited opposition between a text's surfaces and its deeper meanings. As Stephen Best and Sharon Marcus put it, "We take surface to mean what is evident, perceptible, apprehensible in texts; what is neither hidden nor hiding. . . . A surface is what insists on being looked at rather than what we must train ourselves to see through."[7] Surface readings adopt a greater sense of deference toward their textual objects, taking the direction of their analyses from the features of the texts themselves. Sometimes, as Best and Marcus suggest, political content is not hidden in a text: it is visible, especially in writings that plainly document the violence of their times or present us, as so many works from our current moment do, with clear images of catastrophic abandonment, destruction, and torture.

What if images of catastrophic abandonment and violence have always been visible in the literature that documents colonization? And what if we approach ballad texts in the same way we read *corridos* and sorrow songs, as literary masterpieces that both appeal to timeless structures of human feeling but also offer cogent commentary on their own historical moments? Or, to put it more simply, what if we take "Edward" at its word? Perhaps there are new insights to be gleaned from appreciating the tree as a historic story element that "insists on being looked at rather than . . . see[n] through." After all, it is not uncommon for oral-traditional cultures to mobilize significant elements of their ecological environments, not necessarily because they carry deeper symptomatic meaning but because they orient individuals to their physical environments and offer commentaries crucial to survival and good stewardship.[8] Every traditional story is in some respects a story about the land. The plants and animals of "Edward"—deer, hounds, hawks, corn (the term was used in early modern England to refer to wheat), hogs, hazelnut, and holly—connect its Anglo-American singers to the subsistence ecologies and economies of rural England.

Even more significant it seems is that the plotline of "Edward" memorializes the betrayal and abandonment of those physical and social environments. As Sean Wilentz and Greil Marcus have written of the American murder ballad, "No matter what form the ballad takes, more than one life is always at stake."[9] "Edward" tells the story of three intertwined deaths: the death of a tree, the death by murder of the younger brother who killed the tree, and the social death by emigration of the older brother responsible for the crime. The ballad—a centuries-old masterpiece of the Anglo-American folk-traditional canon—points to the role of environmental destruction, particularly deforestation, in the displacement and outmigration of hundreds of thousands of peasant English, among them the ancestors of Davy Crockett and Lina Ward, and my Brooks ancestors as well. For if we listen to Lina Ward's voice and take her words as a path into Anglo-American peasant history, we may discover that damaged environments and unraveling social relations are among the reasons why we left.

IT IS DIFFICULT to locate a reliable genealogy of the ballad we now call "Edward," for the tale of fratricide and exile it tells is an ancient element of Anglo-Nordic culture. Folklore scholars have located the earliest known record of the ballad in circulation in Sweden in 1640, with other versions known to be in oral circulation in Scotland and England in the seventeenth and eighteenth centuries, making the crossing to North America with early English and Scots-Irish peasant migrants.

One of the first print snapshots we have of this stream of oral tradition is the appearance of "Edward" in print in the *Reliques of Ancient English Poetry* (1765), a three-volume collection of 183 ballads developed by the Anglican bishop Thomas Percy. Percy himself stressed the antiquity of the collected ballads, a claim that greatly influenced those who studied and treasured *Reliques,* including Samuel Taylor Coleridge and William Wordsworth. Consequently, Percy's *Reliques,* along with James Macpherson's *Ossian* (1765), has been credited as a source of inspiration for the Romanticist movement, the general turn of English literature from a polite to an imaginative orientation, and the advent of ethnography.[10] Notwithstanding its ancient pretensions, Percy's collection was a modern assemblage of ballad texts (many less than one hundred years old) culled from oral, manuscript, and print sources including the Samuel Pepys broadside ballad collection, shaped with input from literary figures like Samuel Johnson, James Boswell, and William Shenstone, and emended and stylized by Percy himself, a move for which he was criticized by British antiquarians.[11] The ballad "Edward" was sent to Percy by Sir David Dalrymple, Lord Hailes (1726–92), a Scottish jurist and historian. It appeared in the 1765 *Reliques* as follows:

Quhy dois zour brand sae drop wi' bluid,
Edward, Edward?
Quhy dois zour brand sae drop wi' bluid?
And quhy sae sad gang zee, O?
O, I hae killed my hauke sae guide,
Mither, mither:
O, I hae killed my hauke sae guide,
And I had nae mair bot hee, O.
Zour haukis bluid was nevir sae reid,

Edward, Edward.
Zour haukis bluid was nevir sae reid,
My deir son I tell thee, O.
O, I hae killed my reid-roan steid,
Mither, Mither:
O, I hae killed my reid-roan steid,
That erst was sae fair and free, O.
Zour steid was auld, and ze hae gat mair,
Edward, Edward:
Zour steid was auld, and ze hae gat mair,
Sum other dule ze drie, O.
O, I hae killed my fadir deir,
Mither, mither:
O, I hae killed my fadir deir,
Alas! and wae is mee, O!
And quahatten penance wul ze drie for that,
Edward, Edward?
And quahatten penance wul ze drie for that?
My deir son, now tell mee, O.
Ile set my feit in zonder boat,
Mither, mither:
Ile set my feit in zonder boat,
And I'e fare ovir the sea, O.
And quhat wul ze doe wi' zour towirs and zour ha',
Edward, Edward?
And quhat wul ze doe wi' zour towirs and zour ha',
That were sae fair to see, O?
Ile let thame stand til they doun fa',
Mither, mither:
Ile let theame stand till they doun fa',
For here nevir mair maun I bee, O.
And quhat wul ze leive to zour bairns and zour wife,
Edward, Edward?
And quhat wul ze leive to zour bairms and zour wife,
Quhan ze gang ovir the sea, O?
The warldis room, let thame beg thrae life,
Mither, mither:
The warldis room, let thame beg thrae life,
For thame nevir mair wul I see, O.
And quhat wul ze leive to zour ain mither deir,
Edward, Edward:

And quhat wul ze leive to zour ain mither deir,
My deir son, now tell mee, O.
The curse of hell frae me fall ze beir,
Mither, mither:
The curse of hell frae me fall ze beir,
Sic counseils ze gave to me, O.[12]

Percy made several innovations to the ballad, among them its highly stylized orthographic rendering of Scotch-Gaelic dialect and the resignification of the murder as a patricide rather than a fratricide. It seems he made these changes to foreground a father-mother-son triangle and thus vest "Edward" with an even more dramatic Oedipal quality. But because Percy's is the only documented version of "Edward" to tell the story as a patricide, scholars have judged it to be a stylized divergence from rather than a reflection of existing oral tradition. And despite its popularity in England as a printed text, Percy's *Reliques* and its version of "Edward" have had no influence on the ballad's rendition in Anglo-America.[13]

The Scottish sheriff and folk researcher William Motherwell (1797–1835) also included a version of "Edward" in his *Minstrelsy Ancient and Modern* (1827). Rather than relying solely on second- and thirdhand reports of folk content, as did Percy, Motherwell conducted his own systematic field research between 1825 and 1826 in and around Renfrewshire, Scotland, in an attempt to document what he promoted as an unsullied and endangered oral tradition. It was a somewhat romantic quest, given the ready availability and broad circulation of print ballads from the late sixteenth century and the role that print materials have traditionally played as mnemonic devices for oral tradition.[14] Still, his version of the ballad as sung by Mrs. King of Kilbarchan, Scotland, has been regarded as a better representation of the Scottish "Edward" tradition:

"What bluid's that on thy coat lap?
Son Davie! Son Davie!
What bluid's that on thy coat lap?
And the truth come tell to me O."
"It is the bluid of my great hawk,
Mother lady! mother lady!

It is the bluid of my great hawk,
And the truth I hae tald to thee O."
"Hawk's bluid was ne'er sae red,
Son Davie! Son Davie!
Hawk's bluid was ne'er sae red,
And the truth come tell to me O."
"It is the bluid o' my grey hound,
Mother lady! mother lady!
It is the bluid of my grey hound,
And it wudna rin for me O."
"Hound's bluid was ne'er sae red,
Son Davie! Son Davie!
Hound's bluid was ne'er sae red,
And the truth come tell to me O."
"It is the bluid o' my brother John,
Mother lady! mother lady!
It is the bluid o' my brother John,
And the truth I hae tald to thee O."
"What about did the plea begin?
Son Davie! Son Davie!
What about did the plea begin?
And the truth come tell to me O."
"It began about the cutting o' a willow wand,
Mother lady! mother lady!
It began about the cutting o' a willow wand,
That would never hae been a tree O."
"What death dost thou desire to die?
Son Davie! Son Davie!
What death dost thou desire to die?
And the truth come tell to me O."
"I'll set my foot in a bottomless ship,
Mother lady! mother lady!
I'll set my foot in a bottomless ship,
And ye'll never see mair o' me O."
"What wilt thou leave to thy poor wife?
Son Davie! Son Davie!
What wilt thou leave to thy poor wife?
And the truth come tell to me O."
"Grief and sorrow all her life,
Mother lady! mother lady!

Grief and sorrow all her life,
And she'll never get mair frae me O."
"What wilt thou leave to thy auld son?
Son Davie! Son Davie!
What wilt thou leave to thy auld son?
And the truth come tell to me O."
"The weary warld to wander up and down,
Mother lady! mother lady!
The weary warld to wander up and down,
And he'll never get mair o' me O."
"What wilt thou leave to thy mother dear?
Son Davie! Son Davie!
What wilt thou leave to thy mother dear?
And the truth come tell to me O."
"A fire o' coals to burn her wi' hearty cheer,
Mother lady! mother lady!
A fire o' coals to burn her wi' hearty cheer,
And she'll never get mair o' me O."[15]

The Percy and the Motherwell versions of "Edward" are but print snapshots of a living, moving tradition of folk knowledge and literature that carried this ballad to North America on the great waves of seventeenth-century English and eighteenth-century Scotch-Irish peasant migration. In fact, it appears that these early migrants were among the most important keepers of the "Edward" tradition, for the song settled in among Anglo-American singers of the Appalachians, even as it virtually disappeared from the Scottish and English repertoires.[16] As it did with so many other Anglo-American ballads, the process of crossing the ocean and removing the song from a print-rich context in England—where cheaply printed broadside ballads circulated by the thousands—led to an oral condensation of the ballad and a distillation of what folklorists call its "emotional core." Prologue and concluding verses dropped away. Details of characterization dropped away. Highly stylized dialect dropped away. What remained at the core of the ballad was plot: an unstable situation and the dramatic act that led to its resolution.[17] As "Edward" crossed time and space and settled into the Anglo-American folk repertoire, it developed an economy of expression that better radiated the core emotional impact of the fratricide and its discovery.

The most distinctively Anglo-American versions of Edward sound like the one sung by Lina Ward, or this by Emma Dusenbury, in Mena, Arkansas, in 1936:

What blood, what blood on the point of your knife?
My son come tell to me.
It is the blood of my old gray horse
That plowed my corn for me.
What blood, what blood on the point of your knife?
My son come tell to me.
It is the blood of my old gray hound
That run the deer for me.
What blood, what blood on the point of your knife?
Dear son come tell to me.
It is the blood of my old gray sow
That eat the corn for me.
What blood, what blood on the point of your knife?
Dear son come tell to me.
It is the blood of my youngest brother
That fall to battle with me.
What did you and brother fight about?
Dear son come tell to me.
We fought about the holly bush
That grew by the merry tree.
What will you do when your father comes home?
Dear son come tell to me.
I'll put my boots in a bunkum boat
And sail across the sea.
What will you do with your pretty little wife?
Dear son come tell to me.
I'll put her in the bunkum boat
To sail along with me.
What will you do with your pretty little babes?
Dear son come tell to me.
I'll leave them here with you
For to bundle on your knee.[18]

This Anglo-American "Edward" differs significantly from English print versions. Gone are the stylized courtly pretenses we find in the Percy and Motherwell versions, flourishes most likely introduced by folklorists to support their romantic view that the ballad tradition was the property of a select band of medieval minstrels rather than common people. In most American versions, blood is discovered not on Edward's "sword" but rather on his "knife," as Emma Dusenbury of Arkansas sang it, or even more humbly on the sleeve of his "coat," in the version sung by Lina Ward. The cast of animal characters shifts as well from the falconer's "hawk" and the foxhunter's "grey hound" to the "gray mare" that plows the corn and the "gray sow" that eats it. Anglo-American singers maintained a version of Edward that resembled the lives of common rural people.

Gone too from most Anglo-American versions of "Edward" are the elements of Oedipal intrigue suggested by the Percy version. Edward has not murdered his father but rather his brother. Nor does he blame his mother for motivating the crime, as Percy suggested. Gone are concluding stanzas in which he levies a set of curses on his mother. In fact, the mother appears to collaborate with her son in planning his necessary escape from his father's wrath. She emerges in the Anglo-American versions of "Edward" as the sorrowful sole witness to a world-shifting act of violence and its consequence, the repository of family secrets, and the keeper of the grandchildren. For Anglo-American singers, the emotional core of "Edward" shifts to the conflict between two brothers and its destructive resolution.

Another important change in the Anglo-American versions of "Edward" is the emphasis on Edward's ocean crossing and permanent exile. Some early English, Scottish, and Scandinavian versions of "Edward"—including the Motherwell version—indicate that for his punishment Edward will take to a "bottomless boat." It was, in fact, customary in Anglo-Saxon times to punish kin-murderers by setting them to sea in boats that had been scuttled, with holes drilled into their hulls. The *Vita Offae Secundi,* the life of King Offa of Mercia (757–96) as chronicled by the thirteenth-century English Benedictine monk Matthew Paris, relates that Offa's wife Cynethryth had been punished for an unnamed crime: "in navicula armamentis carente apposita victu tenui ventis et mari exponitur condemnata," or, in translation, "having been placed in a little boat lacking oars (or tackle) with a bit of food, she was exposed to the winds and sea, condemned."[19] (Cynethryth evidently outwitted her death sentence.) The kernel of the old phrase about the "bottomless boat" is sometimes preserved in the Anglo-American traditional "Edward" with the substitution of the phrase "bunkum boat," as in Emma Dusenbury's version, "bunkum" being a nineteenth-century coinage for "nonsense," after an ill-conceived and ill-fated political speech attempted in 1820 by Lewis Walker, the congressman representing Buncombe County, North Carolina. Perhaps to the nineteenth-century singers of "Edward" the idea of a "bottomless boat" did seem like nonsense, especially since the Anglo-American tradition had shifted emphasis to the murderer's attempt to escape the wrath of his father by fleeing across the ocean, sometimes taking his wife, but always abandoning their children. This act of self-willed exile is depicted as permanent, and its permanency underscored by the deletion in many Anglo-American versions of "Edward" of concluding stanzas in which the mother asks her son if he will ever return. It is as though the ballad and its singers in moving further in time and space from their ancestral home in England underscored the permanent effects of their own outmigration.

Over thousands of miles and hundreds of years, Anglo-American singers carried "Edward," and as they did the song as a document of living memory shifted to reflect the emotional core of their own experience as the descendant of peasants who had long ago fled a no longer inhabitable home place. In their minds and in their mouths, the song became situated in the social economies of rural subsistence living, and it emphasized the intragenerational conflicts that threatened to tear those societies apart. The Anglo-American singer, voicing the role of the mother in "Edward," initiated a dialogue probing the nature of the conflict long after the fact. And yet across all the changes and in almost all the documented Anglo-American versions of "Edward," there persisted a seemingly unlikely detail: that what had motivated the original crime—a brother murdering his own brother—was the destruction of a young tree.

It is a detail that has puzzled and irritated the folklorists who studied "Edward" over the years. In his 1931 book-length study of the Edward ballad and its Scandinavian relatives, Archer Taylor wrote, "This explanation may be a fragment, a substitute for some more intelligible motive, or even the original form."[20] In 1933, Phillips Barry reported that an English informant had once told Cecil Sharp that "a little bush" was a kenning—an Anglo-Saxon trope—for a young girl and concluded that the motive was incest.[21] Following Barry, folklorist Tristram Coffin also ruled out tree-vengeance as a precipitant for the murder. Writing in 1949, Coffin inveighed:

> In the first place, as such, it is scarcely a sufficient cause for fratricide, especially ballad fratricide, unless some well-known and well-established rivalry already existed between the brothers. In the second place, it has too many of the rural characteristics of the degenerate modern tradition of the song, and too few of the courtly traits of the version that Taylor classified as the original. And most important of all . . . the "breaking of a little bush" is a kenning which refers to a little girl, according to the intrepretation of a singer known to Cecil Sharp.

Because Coffin took the romantic but then still prevalent view among folklorists that English and Anglo-American folk ballads were but the degraded remnants of medieval minstrels' repertoire rather than manifestations of a living tradition of vernacular artistry and memory, he dismissed the tree-vengeance motive because it was too "rural," and "rural" meant inauthentic. Instead, following Barry and setting "Edward" within a subgenre of ballads where fratricide is repayment for sexual betrayal, he concluded, "I think that the tree incident, as such, may justifiably be dismissed, and that the incident may be fused with the other two possible motives: sweetheart jealousy and incestuous relationship." What motivated Edward to kill his brother, the experts concluded, was incest.[22]

That's a perfectly timeless and Lévi-Straussian theme. But in the decades since, folklore scholars have moved away from modes of interpretation that aim recursively for original meanings as articulated by original *auteurs*. Instead, like other scholars of culture, they have emphasized the role everyday contexts and communities play in the construction of meaning over time. Roger Renwick in his classic *English Folk Poetry* (1980) argued that local contexts and histories create the semantic fields in which the phrases and figurative language of ballads take shape. Following Renwick, Barre Toelken emphasized the power of shared experiential and historical contexts in generating figures of speech that were capable of registering and projecting the "complexities and ambiguities of human affairs."[23] He wrote:

> Folksongs do not use a secret language of the sort Robert Graves argued for the druidic poems of Wales. Rather, folksongs participate in the local, functional, connotative systems that exist in the everyday lives of any group (for example, students, women, soldiers

> or farmers). . . . Vernacular language articulates, not explains, the shared values, assumptions, logic, and the sense of the normal and discrepant that constitutes any culture's system of meaning.[24]

Toelken suggests that we view folk songs as a sort of a living "fossil record" containing "suspended forms" that can provide rich insights into historical and contemporary cultures.[25] Adam Fox has emphasized the value of English oral literature as a repository of local history.[26] Most recently, David Atkinson has posited "primogeniture, inheritance rights, and killing in self-defence" as alternative motives for the murder based on stories told by other traditional singers of "Edward." And Atkinson concluded finally that it is impossible to reconstruct some original meaning of "Edward" because all meaning is produced "intertextually," with "scholarly commentary" participating equally in the "construction of meaning for a work of art."[27]

Approaching "Edward," then, not only as an artifact of a primeval human struggle but also potentially as a document that took shape from historical contexts and vernacular semantic fields opens the possibility for a more literal reading of the tree that other scholars have long puzzled over. What if the tree hewn down before its time was a figure familiar to Edward's seventeenth- and eighteenth-century Anglo-American peasant singers? Surely such an interpretation would complement the trajectory of the song in the Anglo-American folk tradition away from courtly pretenses and toward a firmer contextualization within the everyday economies and tensions of rural life. If we attempt to read the tree-vengeance motive as literal, to locate this figure in an actual field of historical experience, what paths might it offer into understanding the forces that animated Anglo-American outmigration, or even into the "emotional core" of the Anglo-American peasant emigrant experience? It may be possible, after all, to see the forest for the trees.

THE WORLD MY BROOKS ANCESTORS and other Anglo-American peasants left had been from primeval times a land of forests: oak, hawthorn, hazel, beech, willow, yew, and alder. Forest coverage gradually diminished during Anglo-Saxon times as population and agriculture grew, and along with it demand for charcoal and wood fuel to fire iron smelters. Still, trees far outnumbered people, and access to forest—including hunting of red deer, roe deer, boar, and hare, birding, fishing, gathering of wood, peat, grass, and clay for building and fuel, pasturing of cows and sheep, pannage of pigs, gathering of honey, wax, berries, nuts, and medicinal plants—was enjoyed equally by kings and commoners. The land may have been understood as the domain of the king and tribute including service in the king's army expected, but access to forest resources was governed primarily by ancient customs, traditions, and privileges residing with and enforced by local lords, clergy, and clans. In an Anglo-Saxon court, a peasant could defend his or her right to hunt a particular tract of land by declaring that his or her family had always hunted that land, provided of course that he or she could muster the genealogy to prove it. Locally generated seasonal regulations for preventing resource depletion were well known and observed, including the punishment by hanging of proven poachers and thieves.[28]

With the Norman Conquest in 1066 came the imposition of a royal forest system based on Norman values and customs and designed primarily to preserve and promote the supply of venison in the service of royal hunting. The *Anglo-Saxon Chronicle* recorded of William the Conqueror:

> He was fallen into avarice,
> and he loved greediness above all.
> He set up great beast-woodlands, and he laid down laws for them,
> that whosoever killed hart or hind
> he was to be blinded.
> He forbade hunting the harts, so also the boars;
> he loved the stags so very much,
> as if he were their father;
> also he decreed for the hares that they might go freed.
> His powerful men lamented it, and the wretched men complained of it
> but he was so severe that he did not care about the enmity of all of them.[29]

Large tracts of forest were restricted to royal usage: hunting of harts and hares was forbidden in royal chases and warrens on penalty of death or dismemberment, local dogs required to be declawed, and rights to take "vert" for fuel and building curtailed. Even traditional access and the taking of grass, wax and honey from beehives, or fish and birds was criminalized for all but freeholders who lived in the forest as employees of the king.[30] An intricate system of forest courts, or swanimotes, officers, and systems of tribute developed to support the forest system. Under King Henry III, penalties for offenses were softened from the mutilation or amputation of body parts to the levying of substantial fines or the "attachment" (seizure) of property, including oxen necessary to agricultural labor.[31] Still, common people could be brought up on charges including gathering acorns and apples for market sale, grazing animals on pastures, and digging clay or mining coal without license.[32] Conditions led to the complaint in King Edward I's "Ordinance of the Forest" (1306) that "the people of our Realm are, by the Officers of our Forests, miserably oppressed, impoverished and troubled with many wrongs, being everywhere molested."[33] Bands of armed locals regularly overpowered forest officers to take venison and vert as they pleased, and royal attempts to reassert control included the passage and application of laws forbidding the keeping of dogs by smallholders and peasants and hunting in disguise or by night.[34] Control of the forests was a decisive element of the conquest of the indigenous Anglo-Saxon by the invading Normans, and it had long-term impacts on the English concept of the forests as well as the daily practices of hunting and gathering on which many if not most peasants (even those who were also small-scale farmers) depended for survival and understood as their common right. The Norman Conquest had spurred a shift in the English concept of the forest from common resource to the hunting grounds of kings.[35]

In early modern times, that concept shifted once more from forests as habitat to supplier of salable commodity. Population growth increased demand for wood to construct homes and buildings, fire iron smelters and blast furnaces, and burn as charcoal. (Charcoal production drove deforestation across early modern Europe.) Deforestation accelerated. Beginning in 1483, the Crown instituted a number of forest-management measures promoting traditional sustainable wood-harvesting practices like coppicing and pollarding, which entail the removal of only branches or trunks and allow for regrowth. "Offenses against the vert" such as digging up young holly, hawthorn, and hazel trees, lopping off large branches, and taking acorns were made punishable by fines.[36] Still, such measures did not substantially change the trajectory of forest depletion. Norman Cantor expertly summarized the broader European situation:

> Europeans had lived in the midst of vast forests throughout the earlier medieval centuries. After 1250 they became so skilled at deforestation that by 1500 they were running short of wood for heating and cooking. They were faced with a nutritional decline because of the elimination of the generous supply of wild game that had inhabited the now-disappearing forests, which throughout medieval times had provided the staple of their carnivorous high-protein diet. By 1500 Europe was on the edge of a fuel and nutritional disaster from which it was saved in the sixteenth century only by the burning of soft coal and the cultivation of potatoes and maize.[37]

According to Cantor's view, only the colonial importation of American indigenous plant staples saved Europe from demographic collapse due to deforestation.

Yet imperialism would prove to be one of the major contributors to further acceleration of deforestation in England, just as it had in sixteenth-century Venice and Spain. With the dawning of the era of circumatlantic mercantilism came a tremendous demand for shipbuilding. In the early sixteenth century, Kings Henry VII and VIII judged that Great Britain's naval needs could no longer be served through the temporary impressment of merchant ships and authorized the building of a freestanding Royal Navy. Shipbuilding was also commissioned by would-be merchant-adventurers, colonizers, privateers, and slave traders looking to the high seas as well as by domestic merchants trying to move domestically produced raw materials down the Thames and other rivers to market and export. Because ships could not be built with sustainable harvesting techniques like pollarding or coppicing, the early sixteenth century saw the first large-scale felling of trees in England. Hedgerow oaks from the southern woodlands were judged to be especially well suited for naval purposes. As naval historian G. J. Marcus writes, "From these gnarled and crooked hedgrrow oaks were fashioned the curved frame timbers indispensible to the construction of wooden ships. The great compass timbers were shaped from oak trees at least one hundred and fifty years old."[38] It is estimated that each naval ship took about two thousand oaks at least a century old to construct.[39] With each acre of woodlands capable of supporting twelve to twenty oaks, each seafaring ship constructed would have caused the clear-cutting of at least one hundred acres of woodlands. Massive amounts of wood fuel were also consumed in the casting of naval munitions and iron cannons in blast furnaces. Finally, woodlands served as a source of revenue for the Crown in its efforts to finance its ongoing contest for domination of the Atlantic world. Kings looked to the forests not as pleasure grounds but as fungible resources. For example, in 1607 and 1608, King James I commissioned the first Great Survey, a comprehensive survey of forests designed not to protect them but to effect their utilization. He assessed that they might yield three hundred thousand loads of timber, two-thirds of which—between sixty thousand and one hundred thousand mature oaks—could be used to build ships.[40] The shift to modern imperial statehood had hastened an equally bureaucratic and rationalistic approach to the forests.[41]

Britain's emergence as a modern military and economic power was fueled by wood. Just as navies and merchant marines built of timber and wood-fired iron advanced colonization overseas, an internal colonization transforming England from subsistence economy to industrial and mercantile export economy was taking place at home, and that transformation consumed massive amounts of wood and acreage of woodlands as well. From the time of Queen Elizabeth onward, deforestation and disafforestation—the transfer of royal forest lands to individual landowners—accelerated as the Crown sought revenue from the sale of raw materials like wood to ironworks and other industrial producers as well as from leases of land for use in farming and wool growing.[42] Nonroyal woodlands were also enclosed and transformed into wood plantations to supply industrial demand for firewood as well as arable and pasture lands to feed and clothe the growing and urbanizing English population. Between 1560 and 1590, tens of thousands of oaks were felled in Duffield Forest; during the same time period, a million cubic feet of wood was produced from St. Leonard's Forest.[43] Writes historian Robert Albion, "This reckless cutting was prevalent throughout the land, and in spite of the large amount of timber offered for sale, prices more than doubled during this period."[44] As early as 1577, William Harrison lamented in his *Historicall Description of the Iland of Britaine* (included in Holinshed's *Chronicles*):

> Howbeit thus much I dare affirme, that if woods go so fast to decaie in the next hundred yeere of Grace, as they haue doone and are like to doo in this, sometimes for increase of sheepwalks, and some maintenance of prodigalitie and pompe (for I haue knowne a well burnished gentleman that hath burne threescore at once in

> one paire of galigascons to shew his strength and brauerie) it is to be feared that the fennie bote, broome, turfe, gall, heath, firze, brakes, whinnes, ling, dies, hassacks, flags, straw, sedge, reed, rush, and also seacole will be good merchandize even in the citie of London, whereunto some of them even now have gotten readie passage, and taken up their innes in the greatest merchants parlours. . . . Certes euerie small occasion in my time is enough to cut down a great wood, and euerie trifle sufficeth to laie infinite acres of corne ground vnto pasture.[45]

A modern ideology of improvement soon took hold, implanting in modern English minds a concept of woodlands not as domain, habitat, or environment but as a resource to be transformed through labor into profit. Improvement was the reason given for the enclosure over the course of the sixteenth century of about 50 percent of open fields.[46] In the 1610s and 1620s, King James raised money to pay debts by disafforesting and leasing woodlands to improvers, a pattern that would continue throughout the Restoration.[47] Outright sales of royal forests to improvers began under King James and steadily increased throughout the Stuart era, until 1657 when Parliament repealed the sale of the Forest of Dean to Sir John Wintour. But the halt of forest sales did nothing to deter the widespread destruction of timber, which continued apace.[48] All forms of manufacturing, from tanning to glassmaking to sugar refining and brick manufacturing, required hardwoods or wood products.[49]

With a need for wood both fueling and being fueled by capital accumulation and overseas expansion, British forests were already showing signs of serious depletion by 1600. Remaining forest areas became home to increased industrial activity including iron and coal mining and a growing population of landless and displaced peasant workers.[50] This growing and newly proletarianized population of forest residents demonstrated an increased vigilance in protecting forest resources against for-profit utilization and export. Forest dwellers rioted, tore down enclosures, and even mutilated forest resources to prevent them from being carried away to mills and forges. In 1594, Forest of Dean inhabitants cut fifteen tons of timber into pieces too small to be used in order to prevent the forest's exploitation by wealthy lords and outsiders.[51] Both the Midlands Revolt of 1607 and the Western Rising of the 1630s took place in forests or were led by forest dwellers. Village riots led to legislation against the "unlawful cutting or stealing or spoiling of wood and underwood and destroyers of young trees" in 1663.[52] But they also earned the forests a reputation as a zone of lawlessness and savagery openly resistant to improvement.[53] One observer wrote in 1610 that the forests and woods were "the verye nurseryes of Idlenes Atheisme Beggerie perfidiousness and mere disobedience to goes and the lawes of the kingdom. . . . For poverties sake, havinge noe other meanes, [forest residents] thruste themselves into theis obscure places (as they thincke) out of the view of god or men whoe become *Rudes et Refractorij,* Lyving most baselie, prophanlie and by thefte, A peste in a Comonwealth."[54]

Concern about diminished forest resources also came from the merchant and gentry classes. Supply depletion led to the doubling of wood prices between 1618 and 1670.[55] By 1620, England's shipbuilders were already looking to imports from the Baltic, especially for masts; wood also had to be imported for rebuilding the city of London after the Great Fire of 1666. The domestic timber shortage had long-term impacts shaping Britain's presence and dominance as a political and economic power in the Atlantic world.[56] Historians Stephen Bunker and Paul Ciccantell explain, "British access to critical raw materials depended on a navy that was first predatory and then imperial. That navy greatly expanded British needs for raw materials, and was thus both an instrument and a cause of military and colonial conquests."[57] A few voices within Britain called for greater conservation, including John Evelyn, the diarist and author of the anti–air pollution tract *Fumifugium, or The Inconvenience of the Aer and Smoak of London Dissipated* (1661), who was commissioned by the navy to write *Sylva, or A Discourse of Forest Trees, and the Propagation of Timber in his Majesty's Dominions* (1664), one of the first published forestry texts, and a book credited with inspiring the planting of millions of trees by sympathetic members of the landed gentry. Statutory limitations on forest sales and leases and timber harvest were also imposed piecemeal by Parliament. But neither replanting nor conservation measures answered the ever-increasing industrial demand for wood supply.[58] England thus turned to its colonial possessions, there instituting practices of land improvement and wood harvesting as other European imperial powers had in their colonies. The Portuguese deforested the island of Madeira and Brazil to develop sugar plantations and fuel sugar processing; they also exported Madeiran wood to Portugal to build ships. The Spanish colonization of the Philippines also extracted hardwoods for the building of Spanish galleons.[59] North American forests provided wood for English shipbuilding as well as for industrial and consumer use in other English colonies such as the West Indies.[60] But to address its persistent domestic shortages, England finally turned to domestically produced coal. Environmental historian Paul Warde writes, "Eighteenth-century England mined and consumed a multiple of the amount of coal consumed by the rest of the world put together."[61]

More than for any other form of habitat, control and exploitation of woodlands served as a central front first in the imperial domination of England and then in its own transformation into a modern imperial power. There is no question that economic modernization caused serious forest depletion on a scale as yet uncalculated by contemporary geographers and historians.[62] To give some idea of the extent of the depletion, consider this one point of data: a survey of oaks in six royal forests conducted in 1608 and again in 1783 shows that the number of mature oaks in royal forests declined from about 230,000 to about 51,000, a loss of more than 75 percent.[63] England (along with the rest of imperial Europe) deforested itself, setting off a chain of ecological and economic consequences perhaps best conceived of as a serial deforestation that has played out across the globe. And as we observe the consequences of deforestation in places like Brazil, Haiti, and Malawi, we can begin to imagine the consequences of the deforestation of England for my Brooks ancestors and other migratory peasants. What happens to a people when the forests they have built their livelihoods around for centuries upon centuries are destroyed? Massive changes to the land ensue. Soils lose their ability to hold water. Flooding follows. Soils erode. Water sources become fouled. Fish lose habitat, as do large and small game crucial to the food supply. Access to centuries-old sources for fall acorn pannaging of domestic hogs and the winter provisioning of livestock disappears. Birds and honeybees lose habitat. And peasants lose the ability to subsist in the land that has always been their home and instead come to rely for their subsistence on high-yield cereal grains sold at market for a profit—along with everything else. If deforestation played a pivotal role in the internal colonization and economic modernization of England, imagine too its impacts on the cultural and social lives of English peasants. Historian Carl Griffin writes, "Forests were refuges of what was arcane in the wider net of rural England."[64] To the dislocated rural proletariat that took refuge there and to the peasants who continued to remember them in their oral traditions, forests held meaning as outposts of English resistance to imperial modernity.

Perhaps it is not so farfetched to imagine that in an arboreal culture that from Anglo-Saxon times had maintained strong customs governing the sustainable harvesting of wood, a culture that had instituted stiff—even capital—punishments for the reckless destruction of young trees, a culture that had witnessed deforestation on an utterly transformational scale, a man might indeed be angry enough over the destruction of young trees (and the assault on land and lifeways that destruction represented) to kill his own brother. Perhaps it is not so farfetched to imagine that people experiencing that degree of dislocation, disorientation, and alienation might seek to flee and hide themselves on the other side of the ocean. Perhaps the traditional singers of "Edward" knew what they were talking about after all.

WHAT DID LINA CROCKETT WARD REMEMBER of the reasons her ancestors (and mine too) left England in the seventeenth and eighteenth centuries? Were she to look in popular American histories of colonization, she would find confident and celebratory accounts of conscience-bound Puritans and courtly Virginia adventurers. Her own repertoire of folk memory and the "Edward" ballad in particular assumed a far more interrogative and mournful disposition toward history. History, it remembered, had begun in an act of senselessness and wastefulness, the betrayal of one brother by another, in this instance, over the destruction of a hazel tree:

> What'd you and him fall out about
> My son come tell unto me
> Bout cutting down yon hazelnut tree
> What caused it for to be
> What will you do when your daddy comes home
> My son come tell unto me
> I'll set my foot in yonder ship
> I'll sail across the sea.

What could it have mattered, this hazel tree? What *can* it mean if we set aside the impulse to read through the tree and look directly at it instead: if we look directly at the environmental destruction and colonial violence hidden in plain sight in American folk memory. In the English woodlands, hazels constituted the undergrowth of the oak forest, growing as tall as thirty feet. Hazel rods were prized material for crafting essential household items, constructing fencing, and house building; rods were split and woven into hurdles for wattle-and-daub houses.[65] For this reason, hazels were carefully coppiced only once every four to eight years. Improper cutting of hazel "saplings, branches, or drywood" was reason, under medieval forest codes, for appearance before the court.[66] Moreover, hazelnuts were an important winter crop, as they could be stored, ground, and mixed into flour to make bread when winter grain supplies ran low.[67] In the early nineteenth century, a local historian described the traditional use of hazel in central south England:

> The Woods consist chiefly of hazel, which produce nuts in great profusion, to the relief and benefit of all the hamlets and villages for miles around it. It is their second harvest; for when all the corn hath been got in, and the leasing of the fields at an end, the inhabitants betake themselves to the woods; whole families from distant places flock to the Chase; bring their little cots, provisions, utensils, and every necessary for their comfort that they can provide themselves with, and make their abode there for whole weeks at a time if the weather will permit. . . . Fuel they have at hand in great plenty; and after the fatigue of the day, they make large fires, which they sit round, eat their scanty meal, then slip from the green shells their day's gathering, talk over their success, crack their jokes as well as their nuts, and clothed with innocence and simplicity, are much happier than most of the Princes of Europe.[68]

Setting aside the historian's unwarranted romanticization of peasant life, his description still conveys the sense that hazelnuts had been from premodern times a source of winter subsistence. The reckless destruction of a hazel tree, then, could be understood as a flouting of if not an open assault on traditional subsistence economy. In cutting down a hazel tree—either before its time, as some versions of the ballad suggest, or completely and without the traditional coppicing techniques developed by peasants to safeguard forest continuity—the younger brother demonstrated an open disregard for the body of customs that had maintained his family on the land. Like those who clear-cut the oak forests to sell for gain, to finance war, or to construct merchant-imperial vessels, the younger brother's actions proved him a threat to the lifeways of his own class. For just as in its subsistence value the hazel tree also provided habitat for intergenerational rituals of social bonding, the destruction of a hazel tree could not be separated from the dissolution of family bonds and social ties.

Perhaps the significance of the hazel tree in the "Edward" ballad and of trees in general to English and Anglo-American peasants goes even further, into a domain we might describe as spiritual. For it bears remembering that my Brooks ancestors, like the majority of English and Anglo-American peasants, were not entirely Christian. Instead, they practiced what historian James Horn describes as "an eclectic form of popular belief that drew upon a hotchpotch of sources and traditions—Protestant, Catholic, pre-Christian, and occult."[69] Among the ancient Celts, the hazel held significance as a tree of wisdom and a symbol of fertility; hazel rods were used in divination and dowsing through the eighteenth and nineteenth centuries. But even more significantly, according to folklorists, the ancient Anglo-Saxons regarded forests as the habitat of the souls of the dead. By some accounts, the souls of the dead pass into trees themselves. Traditional English folk literature and ballads are replete with such references, all of them remnants and residues of premodern and pre-Christian sensibilities: in many ballads, the woods are sacred or taboo spaces of encounter with powerful beings; in some ballads, plants and trees spring from the graves of the dead; in others, characters swear by "oake and ashe and thorne"; and some give birth near the trees as in the ballad "The Cruel Mother."[70] In such a cultural context, residual as it might have been, the killing of trees is tantamount to the murder of the dead, the severing of relationships between the ancestors, the earth, and the living. Where do the dead go when they are made homeless? Is there a more complete form of dispossession than to sever a people from its dead? And is this profound experience of dispossession, placelessness, alienation, and anonymity one of the fundamental bases of modernity?

Historical fact demonstrates that the lifeways of English peasants were substantially transformed by the deforestation and industrialization of England. Those real-world contexts give new meaning and force to forests in early modern literature, like Arden and Athens in William Shakespeare's plays.[71] Folk literature too, like the ballad "Edward," captured a sense of the forest's imperilment and connects that imperilment to the dispossession and outmigration of English peasants. "Edward" documents a profound sense of loss at the emotional core of colonial outmigration. Cut off from their homelands—and from a knowing relationship to land itself—English peasant migrants came to North America. Upon their arrival, they found themselves once again in thick forests, with trees growing as much as one hundred feet taller than their familiar oaks.[72] But if their ancestors had once rioted against the destruction of forests, they themselves being transformed by dispossession into rootless and anonymous modern men knew the land must also be transformed from indigenous home into capital resource. Grimly, they set to work in America the way they had been set to work on the lands they used to call home in England.[73] With no foresters or swanimotes to defend customs of forest management and sustainable harvest, no coppicing or pollarding, no common understanding that young trees must not be felled, and no particular affinity or intimate knowledge of American tree species, and having left both their watchful ancestors and ancestral customs an ocean behind, they set bounds, imposed borders, and instituted a rational system of land appropriation, doing unto indigenous American people what had been done unto them in the centuries before.

CHAPTER THREE

Two Sisters and a Beaver Hat

Desire and the Story of Colonial Commodity Culture

On August 15, 1932, a young and enterprising literature scholar named Arthur Kyle Davis Jr. set up his Speak-o-Phone recording device in the tiny parlor of the home of Horton Barker in St. Clair's Bottom, Virginia. Barker had been born in 1889 in Laurel Bloomery, Tennessee, in the eastern foothills of the Blue Ridge Mountains, into a family of tenant farmers and domestic servants in a mountain mining and iron mill town; he became blind when he was just a small child. Over a lifetime of listening—to his mother, to the music teachers at the Virginia School for the Deaf and Blind, and to hymn singers during his years on the road with a traveling preacher—Barker had developed a mastery of the canons of Anglo-American traditional music. He had also cultivated a lucid and angular tenor voice, the desired object of many folk song collectors then combing the highways and byways of the American South. Among folklore enthusiasts, Barker, who sometimes made a living as a broom salesman, came to be known as an "aristocrat of singers."[1]

Barker probably had little use for such adulation, or for the romantic attitudes Davis and other eager young salvage ethnographers brought into the Blue Ridge Mountains. By all accounts, he was a bit of a rascal, as happy to tease would-be scholars by singing only popular tunes of the time, rather than the ballads made famous by British folklorist Francis James Child that could be traced back to sixteenth- and seventeenth-century England. Barker, whose mother was a multigeneration mountain woman—the name of his father, who died early, does not survive—could probably trace his ancestral roots back that far too, had anyone bothered to keep up the records.

Either it was an especially muggy August day in the bottomlands near Chilhowie, Virginia, or something about the earnest young scholar with the fancy recording device made Horton Barker feel obliging. For when Davis turned on the Speak-o-Phone, Barker delivered a stellar version of one of the most ancient and familiar ballads in the English and Anglo-American canons:

There was an old woman lived on the seashore,
Bowing to me,
There was an old woman lived on the seashore,
Her number of daughters, one, two, three, four,
And I'll be true to my love,
If my love will be true to me.
There was a young man came there to see them,
Bowing to me,
There was a young man came there to see them,
And the oldest one got stuck on him.
And I'll be true to my love,
If my love will be true to me.
He bought the youngest a beaver hat,
Bowing to me,
He bought the youngest a beaver hat,
And the oldest one got mad at that.
And I'll be true to my love,
If my love will be true to me.
"O sister, O sister, let's walk the seashore,"
Bowing to me,
"O sister, O sister, let's walk the seashore,
And see the ships as they sail o'er."
And I'll be true to my love,
If my love will be true to me.
While these two sisters were walking the shore,
Bowing to me,
While these two sisters were walking the shore,
The oldest pushed the youngest o'er.
And I'll be true to my love,
If my love will be true to me.
"O sister, O sister, please lend me your hand,"
Bowing to me,

"Sister, O sister, lend me your hand,
And you may have Willie and all of his land,"
And I'll be true to my love,
If my love will be true to me.
"Oh no, I'll never lend you my hand,"
Bowing to me,
"Oh no, I'll never lend you my hand,
But I'll have Willie and all of his land."
And I'll be true to my love,
If my love will be true to me.
The miller he got his fishing hook,
Bowing to me,
The miller he got his fishing hook,
And fished the maiden out of the brook.
And I'll be true to my love,
If my love will be true to me.
"O miller, O miller, here's five gold rings,"
Bowing to me,
"O miller, O miller, here's five gold rings,"
To push the maiden in again.
And I'll be true to my love,
If my love will be true to me.
The miller received those five gold rings,
Bowing to me,
The miller received those five gold rings,
And pushed the maiden in again.
And I'll be true to my love,
If my love will be true to me.
The miller was hung at his own mill gate
Bowing to me,
The miller was hung at his own mill gate,
For drowning little sister Kate.
And I'll be true to my love,
If my love will be true to me.[2]

The song Horton Barker sang for Arthur Kyle Davis Jr. is called "The Two Sisters," and just like the ballad "Edward," it tells an ancient saga of sibling rivalry and betrayal. A young man, often a sailor, comes to visit a family and falls in love with the younger sister. He offers her as a token a "beaver hat," incurring the older sister's jealousy. The older sister invites the younger to walk down by the seashore, then tries to drown her. The younger sister tries to allow the older sister to have her new love as well as his land, but the eldest sister refuses to extend her hand, so the younger sister washes downstream until she reaches the miller's pond. The miller takes gold from the younger sister and pushes her back into the pond, where she drowns. Even if we recognize how important fraternal and sororal loyalty were to the ballad tradition, the apparent whimsy and cruelty of the eldest sister and the miller in "The Two Sisters" still have the power to startle, especially when set against the chorus: "I'll be true to my love, / If my love will be true to me." As I listen, so too does Horton Barker's sweet, bright, unaccompanied tenor startle as it pushes through the story of murderous betrayal, reaching gladly for high notes and leaning full-throated into the chorus. As with Lina Ward's singing of "Edward," Barker's singing is spare and sinewy. Dark though the betrayal may be, he sings it as though it would be extravagant to sentimentalize such a familiar story.

Variants of the "Two Sisters" ballad have been documented and collected by folklorists not only in England but also in Norway, Sweden, Iceland, and the Faroe Islands.[3] But it was among the Anglo-American folk singers of the southern United States that the ballad achieved its greatest popularity. In the first decades of the twentieth century, ethnographers working in small communities from Virginia to Arkansas transcribed and recorded dozens of versions of "The Two Sisters." Almost all of them share the same narrative bones: two sisters, a suitor, a coveted gift, a murderous betrayal, and a final act of desecration. A few Anglo-American singers set the ballad in mythic time, as did their English and Scandinavian forbears, describing the sisters as daughters of a "king" or a "lord," the suitor as a "knight," and the gift as a "fine gold ring" and "silken dress."[4] Most, however, vest the story with a close familiarity, describing the sisters as daughters of an "old woman" or a "man in the west," the suitor as a commoner, either a sailor or a boy named "Willie" or "Johnny," and the gift as a "beaver hat," and sometimes a "gay gold ring" as well.[5] The most significant variations in story concern the behavior of the miller. In the version of the ballad as sung by Horton Barker and others documented in rural Virginia between 1913 and 1915, the younger sister manages to swim downstream until she reaches the miller's pond, where she offers him her gold to rescue her, but the miller robs her and throws her back in the pond to drown instead.[6] In others, as in the version sung by Jean Ritchie, in Viper,

Kentucky, in 1946, the younger sister drowns, then the miller fishes the younger sister's dead body out of his pond—thinking, fancifully, it is "either a mermaid or a swan"—robs her of her "gay gold ring," and pushes her dead body back into the water.[7]

Across almost all of these variants, one image recurs: the beaver hat. As curious as it seems that a sister should murder her sister over a hat, the wide distribution of this image across the Anglo-American "Two Sisters" tradition suggests that it is no incidental detail.[8] In fact, the version sung by Sam Pritt in Alleghany County, Virginia, in November 1924, underscores the importance of the hat by relating that the older sister is so jealous of the "beaver hat" that she "mashed it flat" before pushing her sister in the water.[9] Do sisters really kill their sisters over beaver hats? Do brothers really murder their brothers over the destruction of young trees?

Here, again, we face the same questions as we did in examining the ballad "Edward." Folklorists have not spent as much time arguing over the meaning of "The Two Sisters" as they have over the ballad "Edward," nor have they tried to transpose the sisters' rivalry into some more Lévi-Straussian frame. But as the example of "Edward" shows, the apparently surface details of oral literatures anchor them in specific historical environments. It pays to look at rather than strive to see through the details. It pays to read them not as symptoms pointing to hidden and therefore supposedly more timeless and meaningful texts of human experience but rather as paths into particularly pivotal moments in human history. If we follow the destruction of a young tree, for example, at the heart of "Edward," the story opens outward to a broader history of deforestation in England, a history that proved decisive in the economic, social, and spiritual dislocation of an entire class of common English people and thus to the colonization of the Americas. When we grasp the extent of the impact of deforestation on English lives, the grim and fatal tone of the "Edward" ballad no longer seems so puzzling. What we have, then, is a ballad that serves as a commentary on its times, or, in the words of folklorist Barre Toelken, a "fossil record" of historical feeling.[10] Could "The Two Sisters" be the same?

Like "Edward," "The Two Sisters" is a narrative that suggests a fatal introduction of disorder into community and family. Especially in the version of the story first deployed in seventeenth-century England and refined over centuries by Anglo-American folksingers, the ballad depicts a world where social guarantees and norms are upended. Sisters murder sisters; millers pillage corpses; bodies foul the waters. As underscored by the choral refrain—"I'll be true to my love / if my love will be true to me"—the norms of decency and reciprocity that distinguish a well-ordered society collapse and in their place emerge a host of intimate cruelties. What sets this crisis narrative in motion? The introduction of a single beaver hat. This chapter will look at rather than strive to see through the beaver hat. For if we listen to Horton Barker, and the hundreds of other Anglo-American folk singers of "The Two Sisters" who preserved this oral literary masterpiece over more than two centuries, if we take their words as a path into Anglo-American peasant history, we may find that an apparently simple transaction like the gift of a beaver hat can incur world-reshaping consequences. The story of colonial commodity culture and its consequences is an important dimension of the Anglo-American colonial story. The hunger for status goods both reflected and created powerful economic and social transformations in both America and England. It contributed to social and economic conditions that common English men and women like the ancestors of Horton Barker (and my Brooks ancestors as well) found uninhabitable. This chapter will explore the starring role of the beaver hat in this larger story of why we left.

LONG BEFORE THE EUROPEANS even dreamed of North America, fur held pride of place as a status commodity of empire. From ancient times through the early modern period, Viking, Russian, and German feudal overlords had demanded marten, sable, ermine, fox, and beaver pelts as tribute from peasant hunting communities from Lapland to Siberia, then trafficked them (alongside human slaves) to the Roman Empire and the Levant. Smaller, finer furs became part of the distinctive costume of the early modern merchant class, as seen in the fur-lined coat and felt hat of the merchant depicted in the Jan van Eyck painting *The Arnolfini Portrait* (1434) and the fur overcoat on the ambassador in Hans Holbein's *The Ambassadors* (1533). The emergence of a late medieval and early modern merchant class spurred the official regulation of the wearing and display of status goods like fur. The Crown, Parliament, and the Church all passed sumptuary laws designed to restrict the wearing of fur (and other forms of conspicuous consumption) by social rank. For example, King Edward III's 1363 Statute concerning

Diet and Apparel restricted the wearing of miniver and ermine to the aristocracy and upper nobility. Other furs like hare, otter, and fox could be worn by lower nobility, knights, and clergy, while common people wore muskrat, badger, and sheepskin.[11]

Among the most admired accoutrements of the emerging merchant class was a kind of hat made from the soft undercoat of the European beaver *(Castor fiber)*. The beaver has two layers of fur: an outer layer of long, coarse hairs and an inner layer of short, fine, dense ones. As a water-dwelling mammal, the beaver is also equipped with anal glands that secrete castoreum oil to protect and waterproof the fur. It was from the short, fine, and specially lubricated undercoat of the beaver that a special variety of felt was made through a complex multistep process that entailed removing long guard hairs, shaving off short downy wool, and matting the wool into felt sheets that could then be rolled, bathed, shaped, trimmed, tallowed, shellacked, dyed, and decorated. What made the beaver hat special was that, thanks to the water-repellent quality of beaver fur, a beaver hat held its shape in the rain, while lesser felt hats and woolen caps did not. It took pelts from two beavers to make a single beaver felt hat. Owing to the intricacy of its production—felt making was regarded as one of the finest arts of textile making—felt had long been regarded as a status good. King Henry III reportedly wore felt hats in the 1260s, as did merchants from the Islamic Levant in the fourteenth century.[12] Flanders became known as a European center of felt hat making; in fact, Chaucer's description of the merchant in the *Canterbury Tales* mentions that the merchant has "a Flaundrish bever hat."[13]

By the late sixteenth century, the beaver hat was enjoying a fashion resurgence, even as supplies of European beaver rapidly diminished. In 1583, Puritan pamphleteer Phillip Stubbes published an antiluxury treatise titled *The Anatomie of Abuses*. In addition to lamenting all manner of extravagant dress and social custom, Stubbes paused to wonder at the emerging craze in beaver hats:

> And as the fashions bee rare and straunge, so are the things whereof their Hattes be made. Some of a certaine kind of fine haire, far fetched and deare bought. . . . These thei call Beuer hattes of xx, xxx, or xl shillinges price fetched from beyond the seas, from whence a greate sorte of other varieties doe come besides.[14]

Stubbes criticized not only the extravagance of expenditure but the confusion of social classes this luxury sowed. Whereas simple woolen caps had always been the headgear of all but the English nobility and gentry, the popularization of the beaver hat introduced an entire new medium of cultural aspiration, expression, and distinction. Especially ornate beaver hats made of rare sable beaver, taffeta linings, and imported silken hatbands might cost up to five times as much as a simple woolen cap: about forty or fifty shillings, or one pound, at a time when the salary for a clergyman was thirty pounds a year.[15] Beaver hat owners also paid as much as twenty or thirty shillings to refurbish or customize their hats with the latest, most fashionable trimmings. Thanks to the hunger of the merchant class to stay up-to-date and their own inventiveness in creating an endless demand for the customizing and refurbishing of hats, haberdashers became among the most wealthy and powerful guilds in the city of London. Some especially prosperous haberdashers reinvested their new wealth in the very merchant venture companies that would initiate the English colonization of North America.

And what a timely investment that was. For by 1600, the European beaver had been hunted into extinction, forcing European haberdashers to look westward for fresh supplies. It was French, Basque, and Portuguese cod fishermen trolling the shores of Newfoundland and New England in the sixteenth century who first bartered with local communities of Micmac and Abenaki for the fur of the American beaver *(Castor canadensis).* Regular networks for trafficking furs from North America to France were established in the 1570s and 1580s. Visiting Paris in the 1580s, colonial promoter Richard Hakluyt reported viewing "divers beastes skynnes, as bevers, otters, marternes, lucernes, seales" imported from Canada.[16] French, Dutch, and English trading companies soon established New World fur-trade footholds: Henry Hudson explored the Manna-hata (now Hudson) River as far north as Albany beginning in 1607; Samuel de Champlain founded Quebec in 1608; and in 1620, yet another fur-post colony was established by Protestant Separatists at Plymouth. When the ship *Fortune* left Plymouth for England in 1621, beaver skins made up 69 percent of its cargo value.[17] It was beaver fur that enabled the Puritans to pay their debts and raise capital enough to finance their religious and civic experiment, even as

Puritan writers like Phillip Stubbes condemned beaver hats and other vanities. By the 1630s, beaver pelts even served as a currency of exchange in North America. The fur trade—driven largely by exchange of a pelt used only to make hats—served as the first economic engine of British North American colonialism.

Refreshed supplies of American furs helped secure for the beaver felt hat an iconic place in the annals of European fashion. The power and expressive range of the hat was modeled by King James's son Prince Charles, who during the 1620s purchased between forty and sixty beaver hats a year, each costing about eighty-five shillings, including fancy trimmings, a sum equivalent to the cost of a good horse or ten weeks' wages for an artisan laborer.[18] Despite its costliness, the wearing of beaver hats was not limited to nobility alone. As Nicholas Bunker writes, "By the 1620s, the beaver hat had ceased to be a foppish, eccentric novelty, and instead it became an almost universal object of codified desire."[19] Over the course of the century, different segments of the English middle class developed their own particular styles of beaver felt hats. Puritans preferred theirs with a high dome, narrow brim, and silver buckle; wide brims and luxurious plumage (a style some historians suggest was first developed in Sweden) were favored by the cavalier, including King Charles II, who supervised the founding of the fur-trading Hudson's Bay Company in 1670.[20] Beaver hats became a symbol of status recognized across all sectors of English society. As had Phillip Stubbes in the 1580s, some critics, like John Evelyn in his book *Tyrannus, or The Mode, in a Discourse of Sumptuary Laws* (1661), expressed concern about the rage for novelty and luxury across the English social classes. Evelyn proposed the reintroduction of sumptuary laws not only to preserve the social order but to discourage the unnecessary expense of luxury goods and to consolidate the economic and national identity of England:

> How glorious to our Prince, when he should behold all his subjects clad with the Production of his own Country, and the people Universally inrich'd whilst the Species that we now consume in Lace, or export for forreign Silks, and more unservicable Stuffs would by this means be all sav'd, and the whole Nation knit as one to the heart of their Soveraign, as to a Provident and Indulgent father?[21]

Evelyn was not entirely wrong in worrying about the political costs of the rage for beaver felt. As the beaver fur trade continued to grow and expand across the North American continent, tensions over the trade impacted the political relationship between France and Great Britain, leading even to open military conflict in the Beaver Wars, which concluded with the Treaty of Utrecht in 1713 and the cession of Hudson's Bay, Newfoundland, and Nova Scotia to England.[22] The impacts of the rage for beaver radiated far beyond the fashionable circles of Europe.

Historian William Cronon and anthropologist Eric Wolf have tracked the world-reshaping effects of the beaver trade among the indigenous nations of North America, from the Abenaki of Maine, to the Algonkians, Hurons, and Iroquois, to the Anishinaabeg people of the Great Lakes, and further west. The trade touched every dimension of Native life. Interaction with European traders brought disease and population decline and created incentives for the reorganization of traditional subsistence-based societies into new, smaller, and more mobile family hunting units. Redirection of economic activity away from horticulture and toward hunting changed Native diets, increased dependence on grains obtained from neighboring tribes, and diminished women's traditional political and economic powers, which in many communities had been closely tied to land and its cultivation. Elimination of the beaver in overhunted areas left lasting ecological consequences, especially inasmuch as beavers and their dam-building habits had played decisive roles in shaping landscapes, meadows, and waterways. Trade routes opened the way to missionary incursion; fur-trading posts were soon converted into forts. The fur trade also introduced a new intertribal lingua franca and spurred the intertribal adoption of formerly local cultural practices like gift exchange. It decisively shaped political confederations and alliances among the Iroquois and Algonkians, as well as intensifying practices of warfare. It redefined notions of kinship and tribal affiliation and spurred new patterns of settlement and resettlement across New York and the Great Lakes. Religion, political organization, gender roles, family life, warfare, diet—all of these were profoundly and decisively reorganized by the advent of the beaver fur trade.[23] The trade, according to Wolf, "deranged accustomed social relations and cultural habits and prompted the formation of new responses—both internally, in the daily life of various human populations, and externally, in relations among them."[24] He continues:

> Native Americans themselves came to rely increasingly on the trading post not only for the tools of the fur trade but also for the means of their own subsistence. This growing dependence pressured the native fur hunters and pemmican suppliers to commit ever more labor to the trade in order to repay the goods advanced to them by the trader. Abandoning their own subsistence activities, they became specialized laborers in a putting out system, in which the entrepreneurs advanced both production goods and consumption goods against commodities to be delivered in the future. Such specialization tied the native Americans more firmly into continent-wide and international networks of exchange, as subordinate producers rather than as partners.[25]

What can be said of the European communities who participated as the trading partners and primary consumers of the fur trade? It seems scarcely possible to believe that a trade that had such powerful impacts on so many dimensions of life in indigenous America should not also exert pressures in European communities as well. If the transition from subsistence to mercantile economics, in Wolf's words, "deranged accustomed social relations and cultural habits" in North America, what impacts must it have had on the English? Perhaps that is the story that "The Two Sisters" is trying to tell.

IF WE WANT TO BEGIN TO ASCERTAIN how the beaver trade registered among the common people of England, we need look no further than the rich body of ballads that grew up over the seventeenth century. As early as the 1630s, when the beaver hat was still out of financial reach for all but nobility and the upper merchant classes, English popular oral culture began to document the impacts of the beaver hat craze on social relations and culture in English peasant-class communities. In the ballad "Well Met Neighbor: Or, A dainty discourse betwixt Nell and Sisse, of men that doe use their wives amisse," published (scholars estimate) sometime between 1633 and 1669, two friends on their way to attend another woman's labor exchange a long litany of reports of abuses doled out by local men to their wives. A beaver hat plays a starring role in one of the most gruesome cases:

> Know you not Sam the Turner,
> o hee is as good as ere twanged,
> He throws his wife ith fire to burn her

O such a Rogue would be hangd.
I Pray you how happened that,
what should be the cause of this strife?
A man brought a new Beaver hat,
unto his next neighbours wife,
And she spoke unto her good man,
to buy such another for her,
Which made him to curse and to ban,
and thus began all the stir.[26]

These lines reflect the social dynamics that drive the economics of fashionable status goods: display leads to desire; emulation follows consumption. But in this ballad, the introduction of a beaver hat to the village community leads to negative social consequences as well: inequality leads to desire, which foments resentment and anger, which culminates in violence. The hat precipitates social strife and disorder.

Within a few decades, more ballads appeared that established a strong association between the allure of the beaver hat and destabilizing or deceitful social choices. In a ballad detailing a marriage proposition from a traveling soldier, "The True-Lovers Holidaies: OR, The Wooing, Winning, and Wedding of a fair Damosel; performed by a lusty Souldier, being one of the Auxiliaries" (published between 1663 and 1674), a young girl promises to leave her home and family and undertake the difficult life of a camp follower, having been lured by grand promises, including that of a new beaver hat: "Il buy thee a new kirtle, wrought wastcoat & beaver / A dainty silk Apron, my minde shall not waver, / So no body else shall enjoy thee but I." Never mind that both by lifestyle and reputation soldiers were a class associated with inconstancy and that a soldier could never have afforded such extravagances.[27]

Similarly, in "The Country Cozen; or the Crafty City Dame" (published between 1672 and 1696), a woman of London schemes to have an affair with her favorite lover by asking him to come to her house dressed in women's clothing. His costume? "A brave new Gown, and a rich Beaver / New Apron, Hose, and Shooes."[28] "Nell's Humble Petition: OR, The Maidens kind and courteous Courtship to honest John the Joyner, whose love she earnestly desired" (1670s) relates the tale of Nell, a forty-year-old former prostitute, who proposes marriage to a younger and far simpler man. When John complains about her age, her "wrinkl'd Brow," her skin like "the Tawny-Moor," and her crooked nose "all awry," Nell tries to woo him with the promise of her "perfect Skill" in lovemaking, as well as with a set of handsome gifts: "I'll buy thee a new Suit and Cloak, / a delicate Beaver too." What finally clinches the marriage proposal is Nell's offer to allow John to keep a younger lover as well.[29]

By the 1680s, all mentions of the beaver hat in popular ballads connect it to the aspirations and untrustworthy (even criminal) behaviors of self-styled cavaliers. "The Town Bully's Bravery: OR, The High-Way Hector's Ample Confession of his Lewd Life; Being a fore-runner of an Ignominious Death" (1680s) tells the story of the exploits of one such shyster, including his execution for his crimes of deceit. His chosen costume, significantly, includes a beaver hat elaborately customized with silk bands and gold wires:

> All the newest Fashions which any Gallants use,
> I do follow to the life, see Spanish-leather Shooes,
> Campaign-wig, of Flaxin-hair, Beaver-hat and Silks I wear
> With Golden-fringes, Drawers scringes when I do repair
> Unto the Tavern, where I do call
> For Sack and other Wine, yet I seldom pay at all;
> A Room I take below, and watch my time to go,
> And thus I leave them and deceive them like a Bully-Bow.[30]

A beaver hat is the costume of the cunning "Citizen" who demeans the rural commoner and schemes to steal his bride in "The Contention Between a Countryman & a Citizen, For a beauteous London Lass, who at length is married to the Countryman" (published 1685–88).[31] It is also the costume of the "Citizen" who travels to the countryside to woo away a young maiden but who is ultimately defeated and cudgeled by a simple plowman in "The Couragious Plow-man, or, The Citizens Misfortune" (published 1674–79).[32] And it is a signature piece of the habit prescribed by the "Fop Master" to his pupils in "The Fop Masters Instructions to All His Beau Schollars, That are desirous to commence Fops" (published 1675–96). "Cock up your Beaver Sir," is the first of the Fop Master's lessons, followed by a long list of others that reveal the character of the fashionable class:

> Draw your mouth like an Ass, Tol.
> Ogle the Ladies now . . .
> Speak like one has the Pox, Tol.

Lisp sometimes when you speak, Tol.
And wear your Shoes that Creak, Tol. . . .
Strut and swear like a huff, Tol. . . .
Never speak what is true, Tol. . . .
Swear Ladies dies for you, Tol.
Lay your head in their lap, Tol.
Vow you have got a clap, Tol.
Sing them a Baudy Song, Tol.
And then loll out your tongue, Tol.[33]

This ballad associates the beaver hat–topped cavalier costume with deceit, disease, and predatory scheming. It is the costume of the merchant-class cosmopolite out to take advantage of country women and men.

Another parallel body of beaver hat ballads depicts the hats as a sign of economic overextension and social ruin. "Ill-gotten Goods seldome thrive. Or, the English Antick" (published 1647–65) tells the story of Dick, a country miller, who comes to town, his pockets lined with "silver," and promptly spends a large part of it on status goods:

a Perry-wig,
a gallant Suit of Clothes,
Which was bestrewd with Musk,
more sweeter then a Rose;
A Cambrick Band and Cuffs,
his Halfe-shirt out before,
His Breeches had of Ribbons
at least a dozen score.

And to finish it off:

A Beaver, and a Feather
The Crowne did over-top,
With Ribbons round about,
Like a Haberdashers-shop.

Soon, Dick is beguiled by a "cunning snap" of a "Lasse" who "rusled" by him in "her Silke," another imperial status good brought to England. Dick pursues her to a tavern, where she rebuffs his sexual advances, but continues to flirt with him, even as Dick continues "smoking of his Nose, / and drinking store of Sack." (It bears notice that both tobacco and sack, a fortified white wine imported from the Canary Islands, were imperial status commodities as well.) Finally, she agrees to go "to bed" with him, but before he can accomplish his ends, the inebriated Dick falls asleep, and the woman steals his clothes (including hat) and abandons him. Unable to pay for his room when he awakens, Dick is unceremoniously ejected from the tavern and driven home to his "Fathers Mill," "naked." The ballad concludes with a warning:

> Ill gotten goods nere thrive,
> take heed you pilferers all,
> Lest you like strutting Dick
> to such mischances fall:
> Then young men have a care
> of painted curled Locks.
> For such, though faire above,
> below may have the Pox.[34]

According to this ballad, the beaver hat was the desired object of the newly rich, many of whom had come to their riches through less than honorable means. It is significant that here Dick, a miller and a miller's son, is described as having "ill gotten goods." Millers were often blamed in the sixteenth and seventeenth centuries for food shortages. Common English people viewed millers as profiting from the enclosure movement: when common lands previously farmed for subsistence by English peasants were enclosed and turned over to farmers who raised staple crops for sale and profit, it was the millers who were perceived to have betrayed the interests of their communities for market gain. Food rioters often accused millers of buying up such large quantities of grain for trade and sale that they left not enough for the poor.[35] Dick's pretensions to fashion and his ability to afford a beaver hat came about because he made gain at the expense of peasant farmers who were, by the middle of the seventeenth century, in extreme economic distress, if they had managed to hold on to their plots and commons at all. The loss of his hat (and the rest of his clothing) as well as his humiliating walk back to the countryside served as a form of comic justice.[36]

A similar storyline animates "The Two-Penny Whore" (1692), which tells the tale of a young man, a "vapouring Gallant," who has "consumd his estate" in frivolous expenditures, including upon lavish clothing. Now ruined, he tries to engage a prostitute he once frequented, though he now has only a "two-pence." She rebuffs him, and he pleads for mercy, reminding her:

> When formerly I in my silks was adorned,
> And about my neck wore a fine flanders lacd band,
> Upon my head was no less than a Beaver:
> What was there then I had not at command?[37]

The ballad concludes with the prostitute relenting and working at reduced rates, but it issues a warning as well to young "gallants" to beware the lavish expenditures that lead to ruin. In not a single one of the ballads produced and circulated among common English men and women in the seventeenth century is a beaver hat associated with strength of character, foresight, prudence, or decency. Rather, it is always a spur to envy and conflict, a symbol of ill-gotten gain, a signature accessory of the false and the predatory.

This is the context in which the ballad "The Two Sisters" was born. The earliest documented English version of the ballad was printed as a broadside by Francis Grove in London in 1656, under the title "The Miller and the King's Daughter":

> There were two sisters, they went playing,
> To see their father's ships come sailing in.
> And when they came unto the sea-brym,
> The elder did push the younger in.
> "O sister, O sister, take me by the gowne,
> And drawe me up upon the dry ground."
> "O sister, O sister, that may not bee,
> Till salt and oatmeal grow both of a tree."
> Sometymes she sanke, somtymes she swam,
> Until she came unto the mill-dam.
> The miller runne hastily down the cliffe,
> And up he betook her withouten her life.
> What did he doe with her brest-bone?
> He made him a violl to play thereupon.
> What did he do with her fingers so small?
> He made them pegs to his violl withal.
> What did he doe with her nose-ridge?
> Under his violl he made him a bridge.
> What did he doe with her veynes so blew?
> He made him strings to his violl thereto.

What did he doe with her eyes so bright?
Upon his viol he played at first sight.
What did he doe with her two shinnes?
Unto the viol they danc'd Moll Syms.
Then bespake the treble string,
"O yonder is my father the king."
Then bespake the second string,
"O yonder sitts my mother the queen."
Then bespake the strings all three,
"O yonder is my sister that drowned me."
"Now pay the miller for his payne,
And let him be gone in the divel's name."[38]

This version of the ballad situates the conflict between the sisters on the ocean shore and gives no motive for the elder sister's betrayal of the younger. Significantly, it also concludes with the miller's grisly dismemberment of the younger sister's body and his use of body parts to fashion a musical instrument, through which, in grand supernatural fashion, the murdered sister reveals her older sister's crime.

Sometime during the seventeenth century, the dynamic street and alehouse ballad culture developed a parallel version of this classic, one that translated the scene of betrayal into far more familiar terms. The king became a common man, or a widowed woman, in the disadvantageous economic position of being a parent to several daughters. Conflict erupts between the daughters when a young man comes to town bearing the gift of the beaver hat, the spoils of the British North American fur trade empire and an iconic and coveted element of English fashion. Envious over the beaver hat gift, the eldest sister drowns the younger. It is this late seventeenth-century version of the ballad, born out of a ballad canon and at a historical moment and milieu wherein beaver hats were associated with deceit and discord, that according to folklore experts served as the source text for "The Two Sisters" that travelled across the Atlantic and became a fixture in Anglo-American folk tradition.[39]

At some point in that ocean crossing and in the centuries that followed, "The Two Sisters" underwent additional changes. Most significant among them is the loss of the final stanzas in which the sister's body is made into a musical instrument—sometimes a viol, as in the 1656 version above, sometimes a harp. The younger sister never manages to speak from beyond the grave to name her older sister her betrayer; the possibility of justice is lost. Story elements of supernatural retribution were a common feature of traditional English ballads, but they disappear almost entirely from American folk music canons. The reasons for this loss of the supernatural are unknown. It may be that the economies of oral tradition pared down concluding stanzas like baggage abandoned because it was too bulky to make the Atlantic crossing. It may also be that the spiritually eclectic Christian-pagan-occult world of many common English people lost some of its richness across the centuries and miles. Perhaps the Anglo-American heirs of the original English ballad singers lost a sensible connection to the spirits of their ancestral lands when they came to North America. Whatever the reason, in American versions of "The Two Sisters," there is no supernatural retribution. In some, the miller is punished for his role in the drowning of the sister. In the version sung by Horton Barker, the younger sister is alive when she reaches the miller's dam and promises him a reward of gold (another imperial status commodity) for rescuing her; the miller takes the gold, but pushes her back in to drown:

The miller received those five gold rings,
Bowing to me,
The miller received those five gold rings,
And pushed the maiden in again.
And I'll be true to my love,
If my love will be true to me.
The miller was hung at his own mill gate
Bowing to me,
The miller was hung at his own mill gate,
For drowning little sister Kate.
And I'll be true to my love,
If my love will be true to me.

Other American versions offer an even more chilling conclusion, as in that sung by Jean Ritchie of Viper, Kentucky, and collected by Artus Moser in 1946:

Into the miller's pond she ran,
I'll be true to my love
If my love will be true to me.
O miller, o miller, go draw your dam,

Bow down,
O miller, o miller, go draw your dam,
Bow your bend to me,
O miller, o miller, go draw your dam,
Here's either a mermaid or a swan,
I'll be true to my love
If my love will be true to me.
He robbed her of her gay gold ring,
Bow down
He robbed her of her gay gold ring,
Bow your bend to me,
He robbed her of her gay gold ring,
And then he pushed her in again,
I'll be true to my love
If my love will be true to me.[40]

Here, the youngest sister is drowned by the time she reaches the miller's pond, for she does not bargain with the miller for her rescue. Rather than recover her body for a proper burial, the miller fishes it from the pond, plunders it of its gold ring (given by the suitor), and then returns the body to the water, leaving it to rot.[41] There is no moral; there is no justice. There is envy, leading to murder, leading to plunder, leading to environmental befoulment. There is, to recall Eric Wolf's descriptions of the impacts of the beaver trade on indigenous North America, the "social derangement" of at least four elements of social order and obligation: first, the young man courts the younger rather than the older sister; second, the older sister tries to murder her younger sister; third, the miller robs the girl rather than rescue her or plunders the body rather than retrieve it for burial; fourth, the miller fouls a common water supply with the corpse. We are left with a chilling, fatal narrative of how people betray one another for gain, a narrative ironically underscored by the chorus: "I'll be true to my love / If my love will be true to me." It cannot be said that the fur trade had the same kind and extent of impact on England as it did on North America, but "The Two Sisters" offers a body of memory dating to the seventeenth century that suggests that the lower ranks of English people perceived the introduction of status commodities like the beaver hat and the broader commercial culture they represented as destabilizing to their own communities as well. If as Nicholas Bunker writes, the beaver hat had become "an almost universal object of codified desire,"[42] working-class ballads featuring beaver hats almost universally comment on the destructive and humiliating consequences of desire unleashed and unregulated.

IT IS IMPOSSIBLE TO KNOW how many beaver hats were actually purchased in England in the seventeenth century. Some idea comes to us from data compiled by the English statistician Gregory King (1648–1712) titled "Annual Consumption of Apparel," wherein he estimates that in 1688 3.3 million hats of all kinds (including beaver, wool felt, and rabbit) were purchased for use in England, as well as more than 1.6 million caps, to cover the heads of about 4.5 million people. Almost everyone had a hat or cap. But it is safe to assume that the hat wealth was not equally distributed, as we may surmise from King's economic census for 1688. According to his calculations, 511,586 English households made an annual average salary of sixty-seven pounds or greater, thus "Increasing the Wealth of the Kingdom," and 849,000 households, including "Common Seamen," "Labouring People and Outservants," "Cottagers and Paupers," "Common Soldiers," and "Vagrants" subsisted on salaries averaging £10.5 annually or less, thus "Decreasing the Wealth of the Kingdom." When we combine King's tables with other sources, including probate records and household account books, we learn that most common laborers earned about ten to twenty pounds per year. Forty pounds per year was considered the bare minimum for middling households, with the most prosperous middle-class households earning about £150 annually, while lesser gentry and especially well-to-do tradesmen might bring in more than £200 in revenue.[43] For lower-rank households, the beaver hat costing upward of fifty shillings, or £2.5, was totally out of reach. At the cost of about two weeks' salary, the beaver hat was also well beyond the reach of most of the middling sort, especially given the fact that in these households food purchase and production amounted to about 50 percent of annual expenses and clothing about 15 percent.[44] Before 1660, it cost about one pound and two shillings to outfit a boy in a respectable middle-class ensemble of hat, coat, shirt, doublet, breeches, stockings, and shoes, and seventeen shillings for a girl's headwear, waistcoat, shift, petticoat, stockings, and shoes.[45] With the median cost of a nonbeaver hat estimated between two shillings and three shillings, the beaver hat at fifty shillings and above was an extravagance on the order of today's Jimmy Choo shoes or even a Hermès Birkin bag.[46] Only the stars (and would-be celebrities) were wearing them.

When we realize how few people were actually wearing beaver hats, it seems clear that their function in the ballads is symbolic. Beaver hats and the trouble they cause are an index to the anxiety common people were feeling about massive economic shifts in early seventeenth-century England. This, after all, is a time when traditional commons are being enclosed and repurposed for commercial agriculture, peasant households displaced, and a new class of landless laborers created. It is also a time of growth in England's commercial and manufacturing activity, growth that was changing the economic and social landscapes of England in profound and permanent ways.

Overseas trade and colonization propelled a significant part of that growth, creating new markets for English goods and manufactures, opening access to new raw materials, and infusing European economies with new capital plundered from the New World. Colonization also reshaped the way England thought of its own role in the global economy from being a producer of raw materials and manufactured goods for domestic consumption and export to playing the role of the middleman in ever more extensive global commercial networks. Such a role would come with an increased standard of living as well, as Richard Hakluyt argued in his case for overseas colonization: "At the firste traficque with the people of those partes, the subjectes of this realme for many yeres shall chaunge many cheape comodities of these partes for thinges of high valor there not estemed; and this to the greate inrichinge of the realme, if common use faile not."[47] Colonization did in fact change the consumption patterns of English men and women, introducing new staple crops such as potatoes and maize, as well as fabrics like silk and calico, and status comestibles like tobacco, sugar, tea, and coffee. By the middle of the seventeenth century, tobacco became an item regularly consumed by more than 25 percent of the English population; tobacco imports for domestic consumption grew a hundredfold from 1620 to 1672, peaking in the first decade of the eighteenth century.[48]

If the advent of imported goods like tobacco changed the daily consumption habits of English men and women, even greater changes came about as a result of the growth of domestic manufacturing during the early seventeenth century. Especially under Queen Elizabeth, a host of new manufacturing projects had been initiated and patented, many offering part-time wage labor in spinning, knitting, pin making, lace making, and so forth to the common sort, including the women and children in rural households and inmates of poorhouses and workhouses. This growth in domestic manufacturing changed the nature of work in many peasant-class English households from subsistence activities like small-scale farming and gathering to a combination of traditional subsistence and specialized wage labor. It also meant that many manufactured goods like pins, paper, and glass formerly imported to England were now produced at home. Consequently, many households did have access to a greater range of domestically produced commodities, thanks in part to the greater price range and variety of goods made available, and thanks in part to wage earnings that put a little cash into the hands of more households.[49] Historian Joan Thirsk argues that a "mass market" for consumer goods such as "stockings, knitted caps, cheap earthenware, nails, tobacco pipes, lace, and ribbon" existed as early as the seventeenth century.[50] By the end of the seventeenth century, many laboring-class households were able to buy pots, pans, dishes, and stockings.[51] This increased domestic consumption fueled the greatest part of English economic growth: by the end of the seventeenth century, production for export was about 7 percent, while production for domestic consumption was 93 percent.[52] This led some political economists who had initially viewed domestic consumption as frivolity to celebrate it as a source of domestic economic growth and capital generation.[53]

Thanks to growth in overseas trade and domestic manufacturing and consumption, the national income of England doubled between the 1560s and 1640s. But the new wealth was not distributed evenly. The commercial shift that brought more English lives into contact with national and international (rather than local) markets was both a source of opportunity and a source of new vulnerability, once that strongly favored the most mobile and educated members of society. New wage laborers working, for example, in cottage cloth and pin-making industries were increasingly vulnerable to interruptions and fluctuations in trade. This vulnerability was compounded by loss of land, livestock, and access for many newly landless laborers to commons, forests, and other sources of traditional subsistence. Writes historian Keith Wrightson: "There was, of course, nothing new about poverty or inequality. But the marked divergence in living standards and life chances between those who gained and those who lost in the decades around 1600, and the sheer growth in the numbers of the labouring poor have led many historians of England and Wales to view this period as one not only of economic expansion, but also of social polarization."[54]

It is against this backdrop of widespread economic insecurity and increasing inequality that the new status consumption of fashionable commodities like the beaver hat emerges. In his classic work on modern cultural economy, Fernand Braudel connected the rise of the fashionable middle class to the overall material "advancement" of European societies, finding in fashion itself an expression of the new "energies, possibilities, demands and *joie de vivre* of a given society, economy, and civilization."[55] But these "energies" and "possibilities" were not equally shared. Those who landed on the right side of England's commercialization could play the status consumption game and chase the latest fashions; all others could not. In seventeenth-century England, the keenest players were not necessarily the wealthiest—gentry, for example—but those whose lives were most linked to the markets like traders, professionals, and wealthy craftsmen.[56] Historian Woodruff Smith writes that for these upper-middling types, the "object" of the game was to "acquire influence and reputation" and to demonstrate "a certain amount of control over the world around them."[57] Keith Wrightson continues:

> The diffusion of new consumption habits certainly spread by example and imitation, but such imitation did not necessarily imply the mimicking of social superiors. Rather, it involved the spread of influence through networks of association of the middle sort themselves. . . . In short, the middle sort were themselves innovators; they helped to initiate new standards of domestic consumption.[58]

The rise of the new status consumption meant the innovation and accumulation of a new strata of social and cultural capital among the middle classes.[59] This new strata of social and cultural capital was not fashioned out of thin air. It was accumulated as surplus from the land, labor, and natural resources of indigenous peoples in the Americas and Africa and from the repurposed lands and natural resources and waged labor of peasant-class Britons.[60] And it came at significant cost, as the beaver hat ballads suggest.

It represented the rise of the city at the expense of the country.

Urbanization played an important role in the spread of demand for status goods. It was in towns and cities that new goods were introduced, marketed, and popularized. Studies of household inventories from the late seventeenth and early eighteenth centuries show that households in London and major towns tended to own decorative and status goods like mirrors, table linens, books, and china in greater proportion than rural households.[61] But the city also represented the end of the line for newly landless laborers. In almost every one of the ballads, the beaver hat is associated with the untrustworthy "citizen" against the honest "countryman," even at a time when greater numbers of countrymen were leaving rural areas for urban employment.[62]

The new status consumption also emblematized the rise of a new modern enterprising individuality at the expense of the many. The seventeenth century witnessed a major power shift from old, exclusive royal-chartered merchant adventurer companies to a new set of enterprising London-based merchants operating as individuals on an unregulated international market.[63] Individualism was also an emerging social logic of the early modern era, and seventeenth-century status consumption presaged the development of a consumer society in which the possession of goods (rather than inherited status, or connection to a community or a place) would play a significant role in establishing the social position of the individual. Lynn Festa has observed in her study of fashionable wig-wearing in the eighteenth century, "The important role played by the wig in establishing, even constituting, the identity of its wearer exposes the dependence of the autonomous individual upon his possessions. If the wig belongs to the wearer, there is also a sense in which the wearer belongs to the wig."[64] The beaver hat emblematized the dawn of a world in which for ever greater segments of society things made and manipulated people, and people belonged to things.

Finally, the plumes and silk bands and rich tastes and textures of the new status consumption emblematized the redistribution of capital from laboring classes to middling classes. To visualize how this shift in resources was experienced, imagine this: a peasant-class household scrapes by in the early seventeenth century by raising food for its own consumption on a tiny garden plot, gathering some household necessaries from forests, taking in some waged work like pin making, and keeping a small number of domestic animals like cows and sheep to graze on local commons. The animals provide a source of the household's milk, butter, eggs, and wool, the opportunity for breeding and therefore increase, as well as the chance to sell surplus milk, butter, and eggs at market. If the commons are enclosed for transformation into commercial farm or pasture, the household loses its ability to maintain livestock: the laboring household loses capital. Many laboring-class households were forced to abandon their livestock in the seventeenth century, and somehow through the workings of the commercial market, that loss translated into a substantial gain for merchant classes.[65] Producer goods were lost by the lower classes, while consumer goods were gained by upper-middling types.[66] Cows, through the magic of mercantilization, somehow became plumed beaver hats.

Thus, what felt to the mercantile class like a new era of possibility felt to many commoners like a new era of insecurity that impacted relationships and the texture of daily lives in families, villages, and towns. It also constituted a major shift in social values and ethics. As historians John Walter and Keith Wrightson explain, "The primacy of local need over individual profit, the obligations of neighbourliness and the traditional interpretation of customary rights were being increasingly denied by a significant element in local society."[67] The beaver hat ballads with their resentment toward millers and other merchants represent a growing focus on those who were perceived to have skimmed the surplus and profited from the impoverishment of others.[68] Thomas Hobbes captures this modern sense of social instability and antagonism in *Leviathan* (1651): "The liberty of the Commonwealth . . . is the same with that which every man then should have, if there were no civil laws nor Commonwealth at all. And the effects of it also be the same. For as amongst masterless men, there is perpetual war of every man against his neighbour; no inheritance to transmit to the son, nor to expect from the father; no propriety of goods or lands; no security; but a full and absolute liberty in every particular man."[69]

Ballads like "The Two Sisters" document a sense of disorder and insecurity and connect it to the introduction of a status commodity culture capitalized on the losses of laboring classes. The beaver hat is the bellwether of the dislocating shift into commercial modernity; it is the lure that sets into motion a chain of events that contributes to the displacement of thousands upon thousands of English peasants to North America. It is this story of desire, deceit, and betrayal that English peasants carried with them across the Atlantic and that persisted with them down through the centuries as an archive of memory. Among the descendents of African slaves kidnapped and brought to North America, there is an oral-traditional story that relates that Africans were lured into the clutches of slave traders with a piece of red cloth.[70] For Anglo-Americans, the oral-traditional story of why we left begins with the allure of a beaver hat.

IN 1933, Horton Barker made his first public folksinging appearance at the White Top Folk Festival in Washington County, Virginia, where his audience included none other than First Lady Eleanor Roosevelt. Like other folk festivals of the time, White Top had been the project of out-of-area folklorists and folk music aficionados who hoped to promote and preserve what they believed to be "authentic" folk traditions; its backers included magnates profiting from the local timber industry and other industrialization in the Virginia mountains. Roosevelt, whose father was among those magnates, had lived in the area decades before, motored to mountain peaks and hiked to local springs, feasted on country ham and beaten biscuits, and was serenaded by local mandolin players and folksingers, among them Barker, who so impressed her that she invited him to sing at the White House one year later. In her speech to the people at White Top, Roosevelt said:

> The study of the folk songs and the early stories of a country are always interesting because they frequently reveal the background on which the customs of a country are built. Very frequently we find explanations for trends in customs and literature of today hidden in some old custom, ballad or legend of many years ago. One thing particularly with regard to the mountains songs is that they go back to our English ancestors. English folklore collectors visiting here have found verses to their ballads that had been lost in England. Historically as well as aesthetically, these folk songs, stories and dances are of value. It is well to encourage a study of folk literature and customs.[71]

Her words conveyed the viewpoints of professional folklorists and scholars like Arthur Kyle Davis Jr. who were professionally invested in the cultural valuation of the ballad form. One wonders, though, what a blind broom seller and generations-long mountain dweller like Horton

Barker thought of it all. Did he feel himself the repository of the foundations of Anglo-American culture? And what are those foundations, exactly? If we look to grim murder ballads like "The Two Sisters" as foundational, how do we reckon with their fatal tone, a fatality made all the more startling by Barker's bright, matter-of-fact rendition of it. Rather than taking a romantic view of the ballads as a confirmation of the continuities of Anglo-American life from Old World to New, ballads like "The Two Sisters" (and "Edward" and others to follow) ask us to reckon with the cruelties and betrayals that stand behind Anglo-American origins and to experience their unsentimental reality to singers like Barker. The story they tell is this one: English peasant migrants did not come here as appointed keepers of ancient customs; we came here as the rejected ones, pushed into the water or across the seas.

"The Two Sisters" suggests the emotional core of a moment when English mercantile imperialism visited English communities with profoundly destabilizing consequences, consequences that ate away at the social fabric of everyday life, the guarantees and obligations that held us in our homes. For the English love of a beaver hat, the lives of hundreds of thousands of indigenous peoples in North America were fundamentally transformed; the lives of English and Anglo-American people were transformed too, propelled away from subsistence economies and into the maw of industrial wage labor, where we were pinioned as the producers of surplus we could only dream of enjoying. Carolyn Merchant has observed of indigenous American involvement in the fur trade: "Furs provided the exchange values needed for the European tools and food required for subsistence. What had begun as adaptation and absorption became dependency."[72] The same might be said for common English people as well. It was only human, after all, to want a taste of the spoils of empire, to want to wear the rich textures and sample the prizes of British colonial mercantilism. And even so we were drawn into a globalizing commercial culture in which we were designated a movable and ultimately disposable class of surplus labor. Adaptation to the modes of global commercial culture led to greater inequality and then dependency. Like the animal whose skins so many craved, we found ourselves dislodged from our traditional homes, and then trapped.

CHAPTER FOUR

To Sink It in the Lonesome Sea

Betrayal and the Story of Indentured Servitude

SOMETIME IN 1949, sixty-seven-year-old Bascom Lamar Lunsford left his home near Leicester, North Carolina, up among the foggy hardwood cove forests of the Great Smoky Mountains, and traveled to the Library of Congress in Washington, D.C. It wasn't the first time Lunsford had visited the District of Columbia: ten years earlier, in 1939, he had played at the Roosevelt White House for the king and queen of Great Britain. But this time, as an honored guest of the Archive of American Folksong, Lunsford gave the recording engineers a sample of the wealth of Anglo-American folk songs he had mastered over the decades. More than a performer, Lunsford was a scholar and curator of the American folk tradition. Growing up in tiny Mars Hill, North Carolina, Lunsford had learned music from his parents James and Arby Buckner Lunsford. During his early years of work as a fruit tree salesman, he also learned traditional songs from the families he visited on their remote farms throughout the region. In the 1920s, Lunsford helped found the Asheville Folk Festival, and he continued to travel, learning and collecting music, including a trip in the 1930s to the government-sponsored Skyline Farms cooperative settlement in northeast Alabama, where he had relearned an old song that he felt deserved a home in the Library of Congress.

"I learned this text from Ada Moss," Lunsford began the recording. "It's the 'Golden Vanity,' or the 'Lonesome Lowlands Low.' I also learned this text from Mr. Murphy of Skyline Farms in Alabama. And it's almost identical." He began to sing:

There was a little ship that sailed upon the sea
And the name that they gave it was the Merry Golden Tree
And it sailed on the lonesome lowlands low
It sailed on the lonesome sea.
There was another ship that sailed upon the sea
And the name that they gave it was the Merry Turk-e-lee
And it sailed on the lonesome lowlands low
And it sailed on the lonesome sea.
There was a little boy that run amongst the men
That said captain, captain what will you give me then
If I sink it in the lonesome lowlands low
If I sink it in the lonesome sea.
Where they'll be money and there will be a fee
Besides my eldest daughter I will marry unto thee.
Then he soothed his breast and off swum he
And he swum til he come to the Merry Turk-e-lee
To sink it in the lonesome lowlands low
To sink it in the lonesome sea.
And he had a little augur all fitted for the use
And he bored nine holes in its old hull and then
He sank it in the lonesome lowlands low
He sank it in the lonesome sea.
Then he soothed his breast and back swum he
And he swum til he come to the Merry Golden Tree
As it sailed in the lonesome lowlands low
As it sailed in the lonesome sea.
And he said captain, captain, let me on board
Or you'll not be as good as you told me
If I sink it in the lonesome lowlands low
If I sink it in the lonesome sea.
There'll be no money and they'll be no fee
Nor my youngest daughter will I marry unto thee
Though you sunk it in the lonesome lowlands low
Though you sunk it in the lonesome sea.
Were it not for the love that I have for your men
I would do unto you as I done unto them
I would sink you in the lonesome lowlands low
I would sink you in the lonesome sea.
Then he smote his breast and down sank he
Singing fare you well to the Merry Golden Tree

As it sailed on the lonesome lowlands low
It sailed on the lonesome sea.[1]

As I listen to Lunsford, I hear in his tone a plainspoken matter-of-factness. He does not linger achingly over the cruelty of the captain, nor does he pine for the lost boy. He presses energetically through the "lonesome lowlands low" of the chorus, and he briskly closes the tale. There is no sentimental lingering. Concluding his song, Lunsford offered a curatorial note: "That was sung in England about the time of Sir Walter Raleigh. There are stanzas with the name Sir Walter Raleigh given in it." And on this Bascom Lamar Lunsford was entirely correct. The ballad he sang—known as "The Golden Vanity" or "The Sweet Trinity"—did have its roots in seventeenth-century English lore surrounding the colonist and courtier Walter Raleigh. The ballad then crossed the Atlantic with the great seventeenth- and eighteenth-century American migration of common English men and women and was absorbed into American folk repertoire.[2]

The bones of the story are these: A ship built (and sometimes commanded by) Walter Raleigh takes to the oceans. It confronts an enemy vessel, and the captain promises land, money, and the hand of his daughter to any sailor brave enough to defeat the rival craft. A humble sailor boy volunteers, takes an augur in hand, jumps overboard, swims across open seas to the enemy galley, bores a number of holes in its hull, and sinks the ship. He swims back to his home vessel only to be refused and betrayed by his captain, who declares that he will not deliver the promised rewards. Over the years, as the ballad was passed down through the centuries and traveled thousands of miles from its English origins, a number of variants developed. In some, the enemy ship was identified as being Spanish, a reminder of England's great sixteenth- and seventeenth-century rivalry with Spain. In some versions, the ship is identified with Turkey: Mrs. J. H. Harris of Prospect, Virginia, described the rival craft as a "Turkish robery," a pirate ship, when she was interviewed by ethnomusicologists in March 1914.[3] Some American singers relocated the battle as taking place not in the lowland seas off the coast of the Netherlands but on the transatlantic crossing: "A Ship Set Sail for North America" is the first line of the ballad as sung by Mrs. Ollie Jacobs of Pearson, Wisconsin, in 1941.[4] A few remembered the battle as being between rival North and South American vessels:

the "North Amerikee" and "South Amerikee," as sung by Maud Gentry Long of Hot Springs, North Carolina, in 1947.[5]

But the most striking feature shared by virtually all of the American variants of "The Golden Vanity" is its conclusion. Not only does the captain refuse to pay the cabin boy his promised reward, but he refuses to take him back on board the vessel, leaving him to drown in the open ocean. The boy contemplates avenging himself by using the augur in his hand to drill holes in the hull of "The Golden Vanity." But out of love for his fellow sailors he refuses to sabotage the craft, and he drowns. As sung by Bascom Lamar Lunsford, "He smote his breast and down sank he / Singing fare you well."

A senseless act of cold-hearted cruelty. A chilling betrayal. A humiliated and humiliating demise. And a revealing look into the ways common English men and women narrated and understood their own role in the imperial expansion of Great Britain. For as all literary texts do, this ballad serves as an archive of feeling, documenting and helping us key into bodies of experience and memory not readily legible in other records like state papers, parish registers, or embarkation logs. How did peasant-class English people regard Raleigh and other venture colonists hailed as the early architects of the British Empire? How did they understand their own position in their great schemes? What did the colonial project cost them, and how did they understand these costs? The aptly titled "Golden Vanity" and its chilling plotline suggest that common English men and women knew that they would see little of the wealth Raleigh and his cohort reaped from empire. In fact, they recognized that in their role as grunt workers of empire they were utterly expendable. It was more likely that they'd be left out to die than it was that they would reap riches, let alone an entrée into the landed classes.

The long thread of memory documented in this ballad suggests a common Englishman's view of colonization as a process that entailed significant betrayal. The economic modernization of England had created a large permanent class of landless workers who were quite literally at the disposal of imperial projects. Mobilized sometimes voluntarily and sometimes by economic necessity or outright conscription in the hard labor of empire, these men and women understood that their interests did not drive imperial expansion. In fact, the whole emerging modern economic order was being capitalized on the extraction of surplus value from the commons and commoners—including their very lives. In such a context, people like the cabin boy mercilessly betrayed by his captain, the ballad singers who identified with him, and even my Brooks ancestors were not wrong in feeling that the imperial venture and its celebrity proprietors (like Raleigh) were coldly arrayed against them. Encouraged at times to indentify strongly with their English homeland and its global ambitions, acculturated to thinking of themselves as English men and women, their loyalties and affections were instrumentalized when they served the purposes of empire and abused when they did not.

High death rates were a daily fact for all who participated freely or unfreely in transatlantic colonization, but no class of participants faced greater exposure to death than the peasants of the Atlantic world. It is a well-known historical fact that about one-third of all captured Africans designated for the slave trade died before reaching their American destinations. Although they came under markedly different circumstances—circumstances that still do not merit the adjective "free"—common English men and women also experienced high rates of death both at sea and on land. Anglo-American sailors working the transatlantic slave trade died at about the same rate as slaves themselves.[6] One-quarter to one-half of new arrivals to the Chesapeake in the seventeenth century died within one year due to the rigors of their "seasoning" or to diseases like dysentery, typhoid, and malaria.[7] Only about 7 percent were able to claim the land promised them in indenture agreements.[8] Life expectancy in American colonies like Virginia was lower than anywhere in England excepting London itself.[9] "For every ex-servant who made it into the ranks of the middling or upper classes," historian James Horn writes, "tens of others, who left barely a trace in the records, died in poverty and obscurity."[10] Empire was a cruel master not only to those it designated its hated objects but also to those it enlisted with vain promises.

Telling the story of imperialism as a betrayal of common English men and women, as "The Golden Vanity" does, encourages us to consider that the act of colonization entailed not only gains to Euro-American colonists but also losses: of trust, of security, of dignity, and of life itself. It also begs a reconsideration of how England's imperial expansion is represented in historiography. Histories of Great Britain at the beginnings of its overseas colonization often focus on the exploits and intrigues of monarchs and elites—a tendency that is replicated in literary historical scholarship as well. Consequently, this kind of historiography replicates and promotes the same dynamics of identification with the architects of empire that we find in the promotional literature that celebrated the original colonial ventures. But what strikes me about "The Golden Vanity" and its two-hundred-year tenure in the American folk repertoire is that it preserves and promotes a sensibility of disidentification with the figureheads of empire. What can be expected from Walter Raleigh and his ilk, the ballad seems to ask, but cruelty and betrayal? And these were not reserved for indigenous people or African slaves alone; common English men and women were not to be excepted. It is only in these archives of memory that I find that hard-bitten sense of unease and distrust that reminds me of the Brooks men I have known.

MAINSTREAM HISTORIES of the life and times of Walter Raleigh present Raleigh (or Ralegh) through the scrim of an Elizabethan lace collar as the dashing, adventurous courtier or, alternately, as the unjust victim of post-Elizabethan political intrigues. But "The Golden Vanity" withdraws the tissue of romance and reckons with the ugly side of the architects of England's imperial expansion. Born in 1552, the youngest son of a moderately well-to-do gentry family in Devon, Raleigh followed the example of his older half brother Humphrey Gilbert (1539–83) in linking his own personal fate and fortune to the establishment and expansion of a British overseas empire. In 1576, Gilbert had published *A discourse of a discourie for a new passage to Cataia,* proposing that the queen sponsor his search for the northwest passage to China, and in 1578 the queen had given him a patent licensing him to colonize anywhere on the face of the earth. When Gilbert's ship the *Falcon* set out on such a mission in 1579, Raleigh served as its captain. For six months Raleigh and a crew that included known pirates sailed the northeast coast of Africa, preying upon random ships—including one bearing a cargo of citrus fruit—that crossed his path, before returning to England for want of supplies. The voyage was regarded a failure, as would be most of the colonial ventures Raleigh undertook over the course of his career.[11]

Next, Raleigh turned to Ireland, England's first colonial theater, the training grounds for the colonizers of the Americas, and a first-stop destination for young men seeking to build wealth and reputation. Gilbert had taken charge of the province of Munster in 1569, after helping put down the FitzMaurice Rebellion, capturing castles and killing all resisters, including children. He symbolically underscored this by posting the severed heads of rebels on pikes in a line that led to the door of his tent.[12] "No conquering nation will ever yield willingly their obedience for love but rather for fear," Gilbert is reported to have said.[13] Raleigh followed his half brother to Munster in July 1580, having charge of one hundred troops, to assist in putting down the Second Desmond Rebellion, an effort by the FitzGerald dynasty of Munster to resist expanding English control. There, Raleigh improved on his half brother's reputation for cruelty. One story relates that when Raleigh discovered an Irish peasant caught gleaning willow branches left behind at an English encampment, Raleigh asked the peasant what he wanted them for. "To hang English churls," the peasant replied. Raleigh had him hung on the spot. Late in the rebellion, Irish rebels and six hundred papal troops sent over by Spain's King Phillip II were surrounded by English forces at the ancient Celtic site of Dún an Óir, or Smerwick. The rebels and their allies raised a white flag and cried "misercordia" (or mercy). Then, Raleigh commanded his soldiers in hanging unarmed captive rebels (including pregnant women), in having the arms and legs of cooperating Catholic priests smashed on anvils by local blacksmiths, and in cutting the throats of and disemboweling Spanish and Italian troops. The slaughter became infamous across Catholic Europe and horrified Queen Elizabeth who, according to one historian, "from her heart detested to use cruelty to those that yielded, wished that the slaughter had not been, and was with much difficulty appeased and satisfied with it."[14] In the months that followed, the occupying English completed their defeat of Munster by ruining half a million acres of Irish lands. Raleigh left Ireland a hero in 1581.

He received as a reward for his royal service a number of trade monopolies, rents, and royalties (including the right to collect customs on all wool exports), was knighted on the twelfth day of Christmas in 1585, and later that year was also appointed Lord Warden of the Stannaries, the large tin-mining districts of Cornwall and Devon that had, by ancient legal custom, their own governments. His appointment and especially his privilege of taking fees from the export of wool was met with outrage by the working people of the Stannaries, as one contemporary observer wrote:

> No man is more hated than him; none cursed more daily by the poor, of whom infinite numbers are brought to extreme poverty through the gift of cloth to him. His pride is intolerable, without regard to any, as the world knows; and as for dwelling among them, he neither does nor means it, having no place of abode.[15]

Once he established himself as Lord Warden of the Stannaries while maintaining his place by Elizabeth's side in London, Raleigh continued to build his status as an absentee landlord when he was given twelve thousand acres of land in Munster as a reward for his service to the queen in 1586. By 1587 he had increased those holdings to forty-two thousand acres, making him the largest single landowner in all of England's colonial possessions. Raleigh is sometimes credited with introducing the cultivated potato (an indigenous South American plant) to Ireland, a bit of folklore subsequently discredited by historians who hold that the Spanish brought the potato from Peru to Europe in the 1570s.[16] Indeed, the most tangible legacy of Raleigh's dominion was not food but famine, a consequence of the scorched-earth policies of the occupying English during the Second Desmond Rebellion. As the poet Edmund Spenser, a soldier in the campaign, wrote in his *View of the Present State of Ireland* (1596):

> In those late wars in Munster; for notwithstanding that the same was a most rich and plentiful country, full of corn and cattle, that you would have thought they could have been able to stand long, yet ere one year and a half they were brought to such wretchedness, as that any stony heart would have rued the same. Out of every corner of the wood and glens they came creeping forth upon their hands, for their legs could not bear them; they looked Anatomies [of] death, they spoke like ghosts, crying out of their graves; they did eat of the carrions, happy where they could find them, yea, and one another soon after, in so much as the very carcasses they spared not to scrape out of their graves; and if they found a plot of water-cresses or shamrocks, there they flocked as to a feast for the time, yet not able long to continue therewithal; that in a short space there were none almost left, and a most populous and plentiful country suddenly left void of man or beast.[17]

During the 1580s, one third of Munster's population died of famine.[18] As the deadly famine unfolded around him, Raleigh the Irish landlord served for two brief terms as mayor of the town of Youghal, maintained a seasonal home at Myrtle Grove, and imported a set of familiar consorts—among them Edmund Spenser, John White, and Thomas Harriot—to complete the transition from traditional Irish governance to entrepreneurial English colonial management. He rarely resided in Ireland and failed to improve on his holdings. Raleigh sold his lands at a loss in 1602.[19]

After his first foray to Ireland, Raleigh had developed an ambitious enterprise to enrich himself and Queen Elizabeth through developing a transatlantic trade empire to rival Spain's. As in almost all things, Raleigh followed the model set by his half brother Humphrey Gilbert, who had been an aggressive advocate of English North American exploration and colonization, including the search for a northwest passage to China. Gilbert also proposed that the problem of the English peasantry could be disposed of through North American colonization: "a great number of men which do now live idly at home, are burdenous, chargeable, and unprofitable to this realm," he wrote, "shall hereby be set on work."[20] Gilbert took "possession" of Newfoundland on August 5, 1583, with a ceremony that culminated in the symbolic handing over of a piece of cut sod, an act long memorialized as the founding of the British overseas empire. He died on the way home on September 9, 1583 when his ship the *Squirrel* sank in heavy North Atlantic seas. Raleigh inherited Humphrey's venture and, surrounded by his coterie of early venture capitalists and publicists—Richard Hakluyt, John White, Thomas Harriot[21]—planned new ones of his own and received, thanks to his avid courting of the favors of Queen Elizabeth (a contemporary observer called him her "dear minion"),[22] exclusive royal support to realize them. From Elizabeth, in 1584, Raleigh received a patent to colonize North America, including the rights

> from time to time and at all times to discover search find out and view such remote heathen and barbarous lands countries and territories not actually possessed by any Christian prince nor inhabited by Christian people . . . the same to have hold occupy and enjoy to his heirs and assigns forever with all prerogatives commodities jurisdictions and royalties privileges franchises and permanancies thereto and thereabouts both by sea and land.[23]

Patent in hand, Raleigh organized an exploratory expedition that sited a potential settlement on the Outer Banks of North Carolina.

A fleet of five vessels and six hundred men, many of them veterans of English colonial wars in Ireland, followed from Plymouth, England, in April 1585, and another party of 117 colonists—including families—left England in 1587, arriving at Roanoke colony, North Carolina, on July 22, 1587. Discovering that earlier colonists had established neither the resources to sustain them nor decent relationships with local indigenous peoples, the Roanoke settlers sent Governor John White back to England for assistance. Help did not arrive—due to the competing demands of war against Spain and piratical haplessness (the captain of one supply ship attempted to take Spanish treasure but was himself captured)—until 1590. By that time, the colony of Roanoke had disappeared. Though the expedition was an entire failure, Raleigh during these years somehow managed to commission a fleet of ships (including the famed *Ark Raleigh,* later renamed the *Ark Royal*), take on new royal appointments and offices, and grow in favor with the queen. Only his marriage to one of her ladies-in-waiting in 1591 slowed Raleigh's rise to power.[24]

As this résumé of failure suggests, Raleigh's ascent had less to do with the outcomes of his colonial projects than with the effectiveness of what Stephen Greenblatt has described as his theatrical self-fashioning. In both Ireland and North America, Raleigh conceptualized bold ventures that he left to others to execute and that resulted not in riches but in ugly dominion or death. Indeed, his greatest yields for the Crown came by way of privateering: the big business of capturing ships and treasure on the open seas from rival European powers. It was through privateering (or piracy, to put it less politely) and his mastery of court politics (including his literary courtship of Queen Elizabeth) that Raleigh amassed power.[25] More than once had the affections of Queen Elizabeth in fact preserved Raleigh from seeing action in dangerous colonial theaters: in 1592, for example, she recalled him home from commanding a naval mission to capture the Spanish treasure fleet, as Raleigh recalled in his poem "The 21st (and last) Book of the Ocean to Cynthia":

> To seek new worlds, for gold, for praise, for glory,
> To try desire, to try love severed far,
> When I was gone she sent her memory
> More strong than were ten thousand ships of war

> To call me back, to leave great honour's thought
> To leave my friends, my fortune, my attempt,
> To leave the purpose I so long had sought
> And hold both cares and comforts in contempt.[26]

Some have suggested that Raleigh was banking on the queen once again recalling him to London after he proposed a British expeditionary search for the golden treasure of El Dorado in the Orinoco River basin in South America. Surely, he stood to gain more and risk less if he traded once again on his powers of influence and promotion rather than on actual accomplishments in the colonial field. But this time the queen did not intervene, and Raleigh embarked for South America with a fleet of four ships in February 1595. He returned in September empty-handed except for a small specimen of gold ore. Understanding well the compensatory value of theatrical self-promotion, Raleigh set out to redeem himself by writing *The Discoverie of the Large, Rich, and Bewtiful Empyre of Guiana* (1596), a fantastical recounting of his travels most memorable for its unbelievable descriptions of indigenous Amazons with "eyes in their shoulders, and their mouths in the middle of their breasts," as well as for what Annette Kolodny has called the most "explicit articulation" of the trope of the New World as a virgin land awaiting sexual exploitation: Guiana, Raleigh wrote, was "a country that hath yet her maydenhead, never sackt, turned, nor wrought."[27] In *Discoverie,* Raleigh also excused his poor outcomes in Guiana by pleading that (although he had never been innocent to violent conquest or plunder) he had in Guiana elected a course of cautious forbearance and "chosen rather to beare the burthen of poverty, then reproch, & rather to endure a second travel & the chances therof, then to have defaced an enterprise of so great assurance."[28] But such elegant reasoning would not be able to carry him along much further. Raleigh's subsequent naval missions against Spain in 1596 failed their purposes, and treasonous intrigues and rebellions disrupted his familiar networks of power at court. Truly hard times came after the death of Queen Elizabeth and the ascension of James I in 1603. Charged by his enemies with high treason, Raleigh was consigned to the Tower of London and condemned to hang, a sentence later commuted by King James to life imprisonment. Over the next twelve years, Raleigh built a library, conducted scientific experiments, and through writing refashioned himself as a statesman.

His five-volume *A History of the World*—a work that without irony lamented the cruelty of war and conquest—was published in 1614. Pinning hopes for a final resurrection of his fortunes on one last voyage to Guiana, Raleigh managed to secure investments enough to launch a fleet of thirteen ships and one thousand sailors in June 1617. It was an utter fiasco, and Raleigh returned to England one year later with just one ship. He was executed in October 1618.

Much of what one now reads about Raleigh focuses on the daring of his exploits, the injustice of his demise, or the ingenuity of his theatrical self-fashioning. Although he maintained influence in royal circles and over his own set of venture publicists like Hakluyt, Harriot, and White, most of the evidence suggests that during his own lifetime, Raleigh was, in the words of Henry Percy, earl of Northumberland, "extremely hated."[29] Some of this strong animosity came from his rivals at court; some, it bears remembering, came also from the common English men and women who suffered under his dominion. As one popular ballad put it, recalling the protests of the residents of the Stannaries:

> Ralegh doth time bestride
> He sits 'twixt wind and tide,
> Yet uphill he cannot ride,
> For all his bloody pride. . . .
> He seeks taxes in the tin,
> He polls the poor to the skin,
> Yet he vows 'tis no sin,
> Lord for thy pity![30]

So too did more democratically minded venture colonists see through the legend of Raleigh to coldly assess the real outcomes of his enterprises. Within just a few years of his death, John Smith concluded his tract *New Englands Trials* (1622) and later his *Generall Historie of Virginia, New England, and the Summer Isles* (1624) with a jab at Raleigh's grand failure in Guiana: "And though I can promise no mines of golde, yet the warrelike Hollanders let us immitate, but not hate, whose wealth and strength are good testimonies of their treasure gotten by fishing. Therefore (honourable and worthy Countrymen) let not the meannesse of the word Fish disates you, for it will afford as good golde as the mines of Guiana, or Tumbatu, with Lesse hazard and charge, and more certaintie and facilitie."[31] Raleigh became for Smith an emblem of the disastrous extravagance of the early years of British global imperial venture.

While during the Commonwealth era, Raleigh's memory was recuperated in the service of various Protestant political causes, the most potent and lasting image of Raleigh fashioned in these years comes to us through the Reverend Thomas Fuller in his *History of the Worthies of England* (1662):

> This captain Raleigh coming out of Ireland to the English Court in good habit (his cloathes being then a considerable part of his estate) found the Queen walking, till, meeting with a Plashy place, she seemed to scruple going thereon. Presently Raleigh cast and spread his new plush cloak on the ground; whereon the Queen trod gently, rewarding him afterwards with many suits, for his so free and seasonable tender of so fair a foot cloth. Thus an advantageous admission into the first notice of a Prince, is more than half a degree to preferment.[32]

Fuller's biographical sketch conveyed to posterity an image Raleigh would have been proud to fashion for himself: that of the dashing courtier profitably enthralled by his Virgin Queen.

But the common people of England—my Brooks ancestors perhaps among them—put little stock in such romance. Their literature on Raleigh, memorialized in oral forms like the ballad, preserved an equally resonant and lasting image of Raleigh as one who made his fame and fortune by betraying the interests of those who bore the brunt of England's rise as a modern global economic power. Sometime between 1682 and 1685, the ballad peddler Joshua Conyers had printed a broadside ballad titled "Sir Walter Raleigh Sailing in the Low-Lands, Shewing how the famous Ship called the Sweet Trinity was taken by a false Gally, and how it was again restored by the craft of a little Seaboy, who sunk the Gally, as the following song will declare." Its lyrics ran as follows:

> Sir Walter Rawleigh ha's built a ship
> in the Neather-lands,
> Sir Walter Rawleigh ha's built a ship
> in the Neather-lands.
> And it is called the sweet Trinity,
> And was taken by the false Gallaly,

sailing in the Low-lands.
Is there never a Seaman bold
in the Neather-lands:
Is there never a Seaman bold
in the Neather-lands?
That will go take this false Gallaly,
And to redeem the sweet Trinity,
sailing in the Low-lands.
Then spoke the little Ship-boy
in the Neather-lands,
Then Spoke the little Ship-boy
in the Neather-lands,
Master, master, what will you give me,
And I will take this false Gallaly,
And release the sweet Trinity,
sailing in the Low-lands.
I'le give thee gold, and I'le give thee fee
in the Neather-lands,
I'le give thee gold, and I'le give thee fee
in the Neather-lands;
And my eldest daughter thy wife shall be,
sailing in the Low-lands.
He set his breast, and away he did swim
in the Neather-lands,
He set his breast, and away he did swim
in the Neather-lands.
Until he came to the false Gallaly,
sailing in the Low-lands.
He had an Augor fit for the once,
in the Neather-lands,
He had an Augor fit for the once,
in the Neather-lands
The which will bore fifteen good holes at once
Sailing in the Low-lands
Some were at Cards, and some at Dice
in the Neather-lands,
Some were at Cards, and some at Dice
in the Neather-lands,
Until the salt water flash'd in their eyes,
sailing in the Low-lands.
Some cut their hats, and some cut their caps,

in the Neather-lands;
Some cut their hats, and some cut their caps
in the Neather-lands,
For to stop the salt-water gaps,
sailing in the Low-lands.
He set his breast and away did swim
in the Neather-lands,
He set his breast and away did swim
in the Neather-lands,
Until he came to his own ship again,
sailing in the Low-lands,
I have done the work I promised to do
in the Neather-lands,
I have done the work I promised to do
in the Neather-lands
For I have sunk the false Gallaly, and released the sweet Trinity,
sailing in the Low-lands.
You promised me gold, and you promised me fee,
in the Neather-lands,
You promised me gold, and you promised me fee,
in the Neather-lands,
Your eldest daughter my wife she must be,
sailing in the Low-lands.
You shall have gold, and you shall have fee
in the Neather-lands,
You shall have gold, and you shall have fee
in the Neather-lands.
But my eldest daughter your wife shall never be
for sailing in the Low-lands.
Then fare you well, you cozening Lord
in the Neather-lands,
Then fare you well, you cozening Lord
in the Neather-lands,
Seeing you are not so good as your word,
for sailing in the Low-lands.
And thus I shall conclude my Song
of the sailing in the Low-lands,
And thus I shall conclude my Song
of the sailing in the Low-lands;
Wishing all happiness to all Seamen both
old & young in their sailing in the Low-lands.[33]

There is no record of a ship named the *Sweet Trinity* built by Walter Raleigh, but we can readily place Raleigh and his interests on the lowland seas. The sea between England and the Netherlands had been the site of naval conflict during the Anglo-Spanish War (1585–1604), and Raleigh (who hated the Spanish) viewed the Netherlands as a key site in England's defense against Spain as a rival imperial power. During the 1580s, Raleigh and his associates had built a fleet of ships to make war against Spain by privateering or seizing Spanish merchant and treasure ships. During an era of rampant nation-on-nation privateering on the high seas, Raleigh's fleet and its captains were known for their ruthlessness and often criticized for capturing and plundering nonenemy French and Dutch ships as well. It was through state-backed piracy—the confiscation of ships and cargoes—that Raleigh secured a great deal of his own fortune as well as treasure for the Crown.[34]

How does an economic enterprise built on ruthless piracy treat its own soldiers? Does it reserve special consideration for the lowly men and women who do the dirty work, or does an ethic of opportunistic betrayal pervade the whole? The ballad suggests that Raleigh and his operatives did not only prey on rival navies and merchant fleets; common people were betrayed in the building of empire as well. The ballad opens by announcing that a ship built by Walter Raleigh has been taken by a rival craft and by summoning a sailor "bold" enough to rescue it. So volunteers a "little Ship-boy," or cabin boy, often the youngest, lowliest, and most vulnerable member of the ship's crew; his size and his rank symbolize his social status and affirm his connection to the English peasantry. The captain promises the cabin boy handsome rewards if he manages to take the rival galley: gold, fee (a medieval legal term indicating land granted to a vassal in exchange for his service), and the right to marry the captain's daughter. Heartened by these prospects, the boy takes his auger in hand, swims across the open ocean, and drills several holes into the sides of the enemy vessel. The vessel, according to the ballad, is populated by a disorderly band of sailors "at Cards and . . . at Dice." Card and dice playing were prohibited in well-regulated crafts; Raleigh himself wrote in his *Orders to be observed by the Commanders of the Fleet and Land Companies* (1617) that "No man shall play at cards or dice, either for his apparel or arms, upon pain of being disarmed, and made a swabber."[35] Surprised by the attack, the sailors cut their clothing to stop up the holes in the ship in a fruitless effort to prevent its sinking, while the "little Ship-boy" swims back to his captain. But despite his "bold" act the "little Ship-boy" returns to discover that he will not reap the promised reward. The captain (while permitting him land and gold) refuses to grant the hand of his eldest daughter, to which the outraged sailor replies:

Then fare you well, you cozening Lord
in the Neather-lands,
Then fare you well, you cozening Lord
in the Neather-lands,
Seeing you are not so good as your word,
for sailing in the Low-lands.

The word "cozening" bears special notice here: to "cozen" is to cheat, deceive, or betray, and the term first emerges as slang in the 1560s or 1570s among England's population of vagabonds, homeless, and unemployed sailors. Here is a word that reflects a notion of decency or honor maintained among those who had eked out a marginal living finding seasonal employ at seas in the service of schemes benefitting the empire and its wealthiest citizens, but for whom such exploits provided no personal gain, not even so much as a home. Some etymologies connect the word "cozen" to "cousin," suggesting an indictment of those who pretend kinship to take advantage of another. Is that not what the ship's captain did, offering, in effect, to make a kinsman of the lowly sailor, but withdrawing that promise after the sailor risked his life to recover Walter Raleigh's ship? Sailors who risked their lives on the open seas in the service of empire yielded no certain benefit from that empire, as the legions of England's homeless and unemployed vagabonds would attest. Indeed, as the use of the medieval term "fee" suggests, shipboard economies only reinstated feudal-type relationships between tyrannical captains and their serf-like sailor crews, a fact often recognized by observers in the seventeenth century.[36]

The severity of the betrayal wrought by Raleigh's ship captain deepened considerably when the ballad crossed the Atlantic Ocean in the mouths and memories of common English people. Virtually all of the documented American versions of the folksong replace the inconclusive ending of the British original with a darkly tragic end. For after the boy bravely swims across open seas, sabotages the rival galley using only a humble carpenter's tool, and swims back, he is met not only with the captain's reneging on his promise of gold, land, and marriage, but with the captain's outright refusal to take him back aboard the ship. In a turn that stuns both the sailor and the ballad audience, the captain in later versions of the ballad unaccountably leaves the sailor to drown in the open ocean, saying: "Neither will I take you on board / Or be to you as good as my word." Why such a murderous act of betrayal against one who risked his life in the service of the ship's mission? The ship captain gives no reason, and neither does the ballad. It is as though such whimsical violence is to be expected as normal conduct by the captains among the privateers. By contrast, in some American versions of the ballad, the common sailor briefly entertains but rejects the idea of using the augur in his hand to sink his own ship as an act of revenge. "If it wasn't for the love that I have for your men," he says, "I would do unto you as I done unto them." Out of solidarity with his shipmates, he refuses treachery.[37] Such solidarity defines the sailor as a member of the vagabond working class, a class that maintained its own notion of honor and loyalty even as the betrayal of common interests came to define the proprietors and principals of empire represented by the ship captain, that "cozening lord," and his sponsor, Raleigh. In fact, the ship-boy sent on a hazardous but profitable imperial errand but abandoned to die can be read as legendary correlate for all of the sailors and settlers who lost their lives in the service of Raleigh's several failed colonial ventures. Were not the colonists at Roanoke basically left to die? Then, applying the legend to a grander scale, can we not read the abandoned and betrayed ship-boy as an embodiment of all the common people whose interests were discarded in the process of economic modernization: the newly landless, unsecured, unemployed class of modern poor whom enterprising thinkers like Raleigh and his half brother Humphrey Gilbert promised to dispose of on the queen's foreign plantations? The American descendents of the original ballad retain a dark and striking sense of the extent of that betrayal, as if to suggest that we abandoned England because England abandoned us. And that we neither identify with nor trust the "cozening lords" who disposed of our lives in the service of their own enrichment. "The Sweet Trinity" reveals a centuries-old tradition of popular countermemory that views supposedly heroic imperial figures like Walter Raleigh as enterprising and coldly mercurial betrayers of common people.

BETRAYAL, OF COURSE, has no historical period. Neither do cruelty or perfidy. But it does bear notice when the most popular stories a culture generates about itself consistently feature themes of betrayal, and even more so, perhaps, when popular narratives identify the perpetrators of social betrayal, as does "The Sweet Trinity," with its specific indictment of Walter Raleigh and his operatives at sea. This ballad (along with the entire class of seventeenth-century ballads this book examines) originated among people who had witnessed a profound economic transformation of their English homeland that had uprooted and unsettled from their native contexts thousands upon thousands of peasants. It was from this new class of landless poor that the engineers of the modern British empire drew expendable bodies to employ as sailors on naval ships and as laborers on overseas plantations. "The Sweet Trinity" reflects the perspective of those common people on the uses to which they were put and the recompense they could expect from their labors, especially their labors at sea.

Karl Marx famously observed that the French smallholding peasantry responded to its own economic and political unsettling by identifying with a strong imperial figure like a Bonaparte. "They cannot represent themselves," he wrote in *The Eighteenth Brumaire*, "they must be represented. Their representative must at the same time appear as their master, as an authority over them, as an unlimited governmental power that protects them against the other classes and sends them rain and sunshine from above."[38] What we find in "The Sweet Trinity" is a decidedly more proletarian point of view: a refusal to identify with Raleigh or principals of empire on the part of English peasants who had not managed to keep their smallholdings. These were the ones who found themselves caught up and carried away by the rush of economic change as flotsam on moving water. That empire-capitalized economic modernization had little regard for their individual fates must have been clear from the beginning to the masses of young men who found themselves adrift in their own country, marked as disposable, conscripted when the Crown and its economic operatives needed them, and discharged to wander as vagabonds when they did not.

Perhaps common men and women identified with the travails of the used and abused sailor boy because they had witnessed in the sixteenth and seventeenth centuries the rise of an entire class of abandoned and landless former sailors in England. Impressment of sailors had been regular practice in England from medieval times: the promises of individual security against seizure and imprisonment in the Magna Carta were not understood to apply on the high seas. Especially after wars against France in 1545 and Scotland and France in the 1560s, those conscripted into naval or military service and then released back into English society came to be seen as a special category of threat to civil life—a new class of masterless men. Wrote William Harrison in his *Description of England* (1577): "It is the custom of the more idle sort, having once served, or but seen the other side of the sea under colour of service, to shake hands with labour for ever, thinking it a disgrace to return unto his former trade."[39] Demobilized troops were left to fend for themselves, even as the economic landscape of England radically shifted and traditional land-based communities that might have reabsorbed them were uprooted. Many discharged sailors took to the highways and byways as vagabond beggars. By the early seventeenth century, historians estimate, one out of five vagrants were discharged sailors or soldiers. Others overwhelmed their home parishes with requests for pension relief. Some rioted, destroying buildings and stealing cattle.[40] The chief remedy proposed for dealing with this large and dislocated class of former seamen was to send them back to sea. The Vagrancy Act of 1597 ordered that all vagabonds and rogues be banished from the realm. Among the reasons for North American colonization framed by Richard Hakluyt was that "Many souldiers and servitours, in the ende of the warres, that mighte be hurtfull to this realme, may there be unladen, to the common profile and quiet of this realme, and to our forreine benefite there, as they may be employed."[41] Following Hakluyt's counsel, Walter Raleigh used impressment to create labor for some of his ventures, as did other merchant capitalists of the day.

Conscripted labor on both merchant ships and naval ships carried out the dangerous grunt work of building England's wealth and territorial expansion. As one historian has put it: "Press gangs made empire."[42] Seventeenth-century naval contests with imperial rivals caused English naval personnel to double between the 1630s and the 1660s and peak at twelve thousand in 1679.[43] Economic conscription and impressment, though privately decried as "tyranny" by naval administrator (and ballad collector) Samuel Pepys, served as the major tools of naval recruitment, inciting widespread fear, resentment, and resistance. As press-gangs scoured seaports and seized working sailors from merchant ships, anti-impressment riots and violence broke out around the Anglo-Atlantic world from the 1690s through the 1760s.[44] Daniel Defoe observed the vulnerable economic situation of impressed soldiers in *Some Considerations on the Reasonableness and Necessity of Encreasing and Encouraging the Seamen* (1728), writing, "The Seamen are but one Species, and are wanted but upon two extraordinary Occasions; in Peace the King has no Occasion for them, the Merchants must employ them, or they starve: in War the King must have them, or the Service is starv'd; and if the King takes them, the Merchant stands still, and the Trade starves."[45] The figure of the impressed sailor became such a fixture in the Anglo-American imagination that Thomas Paine in *Common Sense* (1776) used this figure to represent monarchical tyranny and later in *The Rights of Man* (1791) seized on "the tortured sailor .... dragged through the streets like a felon" as emblematic of the total and arbitrary infringement of monarchy on individual liberty. Tyranny was not all the impressed sailor had to fear: fully half of those pressed into naval service died at sea.[46]

Economic necessity continued to push many Englishmen to sea as labor-intensive transatlantic bulk trades in commodities like tobacco and sugar grew by 2 to 3 percent per year in the late seventeenth and eighteenth centuries.[47] Shipboard order was maintained through the administration of demeaning and frequently disabling forms of physical punishment, including brutal beatings that left some sailors brain damaged and unable to walk—a condition called "falling sickness" by men in the trade.[48] Intimidation tactics such as humiliation, bullying, and hazardous duty assignment were used to single out and make examples of individual sailors.[49] "These were the tactics most frequently employed in a system of authority best described as violent, personal, and arbitrary," writes historian Marcus Rediker. "The system placed violence and discipline at the heart of the social relations of work and reproduced that violence by creating a powerful dynamic of aggression and counteraggression, a strong tendency toward personal vengeance."[50] Shipboard labor served as a brutal tutorial in the class relations of an emerging global-mercantile order. "The tar was caught between the devil and the deep blue sea," Rediker continues. "On one side stood his captain, who was backed by the merchant and royal official, and who held near-dictatorial powers that served a capitalist system rapidly covering the globe; on the other side stood the relentlessly dangerous natural world."[51] Sailors occupied the leading edge of the proletarianization of the newly unsettled and dispossessed English peasantry. When we place the behavior of the captain toward the cabin boy in "The Golden Vanity" into this historical context, we gain a revelatory glimpse into the humiliating modes of discipline practiced within colonizing societies in order to advance imperial agendas.

Ballads documenting the difficult lives of sailors played an important role in maritime culture, and "The Sweet Trinity" was only one of a number of black-letter ballads that memorialized their precarious situation. In 1630, London printer J. Wright published a ballad titled "The praise of Sailors, heere set forth, with their hard fortunes which doe befall them on the Seas, when Land-men sleepe safe in their Beds," which observes that the most dangerous labors are consigned to the most vulnerable members of the shipboard society:

> Our Master to his Compasse goes,
> so well he plies his charge:
> He sends a Youth to the Top amaine,
> for to unsling the Yeards.
> The Boatson hee's under the Deck,
> a man of courage bold;
> To th'top to th'top, my lively Lads,
> hold fast my hearts of gold. . . .
> Our Saylors they worke night and day,
> their manhood for to try,
> When landed men and rustling Jacks,
> doe in their Cabines lye.[52]

The ballad calls out the "master" and "boatson," or boatswain, for hiding below deck while ordering their underlings to prove the stoutness of their "hearts" in hazardous maritime labor. It also characterizes all who do not have to go to sea as partaking in a form of privilege. The phrase "landed men" indicates both those who have their professions at home as well as all who were able to retain their traditional tenure on the land and thus remained invulnerable to the creation of the landless working class from which most sailors were drawn; the term "rustling" (employed in the phrase "rustling jacks") is derived from the sound made by the movement of fine fabrics (like silk) and conventionally used in seventeenth-century English to characterize the dramatic self-presentation of those who could afford to wear such clothing. The "landed men" and silken-clad "rustling Jacks" in many respects contributed to the "hard fortunes" of sailors. The ballad was republished in the 1680s, just as English naval personnel peaked.[53]

Another ballad published in the 1670s or 1680s commemorated the impacts of impressment and maritime conscription on the intimate lives of common English men and women: "The Distressed Damsels: OR, A dolefull Ditty of a sorrowfull Assembly of young Maidens that were met together near Thames-street, to bewail the Loss of their Loves which were lately press'd away to Sea."

> My sweet Sister Sue, ah! what shall I do?
> I fain wou'd be married but know not to who;
> For why, I protest, the young Men are Prest,
> And my sweetheart Robin is gone with the rest
> For a Seaman.
> Then Susan reply'd there's many beside,
> That Fortune this Summer will surely divide;
> Each sudden surprize will cause Lasses cries,
> While Tears they do trickle like Rain from the Skies,
> For our Sweethearts.
> There's Bess at the Bell you know her full well,
> A sorrowful story to me she did tell,
> That Thomas, her Dear, was Prest she did hear,
> And then the poor Creature did tremble for fear
> He should leave her.
> In Thames-street of late, young pretty-fac'd Kate
> Had lost her dear Sweeting, the Bricklayer her Mate;
> He was Prest away, but yet the next day
> They freed him, then Kate she did lovingly say.
> My sweet Johnny.
> There's Doll at the Swan, her true love is gone,
> Poor Heart she with sorrow doth sigh and take on;
> Yet all is in vain, he is gone to the Main,
> She fears that he ne'er will return home again,

To embrace her.
There's Bridget & Joan 'tis very well known,
Of Fourteen young Sweethearts they have not left one
But all Prest on Board for to stand by the Sword,
And this do's much Sorrow and Trouble afford,
At the Parting.
If Pressing goes on, there wont be a Man
To please a young Lass, let her do what she can,
For they will be scarce here in a short space,
Then we shall be all in a sorrowful case,
To be Married. . . .
Young Nancy and Ned last week they were Wed,
And within an Hour of going to Bed,
Just in all their Pride he was Prest from her side,
Before he had dallied one Night with his Bride.
Want it Pity?[54]

Its comedic tone notwithstanding, the ballad presents a social environment so disrupted by the labor needs of England's imperial navy and its mercantile fleets as to tear newly wed grooms from their brides and create crisis for young unmarried women. This same spirit of uncertainty infused other popular genres of early transatlantic literature, giving rise to a number of autobiographical narratives focused on the experiences of common sailors as they passed through captivity after captivity, calamity after calamity, on the high seas and in far-flung colonies of the European empires. The ocean as setting for these ballads and narratives dramatized the vulnerability of newly landless peasants whose interests were just as often betrayed by England's imperial ambitions as they were advanced by them. Given the utter sense of imperilment and tyranny associated in the popular imagination with the life of common sailors at sea, it is no surprise that the earliest identified print progenitor of the slave narrative, *A Narrative of the Uncommon Sufferings, and Surprizing Deliverance of Briton Hammon, a Negro Man* (1760), was in fact a narrative of economic conscription, impressment, and captivity set on the high seas.

OF COURSE not all who crossed the ocean from England to America remembered the deeds of Walter Raleigh in such bitter terms. Within just a few decades of the end of the great Anglo-American peasant-class migration, Raleigh joined the pantheon of heroes celebrated by more elite classes of Americans. Connecticut-born poet Joel Barlow eulogized him in his epic *Vision of Columbus* (1787):

> Great Raleigh, pointing tow'rd the western sun;
> His eye, bent forward, ardent and sublime,
> Seem'd piercing nature and evolving time;
> Beside him stood a globe, whose figures traced
> A future empire in each wilder'd waste;
> All former works of men behind him shone,
> Graved by his hand in ever-during stone;
> On his mild brow, a various crown displays
> The hero's laurel and the scholar's bays;
> his graveful limbs in steely mail were drest,
> The bright star burning on his manly breast;
> His sword high-beaming, like a waving spire,
> Illumed the shrounds and flash'd the solar fire;
> The smiling crew rose resolute and brave,
> And the glad sails hung bounding o'er the wave.
> Far on the main, they held their rapid flight,
> And western coasts salute their longing fight;
> Glad Chesapeak unfolds a passage wide,
> And leads their streamers up the freshening tide;
> Where a mild region and delightful soil
> And groves and streams allure the sites of toil.
> Here, lodged in peace, they tread the welcome land,
> An instant harvest waves beneath their hand,
> Spontaneous fruits their easy cares beguile,
> And opening fields in living culture smile.[55]

A "mild"-"brow[ed]" Raleigh directing a "smiling crew" to the planting of an "instant harvest" in a "welcom[ing]" Virginia? In addition to a loose regard for historical fact, Barlow was also known to have a poor sense of judgment about the trustworthiness of venture colonists, as his dealings with the fraudulent Scioto Land Company in the late 1780s and early 1790s would prove. Decades later, Henry David Thoreau would offer a slightly more canny assessment of Walter Raleigh in a long biographical sketch he wrote in his notebooks and may have hoped to publish in *Dial* in 1844. Having made a study of Raleigh's *History of the World* during the early 1840s, Thoreau was less innocent to qualities that made the archcolonist hated in his own time. But he did hail Raleigh as England's greatest example of "heroic character," lavish attention on Raleigh's literary career, celebrate the diversity of his interests, and excuse the actual failure of his colonial ventures. "He seems to have had, not a profounder or grander but, so to speak, *more* nature than other men,—a great, irregular, luxuriant nature," wrote Thoreau. "Such a life is useful for us to contemplate as suggesting that a man is not to be measured by the virtue of his described actions, or the wisdom of his expressed thoughts merely, but by that free character he is, and is felt to be, under all circumstances."[56] For Thoreau, who in his notebooks would also compare the execution of Walter Raleigh to that of John Brown, Raleigh embodied a personhood of such magnitude as to live outside morality itself. His sketch on Raleigh reads very much in the vein of Ralph Waldo Emerson's *Representative Men* (1850), for what impelled Barlow and Thoreau to eulogize Raleigh in such extravagant terms was that quality the literary classes of the late eighteenth and nineteenth centuries called genius.

But by their measures there were no geniuses among my Brooks ancestors, or among any of the peasant peoples who broke their bodies building the British Empire and the American empires that succeeded it. Thus, it fell to common people to eulogize themselves in ballads such as "The Golden Vanity," and they did so by declaring their own bravery, physical strength, and loyalty to others of their straitened class, even when the landed powers of their home nations marked them as utterly expendable. So too did the Anglo-American descendents of the English peasant migrants of the seventeenth and eighteenth centuries remember Raleigh and his class in a mode that resonates within the broader canon of what one historian has called the English "folk memory of tyranny."[57] It is a canon of memory that preserves a sense of the "cozening lords" who maintained no scruples in betraying their fellow English men and women in the pursuit of gain. And it is a canon that stretches back before the era of colonization, to antienclosure riots and the disorganized rebellion of masterless men, and even to the peasant uprisings of the medieval era. Its literary tradition includes broadsides, speeches, and sung libels, and among its founding texts are these words spoken by the Lollard priest John Ball (1338–81) as an open-air sermon to participants in the Great Peasant Revolt of 1381:

> When Adam dalf, and Eve span, who was thanne a gentilman? From the beginning all men were created equal by nature, and that servitude had been introduced by the unjust and evil oppression of men, against the will of God, who, if it had pleased Him to create serfs, surely in the beginning of the world would have appointed who should be a serf and who a lord?[58]

Brave words, indeed, for which Ball was drawn and quartered before King Richard II.

But as brave as the tradition of folk antityranny commemorated in "The Golden Vanity" may be, I cannot help but get the feeling that in the surviving American version of the ballad as sung by Bascom Lamar Lunsford and his contemporaries something of that rebellious spirit dies with the cabin boy in the Atlantic Ocean. I can't quite cast off the chill those verses give me. How is it that his shipmates do not come to his aid? How is it that one captain could maintain by such cruel betrayals mastery over his far more numerous crew? Certainly, the culture of seventeenth-century shipboard discipline offers some insights here. But perhaps this very plainspoken ballad is also offering a commentary on the larger economic processes that created that imperial and mercantile culture. How is it possible that a few imperial architects and agents could come to compress such outsized wealth from the world's peasant classes? Historians have described the process of economic modernization as one of an intense consolidation of power and resources. Is it possible that the massive dislocations wrought by England's economic modernization so dislocated my Brooks ancestors from their moorings that they became completely submerged in the imperial project? We no longer had the land beneath our feet: only the martial imperatives of the new global economic order on the one side and the treacherous and uncertain ocean on the other.

Of course, we did not completely lose our folk sense of antityranny. That sense flashes up in Bacon's Rebellion and other myriad peasant uprisings of the early Atlantic world. Historians of the early Atlantic world like Marcus Rediker and Peter Linebaugh have documented the role of common maritime workers in fomenting the transatlantic age of revolutions. Sailors were the first modern laborers to go on strike, the word "strike" deriving from the coordinated action of sailors in London's ports in 1768 who hobbled their merchant ships by striking their sails in solidarity with labor demonstrations in the city. But even so it cannot be denied that many of the poor stinted-out newly landless maritime workers and travelers of the early Atlantic world became tools of empire, my Brooks ancestors among them. Whatever forms of dispossession and betrayal had been meted out to us we meted out to the other peasant peoples—indigenous and African—of the Atlantic world. Rather than turning our augurs back on the golden vanity of imperial ambition, we became tools of empire. As Lunsford's brisk and unsentimental singing suggests, we followed orders, and then we died.

CHAPTER FIVE

Seduction of the House Carpenter's Wife

Abandonment and the Story of Colonial Migration

In October 1950, the ethnographer Maud Karpeles sat down with fifty-five-year-old Attie Crane in Limestone, Tennessee, a tiny town on the banks of the Nolichucky River, at the western edge of the Cherokee National Forest—the real-life birthplace of the American folk hero Davy Crockett. Like Crockett himself, Attie Crane was descended from early British emigrants to North America, from the great masses of common peoples dislocated by England's economic transformation into a modern mercantile economy. What did Attie Crane know of that precipitous historical moment that uprooted her ancestors and sent them packing? What body of memory had survived the hundreds of years and thousands of miles from England? What stories did she have to tell? Attie sat forward at the edge of her rocking chair and sang:

> Well met, well met, my own true love
> Well met, well met, says she
> I have just married a house carpenter
> And as you as many as he.
> If you'll forsake your house carpenter
> And go along with me
> I'll take you where the grass grows green
> On the banks of Tennessee.
> She picked up her tender little babe
> And gave it kisses three

Stay here, stay here my tender little babe
While I go sail asea.
They hadn't been gone but about two weeks
I'm sure it was not three
Til this fair lady began to weep
She wept most bitterly.
Are you weeping for my gold?
Or is it for my store?
Or is it for your house carpenter
who face you'll see no more?
I'm neither weeping for your gold
Nor either for your store
I'm only weeping for my tender little babe
Who's face I'll see no more.
What banks, what banks before us now
As white as any snow?
It's the banks of heaven oh love she replied
Where all good people go.
What banks, what banks before us now
As black as any crow?
It's the banks of hell my love she replied
Where you and I must go.
They hadn't been gone but about three weeks
I'm sure it was not four
Till that fair ship began to sink
It sank to rise no more.[1]

Known sometimes as "James Harris" or "The House Carpenter" or "The Demon Lover," this song traveled from England to North America during the seventeenth and eighteenth centuries to become one of the most popular American folk ballads. Early in the twentieth century, ethnomusicologists like Karpeles and her mentor Cecil Sharp documented more than fifty versions of "The House Carpenter" in circulation among singers like Attie Crane in places like Tennessee, North Carolina, and Virginia. It remains one of the most frequently performed songs in the repertoire of American traditional music. As I listen to Attie Crane sing, I hear the clear, direct phrasing I've heard in other traditional singers, but I also hear a touch of longing and sentimentality. She does not press plainly and brightly through the telling of yet another grim tragedy, as did Horton Barker or Bascom Lamar

Lunsford or Lina Crockett, but rather leans into the minor-key tones. She sounds wistful.

All of the documented American versions of the ballad share a basic narrative formula: the wife of a carpenter in England is seduced away by a sailor who promises her great riches across the ocean. She kisses her "tender" young child (or children) goodbye, leaves home, and embarks on the ocean voyage. A few weeks into the voyage, she is beset by remorse at having abandoned her family. Shortly thereafter, the ship sinks, drowning the woman and her lover. Many variants add additional detail to the bones of the "House Carpenter" story. In some, the house carpenter's wife asks her would-be lover, "If I forsake my house carpenter / And go along with thee / What have you got for my support / And to keep me from slavery? / And to keep me from slavery?" a stark reminder that in the seventeenth and eighteenth centuries, common white people understood that their own economic precariousness made them vulnerable to bondage.[2] In the version of the ballad sung by Sam Pritt, in Barber, Alleghany County, Virginia, in November 1924, the wife adorns herself with finery and parades before the neighbors as she leaves home: "she dressed herself in rich attire, / most glorious to behold, / And as she tread upon her road / She shone like the glittering gold."[3] Singer Ada Maddox Allen of Lynchburg, Virginia, in 1950 remembered in more detail the words sung by mother to child: "She picked her newborn baby up / And gave it kisses three / Saying stay at home my darling little babe / And keep your dad company."[4] A version of "The House Carpenter" sung by Mary Sands of Allanstand, North Carolina, in 1916 is especially poignant in recounting the unfaithful wife's remorsefulness: "I'm weeping about my tender little babe / I left a-sitting on the floor / And if I had it's all the gold / That ever crossed the sea, / So free would I give it to see land again / And my tender little babe with me."[5] And some versions of the song conclude with a stanza warning women against seduction, or at least in trusting the words from a "man's lying tongue."[6]

To be sure, this ballad is a classic literary warning against marital infidelity. But as a cultural text generated during the height of the seventeenth-century English migration to North America, it also offers startling insights into how common English people narrated and understood the meaning of that historical moment. As literary texts do, this ballad serves as an archive of feeling, documenting and helping us key into bodies of experience and memory not readily available in legal, shipping, or church records. How did common English people who witnessed their loved ones departing for North America make sense of their own historical moment? And how did they feel, those uprooted common men and women who left their English homes (or had none to begin with) and made the crossing? What did the colonial project cost them, and how did they understand these costs? What is especially telling about the version Attie Crane sang in her house amid the poplar forests near Tennessee's Nolichucky River was that over time and through its travels "The House Carpenter" had evolved into a wistful commentary about her American home place and its false promises. "I'll take you where the grass grows green / On the banks of Tennessee," sings the sailor as he tries to seduce the house carpenter's wife away across the ocean. Land, gold, even a company of servants in America are promised to the deserting wife. But she never reaches America, and what she reaps instead of prosperity is the cataclysmic sorrow that comes from abandoning her baby, and then an early death.

What is additionally significant about "The House Carpenter" is that it opens up the story of the English colonization of the Americas from a distinctly gendered point of view, a point of view that is missing from many conventional histories. Did women view the colonizing enterprise or the advertised promises of America differently than men? How did thousands of young women recruited into colonial ventures understand the benefits and costs of colonization? Were those costs and benefits gendered? By centering on the point of view of a woman seduced away from England to America and turning on the desolation caused by her desertion of her child, "The House Carpenter" suggests that we view colonization as a process of *abandonment:* in its transformation from subsistence to mercantile economy, England abandoned the livelihoods and lifeways of its common peoples, creating a large population of surplus and disposable labor who then abandoned their homelands and families and went to North America. In fact, we can understand one of the sociocultural effects of England's great transformation from subsistence to mercantile economy as the development of a sociocultural capacity or tolerance for abandonment. Scholars today talk about abandonment as an organized surplusing of people, land, and other resources during times of economic structural change and crisis. In times of crisis, it is the most vulnerable classes of society that are surplused, set aside, or disposed of.[7] How did people become accustomed to the idea that people—kin, countrymen, and countrywomen—could be surplused, disposed of, deserted, left behind, as an acceptable sacrifice to profit making? When did abandonment gain acceptance as an expected feature of modern life? Is it possible that the process of colonization hammered out in Anglo-American colonists a capacity for tolerating desertion, loss, and forgetting? Telling the story of colonization as abandonment, as "The House Carpenter" does, encourages us to consider that the act of colonization entailed not only gains to Euro-American colonists but also losses: of family, of community, of home place, of stability, and of humane sensibility. And I find it especially significant that this perspective on colonization as abandonment comes to us through the point of view of a woman.

THE BEGINNINGS of the "House Carpenter" ballad sung by Attie Crane in Tennessee and her American peers have been traced by ballad scholars back to the oral traditions of England and Scotland, where the ballad was known by its alternate titles "James Harris" or "The Demon Lover" and featured an especially dramatic climactic scene wherein James Harris, the sailor-seducer, turns on his lover at sea, sabotages the ship, and as the ship is sinking reveals his cloven foot—a sign of his demonic nature. According to the English diarist and ballad collector Samuel Pepys, the song first appeared in print in London between 1686 and 1688 as a black-letter ballad titled "A Warning for Married Women. Being an Example of Mrs. Jane Reynolds (a west-country-Woman) born neer Plimouth who having plighted her troth to a Seaman, was afterwards married to a Carpenter, / and at last carried away by a Spirit":[8]

> There dwelt a fair Maid in the West,
> of worthy Birth and Fame,
> Neer unto Plimouth stately Town
> Jane Reynolds was her name.
> This Damsel dearly was belov'd,
> by many a proper youth:
> And what of her is to be said,
> is known for very truth:
> Among the rest a Seaman brave,

unto her a wooing came,
A comely proper youth he was,
James Harris call'd by Name.
The Maid and Young-man was agreed
as time did them allow,
And to each other secretly,
they made a solemn vow
That they would ever faithful be,
whilst Heaven afforded life,
He was to be her Husband kind,
and she his faithful Wife.
A day appointed was also,
when they were to be married,
But before these things were brought to pass
matters were strangely carried.
All you that faithful Lovers be,
give ear and hearken well,
And what of them became at last,
I will directly tell.
The Young man he was prest to Sea,
and forced was to go,
His sweet-heart she must stay behind
whether she would or no.
And after he was from her gone,
she three years for him staid,
Expecting of his coming home,
and kept her self a Maid.
At last news came that he was dead,
within a Forraign Land,
And how that he was buried,
she well did understand.
For whose sweet sake the maiden she,
lamented many a day:
And never was she known at all,
the wanton for to play.
A Carpenter that liv'd hard by,
when he heard of the same,
Like as the other had done before,
to her a wooing came.
But when that he had gain'd her love,
they married were with speed,

[A]nd four years space (being man & wife)
they lovingly agreed.
Three pritty Children in this time,
this lovely couple had,
Which made their Fathers heart rejoyce
and Mother wondrous glad.
But as occasion serv'd one time,
the good man took his way,
Some three days journey from his home
intending not to stay.
But whilst that he was gone away,
a spirit in the night,
Came to the window of his Wife,
and did her sorely fright.
Which Spirit spake like to a man,
and unto her did say,
My dear and onely love (quoth he)
prepare and come away.
James Harris is my name (quoth he)
whom thou didst love so dear,
And I have travel'st for thy sake,
at least this seven year.
And now I am return'd again,
to take thee to my wife,
And thou with me shalt go to Sea,
to end all f[?] her strife.
O tempt me not sweet James (quoth she)
with thee away to go,
If I should leave my children small,
alas what would they do?
My Husband is a Carpenter,
a Carpenter of great fame,
I wou'd not for five hundred pounds,
that he should know the same.
I might have had a Kings Daughte,
and she would have married me,
But [I] forsook her Golden Crown
and for the love of thee.
Therefore if thou'lt thy husband forsake
and thy children three also
I will forgive thee what is past

if thou wilt with me go.
If I forsake my husband, and
my little Children three,
What means hast thou to bring me to,
if I should go with thee.
I have seaven Ships upon the Sea,
when they are come to Land,
Both Marriners and Merchandize,
shall be at thy command.
The Ship wherein my love shal[l] sail,
is glorious to behold,
The sails shall be of finest silk,
and the mast of shining gold.
When he had told her these fair tales,
to love him she began,
Because he was in humane shape,
much like unto a man.
And so together away they went,
from off the English shore,
And since that time the Woman-kind,
was never seen no more.
But when her Husband he came home,
and found his Wife was gone,
And left her three sweet pr[i]tty babes,
within the house alone.
He beat hi[s] breast, he tore his hair,
the tears fell from his eyes,
And in the open streets he run,
with heavy doleful cries.
And in this sad distracted case,
he Hang'd himself for Woe,
Upon a tree, near to the place,
the truth of all is so.
The children now are fatherless,
and left without a guide,
But yet no doubt the heavenly powers,
will for them well provide.[9]

This early print version of the "James Harris" ballad sets the story of love, divided loyalties, and betrayal in the town of Plymouth, a historic port at the joining of the rivers Plym and Tamar, one-time home to

English maritime adventurer Sir Francis Drake (1540–96) and ancestral home to Drake's cousin Sir John Hawkins (1532–95), a Royal Navy commander and a trader in the English slave trade. Plymouth was also the point of embarkation for the legendary band of Puritan Separatists who left England for Massachusetts in 1620. It was a town that had played a significant role in the English colonization of the Americas. According to the ballad, Jane Reynolds, a "west-country-Woman" born near Plymouth, meets and makes a "solemn vow" to marry the young James Harris. A seventeenth-century English audience would have understood this solemn vow as equivalent to marriage itself and as a condition for legitimate sexual intimacy between Harris and Reynolds. As historian Keith Wrightson explains, "A promise to marry expressed in words of the present tense in the presence of witnesses constituted a binding marriage, as also did a promise made in words of the future tense, provided that it was followed by sexual union."[10] In fact, the ballad effectively stages an exchange of vows between them—"He was to be her Husband kind, / and she his faithful Wife"—and implies the consummation of their vows by commending their story to other "faithful Lovers."

But after his betrothal James Harris is suddenly "prest to Sea," forcibly recruited into naval service by one of the press-gangs known to scour the taverns of Plymouth town. Jane Reynolds remains behind and stays faithful to her vows for three years until news arrives that Harris is dead and buried in a faraway land. This news brings renewed interest from Reynolds's many would-be suitors, including an unnamed carpenter, who comes "wooing" and marries her "with speed." A happy marriage follows, as do three children over the course of the next four years. But one night, when Reynolds's carpenter husband is away from home on a three-day journey, the "Spirit" of James Harris comes to her window at night and beckons her to come away to sea with him. Jane Reynolds pleads not to go, for the sake of her three young children and her carpenter husband. The spirit, however, indicts her faithlessness by telling Reynolds that he had rejected marriage to a "Kings Daughte" in order to remain faithful to her. The story of the humble English sailor who goes abroad and finds romance with the daughter of a foreign king had been a staple of the English literature of colonization, both imaginative and informational, from at least the fourteenth century. It appeared in the *Gesta Romanorum*, a medieval English compilation of popular stories known by Chaucer, Boccaccio, and Shakespeare, and found new life in ballads such as "Lord Bateman and the Turkish King's Daughter" as well as in the writings of English colonist John Smith, who recorded in his *Generall Historie of Virginia* (1624) his famous rescue by King Powhatan's daughter Pocahontas as well as a previous, lesser-known but equally fabulous near-rescue from slavery in Istanbul in 1603 by a Turkish nobleman's daughter, Charatza.[11] In this telling, the spirit of James Harris uses the then well-known trope of romance with a lady abroad to pressure Reynolds, reminding her that while he has rebuffed the attentions of exotic royalty, she has broken her promises of betrothal to him: "I will forgive thee what is past," he promises, "if thou wilt with me go." Reynolds yields to pressure but demands to know "what means hast thou to bring me to." The spirit replies that he has ships, mariners, and "Merchandize" and promises to transport her across the ocean in a ship with sails "of finest silk / and the mast of shining gold," a ship fashioned quite literally from the spoils of England's global-commercial empire. And Jane Reynolds goes for the spoils; she departs Plymouth. In some early English versions of the ballad, she sings a tearful farewell to her children; in this black-letter version, she goes without so much as saying goodbye. When her husband returns from his errand, he finds the children deserted and out of grief and outrage hangs himself "for Woe, / Upon a tree." Three abandoned children are the legacy of Reynolds's seduction by James Harris, the demon lover.

The demon lover we see in "James Harris" / "A Warning for Married Women" is actually a familiar trope of English folklore known as a revenant, literally meaning "one who returns." In ballads, revenant spirits return from death to exact justice from wrongdoers.[12] They often appear to warn or punish women who transgress marital bonds, serving as a personification of social controls over women.[13] In the case of "The House Carpenter," the spirit of James Harris returns to accuse and punish Jane Reynolds for her faithlessness to their marriage promises seven years earlier, promises that would have been understood according to English custom as the equivalent of a legal vow.[14] Moving beyond these this-worldly social implications of the revenant ballad, when understood on a more metaphysical plane, the appearance of a revenant indicates not only the penetration of this world by otherworldly influences, but the passage of the living into a hazardous or liminal space.[15] As ballad scholar David Atkinson writes, "Revenant ballads represent various unhealthy psychological states and proffer ways of coping with the dangers they present. When taken together as a group in this way, a shared cultural arena becomes evident, in which women (most characteristically) are confronted with dislocations brought about by death."[16] "James Harris" / "A Warning for Married Women" then can be understood to document and dramatize disturbed emotional and relational states of being caused by the wrenching dislocations of a colonial world where newly betrothed husbands are forcibly transported across oceans, undermining and destabilizing the social contexts they leave behind and creating new kinds of social and familial insecurity.

The figure of the revenant takes on another dimension of significance when considered in the context of Anglo-American colonization. The revenant, after all, is identified in the ballad as a "spirit." The term "spirit" was often used in seventeenth-century England to refer to colonial agents who persuaded, lured, intoxicated, or even kidnapped unsuspecting English men, women, and children into the American colonial labor force. Parliament passed "An Ordinance against such who are called Spirits, and use to steal away, and take up children" in 1645. In *Virginia Impartially Examined* (1649), William Bullock explained:

> The usuall way of getting servants, hath been by a sort of men nicknamed *Spirits,* who take up all the idle, lazie, simple people they can intice, such as have professed idlenesse, and will rather beg than work; who are perswaded by these *Spirits,* they shall goe into a place where food shall drop into their mouthes: and being thus deluded, they take courage, and are transported. But not finding what was promised, their courage abates, & their minds being dejected, their work is according.[17]

While the practice of spiriting was never the primary means for securing colonial labor, it was perceived to be widespread enough to constitute a threat demanding constant vigilance and government intervention. In the summer of 1657, for example, word spread in the port of London that the ship *The Conquer* bound for Virginia held many spirited people on board. Port officials interviewed passengers and determined that eleven had in fact been recruited through spirits, and that of these eleven, only two actually wanted to go to Virginia. The rest had been forced or tricked on board.[18] Depictions of spirits, their deceptions, and their victims abounded in the popular literature of seventeenth-century England. Those that focused on the spiriting away of women often intermingled narratives of female sexual licentiousness with abduction into colonial labor, as did Ebenezer Cooke in his satire *The Sot-Weed Factor* (1708) wherein a flirtatious chambermaid tells the poem's narrator she had been "Kidnap'd and Fool'd" into servitude: "These are the general Excuses made by English Women," the narrator responds in a footnote, "which are sold, or sell themselves to Mary-Land."[19] "The House Carpenter" draws on the popular fear of spiriting as well as the association in popular literature between spiriting and seduction. In fact, by identifying the returned lover James Harris as a "spirit," "The House Carpenter" mingles a warning against marital infidelity with a warning against the faithlessness of seductive colonial agents.

A final element that adds to this reading of "The House Carpenter" as a warning against the manifold betrayals of colonization is the length of time between James Harris's impressment and his return to Plymouth. According to the ballad, seven years elapse before Harris returns; seven years was a common length for the contracted bondage of English servants in colonial America. With this in mind, the ballad can also be read from the point of view of James Harris as the tale of someone who returns from a period of colonial contract labor to find his home contexts utterly changed and his relationships destroyed. Just as colonization—especially practices such as impressment and spiriting designed to secure the bodies needed to conquer and capitalize on colonized territories—undermined the ability of wives to count on their husbands, it undermined the ability of husbands to count on their wives. "James Harris" / "A Warning for Married Women," in its English seventeenth-century form, exposes not just the faithlessness of one wife to one husband but a multilayered and interlaced set of social betrayals precipitated by the forcible enlistment of one man into colonial enterprise. James Harris is betrayed by his government through impressment; with no information about her husband's whereabouts, Jane Reynolds abandons her marital vows and forms a new family; confronted by the spirit of James Harris, Jane Reynolds abandons her second husband and their children; and finally the abandoned second husband also abandons his children by committing suicide. In concluding with the image of abandoned children and the dubious hopes that "heavenly powers" will provide for them, the ballad projects forward the social costs of colonial betrayal and abandonment, suggesting that a new form of social insecurity will replicate itself on down through the generations.

The ballad itself also survived down through the generations, crossing the Atlantic Ocean in the mouths and minds of common English people destined for the plantations of the middle Atlantic colonies in the seventeenth and eighteenth centuries, traveling inland with landless and migrant laborers, and finally claiming for itself a secure place in the repertoire of American folk and traditional music.[20] As often happens with ballads that travel orally, "James Harris" underwent some changes along the way, losing some of the ornamentation that only print could afford to carry and becoming a leaner, more action-driven narrative. We can track those changes by examining the first American version of the ballad to make it into print: "The House Carpenter," a broadside issued by H. DeMarsan, a mid-nineteenth-century publisher of popular music, from his shop at 60 Chatham Street in Lower Manhattan sometime between 1858 and 1861.

> "Well met, well met, my own true love,
> Well met, well met!" cried he—
> "For I've just returned from the Salt Sea,
> All for the love of thee!"
> "I might have married the King's daughter dear,—"
> "You might have married her," cried she,
> "For I am married to a House-Carpenter,
> And a fine young man is he."
> "If you will forsake your House-Carpenter,
> And go along with me,
> I will take you to where the grass grows high,
> On the banks of old Tennessee!"
> "If I forsake my House-Carpenter,
> And go along with thee,
> What have you got to keep me upon,
> And keep me from misery?"
> Says he, "I've got six ships at sea,
> All sailing to dry land,
> One hundred and ten of your own countrymen,
> Love, they shall be at your command!"
> She took her babe upon her knee
> And kissed it one, two, and three,

Saying, "Stay at home, my darling sweet babe,
And keep your father's company!"
They had not sailed four weeks or more,
Four weeks, or scarcely three,
When she thought of her darling sweet babe at home,
And she wept most bitterly.
Says he, "Are you weeping for gold, my love,
Or are you weeping for fear,
Or are you weeping for your House-Carpenter,
That you left and followed me?"
"I am not weeping for gold," she replied,
"Nor am I weeping for fear,
But I am weeping alone for my sweet little babe,
That I left with my House-Carpenter."
"Oh, dry up your tears, my own true love,
And cease your weeping," cried he,
"For soon you'll see your own happy home,
On the banks of old Tennessee!"
They had not sailed five weeks or more,
Five weeks or scarcely four,
When the ship struck a rock and sprang a leak,
And they never were seen any more.
A curse be on the sea-faring men,
Oh, cursed be their lives,
For while they are robbing the House-Carpenter,
And coaxing away their wives.[21]

As this broadside documents, the ballad passed through several significant changes in its transit from England to America. First, the title changed from "A Warning for Married Women," "James Harris," or "The Demon Lover" to "The House Carpenter." In fact, it is worth noting that the carpenter husband is not identified as a "house carpenter" until the ballad reaches America.[22] Second, the early stanzas of the story about Jane Reynolds's betrothal to James Harris drop away, as do the ballad's supernatural elements, including Harris's death and his return as a revenant spirit. It was common for English ballads to lose their supernatural elements when they migrated to the Americas. If English folk traditions once relied on spirits to punish the unjust, those spirits, it seems, did not cross the Atlantic, did not leave their ancestral homeland; Anglo-Americans, then, lived in a realm empty of old and familiar spirits, their memories, and their penchant for justice. The dead did not follow, and the new lands were empty of memory and responsibility. With the elimination of the supernatural dimension in the ballad narrative—the betrothal, impressment, betrayal, and vengeance of the revenant spirit of James Harris—the situational center of the story shifts to the seduction of Jane Reynolds by the promises of a lover and the lures of a new world. This represents a third change to the ballad: in its American versions, the narrative refocuses on America as a named destination and as an object of desire. In older English versions, James Harris lures Jane Reynolds away first with promises of wealth, and then, if the destination is named at all, to European places like Italy. But as folklorist Alisoun Gardner-Medwin notes, in the American versions, the seducer first promises passage to America and a new home there, "as if this were the one promise that would persuade the young woman to leave."[23] The final change we note in American versions of the ballad is the elimination of concluding stanzas relating to the fate of the husband and child or children left behind in England. The story leaves England with its female protagonist and stays with her as she discovers the emotional consequences of abandoning her homeland.

What we see, then, as the ballad moved from England to America is a shift in its overall focus from a story of the betrayal of traditional English marriage vows and their punishment to a story about the seductive lure of America and its disappointments. It becomes a story about leaving home, as is underscored by the newly specific characterization of the carpenter husband as a "House Carpenter": Jane Reynolds leaves not only a husband who has a skilled trade, but a husband whose work identifies him with profound investments in the domestic sphere. And as the story drops its early stanzas about betrothal and betrayal and drops as well the final stanzas about marriage and its betrayal, as the setting of the story relocates from England to the ship of passage, the story itself abandons its concern with the past, its ghosts, its attachments, and their emotional reach and refocuses on the future and its disappointments. The version of "The House Carpenter" brought across the ocean by Anglo-American colonists thus enacts the very abandonment of the past it narrates. Gone are the hanged husband and the abandoned children. Gone is all mention of England. The narrative now arcs toward the promise of a new home in Tennessee and its impossibility. With the cataclysmic interruption and termination of the passage to America and the grief wrought by abandonment, the narrative leaves no home undisturbed and casts into doubt the possibility of establishing a home at all in a modern world structured by disruption. The betrayal here is not of husband by wife but of the idea of home, the idea of domestic attachment and belonging, by a new global economic order.[24] What is so striking about this ballad, then, is that it documents a sense of loss and familial disaster associated in the minds of common English people with the project of colonization.

Even as it changes its situational center and its narrative focus, what does not change about "The House Carpenter" in its transit across the ocean is the blame it places on Jane Reynolds for leaving home. From its beginnings as a traditional warning against marital infidelity, the ballad becomes a warning against leaving home for the Americas: both are forms of infidelity punishable by death. It is possible to read the death by shipwreck dramatized in both English and American ballads as an allegorical warning that women who abandon home will experience social death as a consequence: in the case of marital infidelity, a variety of social death Erving Goffman once described as a "spoilage of identity," or in the act of leaving England, a variety of social death sociologist Orlando Patterson described as "natal alienation," a severing from home, kin, memory, and community. We have come to understand this state of natal alienation as a structuring fact of African American slave experience in colonial America; "The House Carpenter" suggests that early Anglo-American colonists also experienced a profound form of alienation crossing to a new land empty of familiar spirits, ancestral memories, and geospiritual home places.

Of course, we are right to resist the narrative implication that women should be punished or blamed for such disastrous changes. For even as common Englishwomen participated in these tectonic social and epistemic shifts that inaugurated modernity, they did not by their individual choices set them into motion. What we see, then, in the accusation and punishment of Jane Reynolds in "The House Carpenter" is a catachresis: the misuse of a trope. Catachresis is an attempt to forcibly ascribe complicated varieties of experiences to common and familiar names: here, for example, by reducing the complex historical forces that impacted common English families in the era of economic transformation from subsistence to colonial mercantile economy to an act of female marital infidelity. Indeed, as postcolonial literary critics have pointed out, catachresis is an act of epistemic violence mobilized with particular and foundational force in colonial contexts. In such contexts, catachresis often operates as the substitution of effect for a cause. Did Jane Reynolds by her individual choices cause the destruction of her marriage and family life, or were Jane Reynolds and her marriage and family life destroyed by the social institution of impressments and by the colonial ambitions for martial, political, and economic dominance that made impressments a common part of English life? Did her home fall apart because Jane Reynolds chose to leave them, or did Jane Reynolds and other common Englishwomen who emigrated to America leave because their homes were already falling apart? Was it the case that the modern Anglo-American capacity for abandonment began in individual acts of social infidelity? Or did men and women cross the ocean and abandon their families because families had already been rendered vulnerable by the massive economic changes of their times? The "House Carpenter" ballad uses a traditional host narrative of infidelity to archive feelings of betrayal, loss, dislocation, and desolation associated with colonization. The ballad reveals that common English men and women understood the lures of colonization to be as false as a lover's promises and the event of leaving home for America to be as devastating as a shipwreck. But to understand the root causes of these feelings, we must move through the catachrestic reversals of the narrative into the more prosaic histories it strives, in its own twisted and ultimately catastrophic way, to make sense of.

INDEED, THE BALLAD NARRATIVE that ascribed familial disaster to one woman's choice to leave home and cross the ocean masked much larger economic and social forces at work in the sixteenth and seventeenth centuries that had rendered families and communities more vulnerable to dissolution. The end of traditional land tenure, the shift from subsistence to mercantile and export economies, the stinting out of traditional subsistence practices, the destruction of forests and habitat, and the creation of a large class of landless migrant wage laborers had contributed to destabilization and transformation in traditional modes of family life, courtship, marriage, and parenthood and undermined the ability of parents to provide for their children in familiar and time-honored ways.

Historians of the English family have linked the economic modernization of England to profound shifts in family structure. With economic modernization and increased subsistence migration weakening local community ties in the late sixteenth and early seventeenth centuries, traditional patronage- and kinship-networked family structures consolidated and recentered around nuclear family units, placing more emphasis on patriarchal authority and economic responsibility, just as economic changes undermined laboring-class men's ability to provide for their own families. The shift from land-based subsistence labor to wage labor in a market economy effected substantial changes in the gendering of authority within the home. The sixteenth-century commentator Judith Drake wrote that, in some laboring-class families, "though not so equal as that of Brutes, yet the condition of the two Sexes is more level, than amongst Gentlemen, City Traders, or rich Yeomen."[25] But this working-class egalitarianism was to come under tremendous pressure. As Allan Kulikoff writes, "Enclosure thus transformed familiar relations among the poor. When peasants lost their land or right to commons, an important buttress of paternal authority—the father's ability to direct family labor—was severed."[26] Few jobs offered wages sufficient to support a family, so many husbands left home as subsistence and betterment migrants in search of decent work. Some men abandoned their families altogether. A vagrancy statute of 1610 deemed such men "incorrigible rogues."[27]

Just as the sixteenth and seventeenth centuries saw the rise of a new class of what Thomas Hobbes and, following him, historian A. L. Beier described as "masterless men"—individual migrant laborers severed from kin and traditional subsistence communities—a new class of "masterless women" also emerged: women left behind by husbands who took to the roads in search of better conditions, or went to sea as sailors, or were impressed into military service or decoyed into colonial indentures. These "masterless women" pieced together their own livelihoods through a combination of wage labor, subsistence practices such as gleaning, poor relief, neighborly aid, selling goods at market, and other practices of the economic margins such as pawning clothes and household items. Theirs was an "economy of makeshifts."[28] And many emergent mercantile industries capitalized on women's economic need to establish cottage operations, even whole villages of textile industry cottages, populated mostly by women living outside the control of patriarchal households. By the mid-sixteenth century, one in three women and children made their living from the cottage cloth industry.[29] Even women who worked in their own homes as the cottage laborers of the textile industry were especially vulnerable, as Patricia Fumerton writes, to "feelings of occasional displacement or unsettledness, given their marginalized work in diverse makeshift jobs both within and outside the home, which exposed them to censure and even accusations of being vagrant."[30] The rise of masterless women fueled common perceptions that adultery, often linked to the work-related travels of husband or wife, was also on the rise.

New economic pressures and uncertainties and new cultures of social and economic mobility generated new anxieties about home, family, and gender roles, much of it focused on women. Consequently, the late sixteenth and early seventeenth centuries saw increased discourse—both high and low culture—aimed to correct incorrigible women and restore patriarchal order. From the pulpits and in printed pamphlets, religious writers inveighed against disorderly, unchaste women and promulgated ideals of piety, chastity, and obedience. Especially in the early seventeenth century, the political theory of patriarchalism, which associated the authority of the king with the authority of the father in the home, gained popularity as men at all levels of society sought to consolidate and preserve their power in a rapidly changing world.[31] Laboring-class literature like ballad broadsides and plays also punished gossiping, adulterous, and critical wives, oftentimes through dramatizing horrific wife beatings.[32] Ballads about sailors and men who worked away from home focused on themes of fidelity, while ballads about women reprimanded those who transgressed the domestic sphere, according to Patricia Fumerton:

> Women in the late sixteenth and especially the seventeenth century were increasingly subject to economic and social sanctions that restricted their "labors"—even the vagrant labors of female hawkers and fishwives—forcing their removal to the domestic sphere of the home. . . . As a consequence, the domestic space became gendered female.[33]

The more the laboring-class home came under pressure from economic changes, the more the domestic sphere was idealized.[34]

The reliability of women as nurturers also became an object of social anxiety, especially with the passage of poor-relief laws that made abandoned children the financial responsibility of taxpayers and local parishes. Such laws incentivized the surveillance and punishment of women and their children. Under sixteenth-century vagrancy statutes and apprenticeship systems, beggar children between five and fourteen could be legally seized and compelled into labor as servants or apprentices. The *Book of Orders* in 1631 ordered that "poore children in every parish" were to "be put forth apprentices to husbandry, and other handy-crafts." In some parishes, 20 to 30 percent of all children aged seven to sixteen were put out to work in the 1620s and 1630s.[35] Anxiety over the financial costs of caring for abandoned children contributed to the removal of more children from their families and homes; the state's attempts to intervene in what was perceived to be a disrupted context for family life only exacerbated the disruption of families. Similarly, anxiety over the failure of maternal care and nurturing fed perceptions that child murder was on the rise and led to new legislation to criminalize infanticide. An Act to Prevent the Destroying and Murthering of Bastard Children, passed by Parliament in 1624, targeted for prosecution the already socioeconomically vulnerable class of unmarried mothers. It focused especially on whether a mother had concealed her pregnancy or the birth or death of an infant; concealment, according to the statute, constituted reasonable grounds for suspecting murder.[36] In legislation ordering the removal of children from laboring-class homes and the criminalization of concealed infant death, we can see how growing state intervention in working-class family life compounded stresses on the intimate and affectionate lives of these families.

Perhaps the best example of how state attempts to regulate newly landless laboring-class families exacerbated family disintegration is the Act for the Better Relief of the Poor of this Kingdom of 1662. Often called the Settlement Act, this legislation attempted to sort out which parishes were to be charged for relief payments to poor and migrant laborers by certifying the parishes to which the poor belonged. Migrant laborers and their families were expected to carry certificates identifying their birthplaces or the places where they had last resided for three years or more; these certificates obliged the home parish to pay for the removal of the poor and their return home to prevent their relief payments being charged to another parish. Consequently, to avoid charges, parishes often resisted issuing settlement certificates, and employers and landowners often hired or rented to nonresidents in order to take advantage of their vulnerability in being far from home places and poor relief. Some parishes even acted to break up families and return poor children to the parishes of their birthplaces—even if different children were born in different birthplaces, as was often the case for migrant laboring families.[37] Government efforts to regulate the movement of the poor only increased the threat of family dissolution. As historian Steve Hindle writes, "It is clear that the very fact of economic need rendered the families of the poor vulnerable to the intervention of the authorities."[38]

The most dramatic steps taken by the state to regulate and dispose of surplused rural laborers and their fragmented families entailed colonization to the Americas. The seventeenth century saw the rise of large populations in London of unsettled and homeless youth, a substantial number of whom were lured, recruited, or forcibly taken to the Americas as laborers. In fact, the term "kidnapping" originates in this historical moment to describe the forcible abduction of children to the colonies. Now infamous are the stories of shipments of orphaned, stranded, and abandoned children shipped to colonial plantations. A few such shipments have been documented in the first half of the seventeenth century. In 1619, several hundred poor children residing at London's Bridewell prison-hospital were exported by the Virginia Company to work as laborers. At least one thousand more were exported in 1627, as were four hundred Irish children in 1653. Orphans made up nearly two-thirds of the young people who left London for America in the 1680s.[39]

Of course, no greater family or household stability awaited laboring emigrants in America, where separation from English extended family networks, frequent migration, and high death rates contributed to the demolition of traditional kinship structures. Marriages among laboring-class emigrants in seventeenth-century Maryland and Virginia lasted on average half as long as marriages in England, due in large part to high mortality rates among emigrants.[40] Even the formation of voluntary, non-blood-related family units was frustrated by incredible rates of population turnover. Some Chesapeake communities witnessed residential turnover rates as high as 80 percent per decade in the seventeenth century.[41]

Laboring-class English families in the sixteenth and seventeenth centuries faced a host of new pressures including fundamental changes to their age-old practices of subsistence living, their livelihoods, their relationships to traditional lands, and the solidity of their kinship networks. England's internal transition from subsistence to mercantile economy forced many families to lose fathers, mothers, and children either to the migrant search for labor or, paradoxically, to state-supported initiatives to manage the laboring poor. The same forces that led to the growth of English colonial ambitions and enterprises dramatically uprooted and destabilized families. And yet, in the popular literature of the time, it is the poor moral choices of individuals and not these tectonic socioeconomic shifts that are blamed for the abandonment of families. Witness the words of the mayor of the port city of Bristol, who observed in 1662:

> Among those who repair to Bristol from all parts to be transported for servants to his Majesty's plantations beyond seas, some are husbands that have forsaken their wives, others wives who have abandoned their husbands; some are children and apprentices run away from their parents and masters; often-times unwary and credulous persons [that] have been tempted on board by men-stealers, and many that have been pursued by hue-and-cry for robberies, burglaries, or breaking prison, do thereby escape the prosecution of law and justice.[42]

In the eyes of the governing classes, the laboring-class English men, women, and children who went as indentured servants to North America were individuals who had "forsaken" and "abandoned" their homes, families, employers, England, even morality itself. No one of this class seemed to entertain the idea that somewhere along the way in its ambition for mercantile power England itself had abandoned its own laboring people.

THE IDEA that colonial emigration to America was an opportunistic betrayal of laboring people akin to sexual infidelity emerged over time in the songs common people sang about America and specifically about the place called "Virginia." For during the disrupted times of sixteenth- and seventeenth-century England, ballads emerged as an important form for communicating social knowledge. "The House Carpenter" was one of several English ballads featuring female protagonists and addressed to female audiences that chart a growing awareness of how colonization contributed to the destabilization of families and social ties and the abandonment of loved ones.

The first ballads about emigration to America directed at women served as promotional literature, publicizing and celebrating the improvements in living conditions women might anticipate as a reward for indentured passage to America. "The Maydens of London," published in the 1650s or 1660s, appeals to "Peg, Nell, and Sisses, Kate, Doll, and Besse / Sue, Rachel, and sweet Sara," promising that if they are "brave" enough to emigrate to Virginia, they will "be fed with good strong fare / according to the season / Bisket salt-Beef, and English Beer / and Pork well boyled with Peason." Warm weather and bounteous natural food supplies also awaited them:

> For victuals when as you come there
> you shall have choice and plenty
> Pigs, Turkies, Geese, Cocks, Hens, and Ducks,
> and other fare most dainty,
> Also be sure that you shall have
> enough sold for your mony
> A good fat Capon for a groat
> and eighteen eggs a penny.

Wages, too, the ballad continued, were much higher in Virginia:

> For every groat that you got here
> you shall have three time double
> For there are Gold and Silver Mines
> and treasures much abounding,
> As plenty as New-Castle Coales
> at some parts may be founding.

In addition to being well paid, the ballad promised, women could expect their labors to eventuate in land ownership, ownership impervious to the English economic policies that had so starkly diminished rural land tenure and stinted commoners out of their traditional subsistence rights in the sixteenth and seventeenth centuries:

Where you shall h[a]ve good ground enough,
for Planting and for Tilling
Which never shal be taken away,
so long as you there are living.[43]

"The Maydens of London" could expect to find in America a land of security and plenty reminiscent of England before its economic transformation.

But soon popular ballads began to register a less sanguine picture of English emigration to Virginia. "A Net for a Night-Raven, Or, A Trap for a Scold," published in London in the 1650s, depicts colonization as a punishment for ill-behaved wives. It begins with an ironic send-up of the genre of colonial advertisement, including a direct lampooning of the sunny claims made in "Maydens of London":

I think there's few that hath not heard
of famous brave Virginny.
Where Capons are so cheap,
and Eggs are in such plenty,
Also Fowl and Fish,
and other things most dainty,
As Pigs, Veal, Lamb and Venison,
if Travellers speak truly,
Which is the cause so many go,
and travels to Virginny.

"A Net for a Night-Raven" gives its audience plenty of reason to doubt whether "Travellers speak truly" about "famous brave Virginny." The narrative action unfolds around a weaver's wife who cheats on her husband and then scolds him, demanding, "When do you pack, / and go unto Virginny?" The husband, tiring of her abuses, approaches the master of a vessel bound for Virginia and arranges to sell his wife. He returns home, tells his wife that he has finally booked his own passage to Virginia, and entreats her to come to port to see him off. Under these pretenses, the wife is decoyed on board ship and taken away to Virginia, where she is resold for fifty pounds. As the ballad ends:

Beware you scolding wives,
if no fair means will win ye,
lest that your Husbands you entrap,
and send you to Virginny.[44]

Instead of naming a promised land for hardy maidens, Virginia becomes a dumping ground for rebellious wives.

The association between marital infidelity or sexual licentiousness and being decoyed to Virginia persists in later ballads. "The Trappan'd Welsh-man Sold to Virginia" (1680–95) recounts the story of a rural Welshman who visits the royal exchange, London's commercial center. There, he is seduced by a "pritty" "Lass" telling stories about the wonders of colonial commerce:

She told a Tale of Ships on th' Ocean,
which the fine Welshman might behold
Who now was quite at her Devotion.

The cosmopolitan "Lass" turns out to be a spirit. She leads the Welshman to the docks and onto a ship named the *Virginia:*

For when they came 'board the Virginny
a Ship most gay and fit for Trade,
There she did sell the harmless Ninny,
to make her Market (like a Jade).

The ballad serves as a warning to rural men and women displaced or dislocated to urban centers about the seductions of colonial commerce and their vicious dangers, betrayals, and costs. Like the "pritty" "Lass" in the royal exchange, venture colonialism preyed upon and profited from the captivity of common English men and women.[45] Virtually the same warning to the rural poor is reiterated in "Love Overthrown: The Young Man's Misery; and the Maids Ruine." This seventeenth-century ballad relates the story of a young woman from rural Herefordshire who comes to London to work as a "Serving Maid" in the household of a wealthy merchant. When the merchant's son falls in love with young "Betty," his mother sells the girl away:

And so away she did her bring,
Unto a Captain of her Kin,
Whose Ship that time lay in the Downs
And he was for Virginia bound.
And so away this Damsel's gone
Unto Virginia, sailing on.
O Heavens unto her prove kind,
And grant she may some comfort find.[46]

In both ballads, Virginia is the name of an intimate betrayal opportunistically wrought upon common and rural people by those of the merchant class.

The ballad that provides the most explicit warning about Virginia's false promises and betrayals is "The Trappan'd Maiden: OR, The Distressed Damsel," which was published between 1689 and 1703. The ballad serves as a warning sent back from a young woman who has been decoyed or "trappan'd" to Virginia:

> Give ear unto a Maid,
> That lately was betray'd,
> And sent into Virginny O:
> In brief I shall declare
> What I have suffered there,
> When that I was weary,
> weary, weary, weary, O.
> When that first I came
> To this Land of Fame,
> Which is called Virginny, O;
> The Axe and the Hoe
> Have wrought my Overthrow.
> When that, etc.
> Five Years served I,
> Under Master Guy,
> In the Land of Virginny, O:
> Which made me for to know,
> Sorrow, Grief, and Woe;
> When that, etc.
> When my Dame says, Go,
> Then I must do so,
> In the Land of Virginny, O;
> When she sits at Meat,
> Then I have none to eat,
> When that, etc.
> The Cloaths that I brought in,
> They are worn very thin,
> In the Land of Virginny, O;
> Which makes me for to say,
> Alas and Well-a-day,
> When that, etc.

Instead of Beds of Ease,
To lye down when I please,
In the Land of Virginny, O,
Upon a Bed of Straw,
I lay down full of Woe,
When that I was weary
weary, weary, weary, O.
Then the Spider she
Daily waits on me,
In the Land of Virginny, O;
Round about my Bed,
She spins her tender web,
When that I am weary
weary, weary, weary, O.
So soon as it is day,
To work I must away,
In the Land of Virginny, O:
Then my Dame she knocks
With her Tinder-box,
When that, etc.
I have play'd my part,
Both at Plow and at Cart,
In the Land of Virginny, O:
Billats from the Wood,
Upon my back they load,
When that, etc.
Instead of drinking Beer,
I drink the Water clear,
In the Land of Virginny, O;
Which makes me pale and wan
Do all that e'r I can,
When that, etc.
If my Dame says, Go,
I dare not say no,
In the Land of Virginny, O:
The Water from the Spring,
Upon my head I bring,
When that, etc. . . .
When the Child doth cry,
I must sing, By a by;
In the Land of Virginny, O:

No rest that I can have,
Whilst I am here a Slave,
When that, etc.
    A thousand Woes beside,
    That I do here abide,
In the Land of Virginny, O:
In misery I spend
My time that hath no end,
When that, etc.
    Then let Maids beware,
    All by my ill-fare,
In the Land of Virginny, O;
Be sure thou stay at home,
For if you do here come,
You all will be weary, etc.
    But if it be my chance,
    Homewards to advance,
From the Land of Virginny, O;
If that I once more,
Land on English Shore,
I'll no more be weary,
weary, weary, weary, O.[47]

In this ballad, the female protagonist sings a song of warning to dispel the celebratory images of Virginia promoted in advertisement ballads. She characterizes her five years' indenture as a time of "sorrow, grief, and woe," of "thin" clothes and beds of straw, of "water" instead of "beer." The protagonist-narrator describes her labors hauling wood and water and calls herself a "slave," reminding us once again (as do the lyrics to "The House Carpenter") that it was not uncommon for servant-class whites in the early seventeenth century to describe their condition as slavery or to worry about falling into a condition of enslavement. That such economic vulnerability also rendered laboring-class women sexually vulnerable to their masters is alluded to in the suggestive line "Five years served I under Master Guy." And the most intriguing image in the ballad, that of the "spider" who spins her "tender web" around the servant's straw bed while she sleeps, also points to the intimate space of the bed as a site of vulnerability, endangerment, and betrayal. The protagonist-narrator moves through the ballad without family or kin, apparently without intimate relationship of any kind to provide comfort or respite. Her only companions are the imagined groups of maids back in London to whom she addresses her warning song.

Traditional Anglo-American ballads about emigration to America narrated from a female perspective preserve this association between colonization and the betrayal, dissolution, or abandonment of family and kinship ties. In "The House Carpenter," as sung by Attie Crane in Tennessee, it is the female protagonist whose emigration to America is rendered as an abandonment of husband and children. An even darker narrative is presented in "Oh mother dear be not severe," an Irish ballad sung by Pearl Jacobs Borusky and recorded by Archive of American Folksong field-workers in Pearson, Wisconsin, in 1941.[48] In this ballad, a young girl pleads with her mother to spare her lover, George Riley, from being murdered by her father. In response to the daughter's pleas—"Oh mother dear, be not severe"—the mother offers £500 to "send Riley to America and purchase there some ground." Riley returns to bring his beloved back to America, and tragedy ensues:

> The storm was loud, the night was dark
> Which grieved their hearts full sore
> And she was locked in Riley's arms
> They were drowned and washed on shore.
> And in her bosom there was a note
> And it was wrote with blood
> How cruel was my father
> When he sought to shoot my love.

This song too ends with an admonition:

> And let this be a warning
> To all young ladies gay
> To never let the lad they love
> sail to America.

As in "The House Carpenter," emigration to America does not improve the fate of the family or the chances for love's survival. It eventuates only in their utter ruin. Whatever promising advertisements colonial venture agents mobilized in seventeenth-century ballads about emigration to America to appeal to young women were soon revised—*thoroughly revised*—to register a sense of disappointment, loss, and betrayal in the colonial enterprise. Even those who survived the voyage to America and their descendents retained in their memory a sense that the passage to America had entailed treacherous losses. Whatever had been lost in England could not simply be regained or re-created through servitude on a different shore. But who could be blamed for such misfortune? When we left our homes, families, kinfolk, ancestors, and country behind, we had no one to blame, finally, for our desolation but ourselves.

IF LOSING WHOLE BODIES OF MEMORY and lifeways to England's economic modernization left my ancestors and other early English colonial emigrant laborers feeling desolated and abandoned, it is not surprising that these feelings found expression in narratives that played out that betrayal on a more domestic, more familiar scale. It is one thing to live through a dislocating shift in history. It is another to have the wherewithal to be able to understand it in its larger global-historical context. It helps, of course, if one can read, which my Brooks ancestors most likely could not. It also helps if one has access to indigenous knowledge traditions that can sometimes foretell such catastrophic turns in history. But my nominally Christianized laboring-class Brooks ancestors probably had little access to the most robust indigenous wisdom traditions of the British Isles. There are even signs that other indigenous wisdom traditions from around the Atlantic world were failing to foretell the great inaugurating catastrophes of the modern era: epidemic diseases spread by colonization and the epic population losses they incurred; forced movements of enslaved labor across hemispheres. As the indigenous chroniclers of Cortez's conquest of Tenochtitlan remarked, the failure of his own holy people and priests to foresee the Spanish invasion cast the mighty Moctezuma himself into despondency.

What I find especially telling about how the dislocated and disrupted society of English laboring people reacted to the way history turned on them was by telling stories that placed the blame on the sexual or romantic transgressions of women. For in doing so, they themselves abandoned an indigenous English oral tradition of celebrating women who transgressed to the benefit of their people. Take, for example, the motif of the female warrior traditional to English, Scottish, and Irish ballads. With their earliest print instances dating to the early seventeenth century, the same moment of inception as "The House Carpenter," female warrior ballads often tell the story of young women who leave home, cross-dress, go to sea or into battle, prove their honor, sometimes find love, and return home heroines. The best-known example of the genre is that of the historical Captain Mary Ambree, who helped liberate the Flemish city of Ghent from Spanish invaders in 1584. Ambree was memorialized in "The Valarous Acts performed at GAUNT, / by the brave Bonny Lass Mary Ambree, / who in Revenge of her Loves death, / did play her part most gallantly," a ballad published in the 1680s.[49] As the ballad relates, Ambree joined the battle at Ghent to avenge the death of her beloved sergeant major. She donned armor, a helmet, and a sword, and led three thousand fighters in battle, before taking a stand on a castle wall and revealing her true identity:

> Why what do you think or take me to be?
> Unto these brave Souldiers so valiant spoke she:
> A Knight Sir of England, and Captain (quoth they)
> Whom shortly we mean to take prisoner away.
> No Captain of England, behold in your sight,
> Two Breasts in my bosom, and therefore no Knight,
> No Knight Sir of England nor Captain, quoth she,
> But even a poor bonny Lass Mary Ambree.

As the ballad further relates, the Prince of Parma heard of the bravery of Mary Ambree and sent her a "Glove and a Ring," which she refused—declaring, "It shall never be said in England so free, / That a stranger did maary with Mary Ambree"—and returned to England a hero whose memory would be preserved in song. Indeed, the ballad not only celebrates the strength of women but links their autonomy to the freedom of England itself. As literary critic Dianne Dugaw observes, Ambree "moves freely between identity as a man and as a woman, actually choosing between the two to her own advantage. Indeed, she is celebrated for negotiating gender as a choice."[50]

Did my Brooks ancestors lose this bolder, more transgressive sense of themselves amid the jarring dislocations of their modernizing world? Did their constrained abandonment of their home places, kin networks, and traditional lifeways lead them to blame women for the sense of desolation and homelessness they felt? And what did the Brooks women of seventeenth-century England feel as they witnessed their families wrecked and scattered not only by the familiar enemies of death and disease but also by massive, nameless new economic forces, by the quotidian betrayals of landlords, bureaucrats, merchants, press-gangs, and spirits? How could we narrate or make sense of all that was happening to us? Failing our traditional narratives, how could we avoid being the ones to blame?

In reaching back across the centuries into the oral traditions of my ancestors, my mind finds a foothold for comparison in the oral traditions I have learned from other civilizations, especially concerning women. It was from American Indian literary scholar Paula Gunn Allen that I learned the Kochinnenako stories of the Laguna Pueblo people of northwestern New Mexico. Like many Pueblo communities and unlike the Anglo-American communities I descend from, the Laguna people have been among the most stable civilizations in the Western world. Laguna oral tradition teaches that the Keres people have lived on their homelands from time immemorial. Archaeological evidence dates back to 3000 BC, and even non-Native historians document tribal history in the area dating back to 1300. Even through the catastrophe of Spanish colonial conquest, including the tumultuous Pueblo Revolt of 1680, the Laguna people maintained a matrilineal and matrifocal social structure that vested women with rights of leadership and property.

They also passed from generation to generation a powerful female-centered story tradition told about and from the point of view of a young woman named Kochinnenako. Kochinnenako means "yellow woman"; in Laguna cosmology, yellow is the color of women, and it is a color vested with particular ceremonial powers and roles. In Yellow Woman stories, Kochinnenako is often characterized as a marginal but exceptional young woman, someone a bit "alienated from the people," as Allen explains.[51] By virtue of her moxie or her independence or her nose for trouble, Yellow Woman finds herself carried away from the village, the people, her family, and her husband (in the versions where she is married) into entanglements with powerful spirits. These spirits are often male, and a sexual relationship is implied or explicitly stated. No blame is placed on Kochinnenako herself, and the sexual relationship is never figured as an act of indecency or immorality. Maybe, as Laguna Pueblo author Leslie Marmon Silko tells it, she was "kidnapped" or she "eloped,"[52] or maybe she just got carried away with herself. What matters is the good things that come back to the people from Kochinnenako's transgression. Maybe she comes back pregnant with twins, or with knowledge of a new way to obtain food for the people, or a change in seasons (meaning a rebalanced cosmos), or maybe just with a good story. Even in the stories that eventuate in Kochinnenako's death, it is clear that the death is not a punishment but an event born of chance and necessity to be honored and mourned by the community. As Silko renders the story in her telling of Yellow Woman and Buffalo Man, Yellow Woman by her sexual dalliance with a spirit discovers a new food source for the Laguna people:

> So that was the beginning—
> the hunters would travel
> far away to plains in the East
> where the Buffalo People lived
> and they would bring home
> all that good meat.
> Nobody would be hungry then.
> It was all because
> one time long ago
> our daughter, our sister Kochininako
> went away with them.[53]

The Yellow Woman stories, then, render women's transgressive choices as

> drastic things which
> must be done
> for the world
> to continue.[54]

Paula Gunn Allen offers a more elaborate explanation:

> The stories do not necessarily imply that difference is punishable; on the contrary, it is often her very difference that makes her special adventures possible, and these adventures often have happy outcomes for Kochinnenako and for her people. This is significant among a people who value conformity and propriety above almost anything. It suggests that the behavior of women, at least at certain times or under certain circumstances, must be improper or nonconformist for the greater good of the whole.[55]

The expression of sexual curiosity and desire, even by a married woman, is portrayed in the Yellow Woman stories as an act that brings strength, necessary change, and regeneration to the people.[56]

I have no doubt that my Brooks foremothers made hard choices as we contemplated the fates of our home places, kin, and children. Maybe some of us participated in the food riots of the early seventeenth century, lashing out against the landlords and merchants who made us pay to eat the fruits of our own land and carried away all the excess. Maybe we tried to hold on to old knowledge about the medicines and foods and stories that came from our forests even as those forests were being cleared to create pasture to feed the textile industry. Even as our familiar ways of feeding, clothing, and warming our children disintegrated, we scraped by: taking in work, selling, growing, pawning, gleaning, even when the law made gleaning criminal. We broke laws, then. Some of us watched our loved ones scatter out across countryside, then ocean, then continent, without having so much as ever seen a map of the places they were headed. Some of us said good-bye to a homeland that had shown itself so ready to dispose of its people. And we crossed the ocean and found that in the new colonial world, as in England, betrayal, abandonment, and memory loss would also govern modernity. We would never again hold on to a place or know the spirits that it belonged to. How could we not feel as though we had been shipwrecked on modernity and all the promises about the future had proven as false as those of a deceitful lover.

For the sad kernel of truth about women's colonial history preserved in the devastating story of "The House Carpenter" is this: it is not so much that our hard choices made history, but that our stinted, intimate choices are the heartbreaking stuff of which history is made.

EPILOGUE

Ballad of the Laboring Poor

I GAVE THIS BOOK THE TITLE *Why We Left: Untold Stories and Songs of America's First Immigrants* because as a literary historian I wanted to call attention to the idea that stories are powerful. The stories we tell about ourselves and about those who came before us shape how we understand history and our responsibility to it. When we talk about the lives of the first mass of laboring-class English emigrants to North America, one story has dominated all others: they came, we tell ourselves, because this was a "land of opportunity." This story, it turns out, was spun and promoted by American industrialists in the early twentieth century. It is not a story that those early migrants would have told about themselves.

Stories early Anglo-American laboring-class colonists told about themselves and why they left and passed down to their descendents were not pretty. In fact, they were quite grim. Betrayal, cruelty, and fatality were their common themes; deceit, environmental destruction, economic inequality, disregard for human life, and regret were their common features. These are the songs of people grappling with world-wrenching economic and social changes, changes they viewed as hostile to their communities and life chances. In documenting this body of alternative stories, it has been my goal to offer a different way of seeing the massive economic and social changes that created the modern world. Alternative stories offer us a point for renewed reflection on what the benefits of globalization have been, and what its costs have been as well. This is a project that leading figures in American studies like Lisa Lowe have urged scholars to undertake: a "productive attention to the scene of loss," as she calls it. She writes, "It is necessary to act within but to think beyond our received humanist tradition and, all the while, to imagine a much more complicated set of stories about the emergence of the now, in which what is foreclosed as unknowable is forever saturating the 'what-can-be-known.'"[1] Lowe points to the fact that some bodies of knowledge are not available to us through traditional social scientific research and that it requires a more imaginative approach to the archives of human experience to cull out the full range of ways our ancestors understood their place in history. This has been my project in *Why We Left*.

Another of my objects in writing this book has been to contribute to the project of critically reexamining the modernizing processes of globalization that began in the early modern period and fundamentally shaped the world we now inhabit. The work of interrogating the costs and benefits of modernity has been assumed in large part by scholars who trace their roots to the world's colonized peoples. My goal has been to contribute an additional perspective to this project from someone who traces her roots to the colonizers, to people who (it can be said) both gained and lost by various colonial projects. Who were we? Did we ever *belong* anywhere on this earth? Did we have oral traditions? Where and how did we acquire the capacity and the inclination to participate through colonialism in the dispossession of others? These are the questions I started asking myself at Paula Gunn Allen's seminar table years ago. I still do not know exactly where on the map of England my Brooks ancestors were from, nor do I expect to find out. But I do know how to locate the historical crises that tore them from their home places and shaped their dispositions.

I hope this book creates an opportunity for humane reflection on what we lost. Chandan Reddy has written that scholars need to "situate the formations of modern knowledge within global histories of contact, collaboration, conflict, and dislocation, examining in each instance how the category of the modern has distorted those global histories, producing unity out of hybridity and development out of displacement."[2] Examined critically, the story that America was to the earliest Anglo-American immigrants a "land of opportunity" disguises the brutal facts of their displacement as a narrative of deliberate and successful choice. It is a narrative that both flatters us and precludes us from understanding how much we have had in common with other peoples pushed about by empire, or from reckoning with how mixed and illusory our gains may have been.

The body of ballads I feature here offers alternative points of entry into English laboring-class colonial history. As a form of what Allison Landberg has called "prosthetic memory," they offer a sensory experience of how that history was lived and remembered by laboring-class Anglo-Americans. The ballads offer what Ann Cvetkovich has characterized as a trauma-related "archive of feelings," and the feelings we find in this archive are stark, unsentimental, and startling. Greil Marcus captures them in his description of the Anglo-American murder-ballad tradition: "The language of the American ballad seeks to make death into a story. . . . It calls upon metaphors from all across the land, reaching back across the Atlantic Ocean, across hundreds of years and uncounted generations."[3] I have grappled with the grim fatality of the ballads, the tone that came to define the classic Anglo-American murder ballad, a staple of Brooks family cultural consumption down through centuries, from seventeenth-century folk songs to the mean and tender Johnny Cash songs my uncles Norm and David—and I—love so well. Now, I can say that death and historical experiences of disjunction and dislocation have been a major force in shaping who we have become. When we enclosed and expropriated indigenous lands, unjustly extracted value from the lives and labors of others, we were operating according to the grim new rules of the modern world we had learned back in England. What we did unto others in America was what had been done unto us.

These are the stories that first took shape as black-letter ballads in England, then crossed the Atlantic in the mouths and memories of early Anglo-American immigrants, and persisted in sung memory and recorded reproduction down through the centuries. The folk revivals of the early and middle twentieth century secured for the ballads a place in a well-commemorated and institutionally valued archive of American folk music, as well as in living repertoires of American traditional music. They are still performed today, albeit in a fashion that betrays little connection to their originating contexts in the massive and often heartbreaking dislocations that created the Anglo-American circumatlantic world. The heirs of those dislocations regard them largely without sentimentality—this much we can hear in the bright, plainspoken, matter-of-fact style adhered to by early twentieth-century ballad singers, the jarring clash of energetic tunes and dark story lines. So pragmatic and unsentimental were those singers that one wonders whether the old ballads would have survived into contemporary memory had it not been for the romantic preoccupations of professional folklorists and ethnographers. Something of that grim sense, however, survived in the murder ballads that became a staple both of the old-time or hillbilly music genre and of its upstart country music cousin. Music kept on moving, and the descendents of the early Anglo-American laboring-class migrants moved with it.

There were a few singers who remembered the spirit of the old ballads and their populist bitterness against the world-making betrayals of modernity. The legendary American folksinger Woody Guthrie, born in the same year and the same town—Okemah, Oklahoma—as my grandmother Dorothy Brooks, was one of them. Guthrie's Dust Bowl ballads like "Talking Dust Bowl Blues" and "Do Re Mi" and his rendition of traditional songs like "Going Down the Road Feeling Bad" secured him a legendary place in American memory as the "Okie Troubadour," but that legend held the most currency among politically progressive audiences on the East Coast. Okies themselves rarely listened to Woody Guthrie. Instead, they favored the kind of country music popularized by Gene Autry, Bob Wills, and Spade Cooley, a music that featured rural good-times nostalgia and cowboy individualism. And by the late 1960s, it was the smugly patriotic Merle Haggard who had emerged as the country music voice of the Okies with his anthem "Okie from Muskogee," which celebrated the Okie penchant for "livin' right and being free," and Oklahoma as a place where the kids "still respect the college dean." (Never mind that in the 1960s high school counselors in the Los Angeles working-class suburbs still discouraged Okie kids like my father from applying to college.)

Historian James Gregory, the finest scholar of Anglo-American migrant laboring-class experience, tracks the emergence of this "tough new populism" in the music of Okies and other Southwesterners in the later decades of the twentieth century. The shift in musical disposition parallels a broader political shift among the migrants and their descendants. They came to subscribe to a complex of cultural values Gregory describes as "plain-folk Americanism"—a "cult of toughness," a willingness to fight, an intolerance of elitism, a dogged individualism—that made for an uneasy (but not altogether impossible) fit with the culture of the labor movement and often aligned with nativism and racism, especially as Southwesterners fought to distinguish themselves from nonwhites who shared their economic class.[4] "Plain-folk Americanist" dispositions stayed with Anglo-American migrants as their class status improved, thanks in large part to jobs provided by the defense industry. In her Okie memoir *Red Dirt,* Roxanne Dunbar-Ortiz remembers a telling encounter with these "defense Okies":

> When I was at UCLA in the mid-sixties, I was well aware that most of the cops in the Los Angeles Police Department were people like me, or like I did not want to be—"defense Okies"—those who came during World War II to work in the war industry.

Dunbar-Ortiz recalls being stopped and threatened by LAPD officers in 1967 for violating curfew.

> They gave themselves away. I recognized the way they moved, the way they talked, not just their Okie accents but as if they moved and talked in slow motion, compared with most Californians I knew, managing to appear humble and arrogant, graceful as cats and that dangerous all at the same time.[5]

Dunbar-Ortiz struck up a conversation with the officers, revealing her own small-town Oklahoma roots and eliciting theirs, which transformed the tense encounter into a friendly conversation. Her characterization of the way the officers moved—in "slow motion," "humble" and "arrogant," "graceful" and "dangerous"—is the nearest I have ever seen my Brooks uncles characterized in print. So too does Dunbar-Ortiz's description of her encounter with these "defense Okies" offer a fitting narration of the way Anglo-American laboring-class dispossession and its companion "cult of toughness" were given over and operationalized in the service of the military state. Plain-folk Americanism directed populism in the service of political conservatism.

It would be nice to think that the older stories of hard luck and dispossession captured in the ballads at the heart of this project might still speak to others who descend from multigenerationally migrant Anglo-American communities. But my experience suggests that the collective identities that once denominated Okies and other Southwestern white migrants have all but dissolved. Those who still claim such identities and their attendant histories typically mobilize them in the service of a politics of distinction—as if to say, "we made it, why didn't you?"—rather than as a critique of political-economic advantage-taking or as a point of commonality with other displaced and migratory peoples. Consequently, my project has been inspired less by a desire to rehabilitate and mobilize social identities derived from landless laboring Anglo-American experience and more by the values these communities shared and transmitted—toughness, plain-spokenness, a touch of pugilism, and even the matter-of-fact way they narrated trouble—values I find reflected in the aesthetically spare, unsentimental, travel-ready archive of cultural memory the ballads entail. Historian Melissah Pawlikowski in a careful and groundbreaking study of late eighteenth- and early nineteenth-century Anglo-American squatter communities locates the roots of these sensibilities in the realities of instability and frequent migration that shaped squatters' relationships to the world of community and property. Anglo-American squatter communities initially formed through kinship networks but absorbed dislocated individuals—widows, orphans, people of color—as they traveled deeper into the backcountry. When it came to community, size meant strength. Fences were not used to enclose private property but to control livestock grazing on collective commons. Clothes were made in one size to fit all and left on pegs near the door of squatters' huts to enable quick migrations. "Objects without an immediate use-value had little to no value," Pawlikowski writes. "The long-term migratory reality of frontier life precipitated only passing attachment or authority over goods."[6]

Perhaps at some point along the way my Brooks ancestors abandoned more elaborate forms of historical memory because it was too heavy or because it had no immediate use-value. I personally came into a very small portion of that memory. I heard from my Uncle Norm a few stories about debtors and mutinies, and I came on my own to piece together the forces behind the history that pushed each Brooks generation farther west. I was not raised with traditional ballads. I was not raised with Woody Guthrie. But I've tried to use my skills as a scholar of American culture to latch onto the ballads as forms of what Allison Landberg calls "prosthetic memory" that can help me better understand our place in history. Just like the singers and storytellers before me, I heard the stories, they spoke to me, and I am passing them on—with my own enlarging stylized and scholarly touches. Inspired by the sense of utility, economy, and tactical community historians trace to early squatter communities, I have written about these ballads because they are common, available, and useful to the scholarly and political projects I care about. As far as I'm concerned, whoever can make use of this body of memory should have and use it. I hope these stories of why we left communicate solidarity to anyone leaving behind catastrophes wrought in the name of economic progress and moving toward that dream of a stateless commons where everyone gets what they need. In the words of Woody Guthrie, the stories I've told in these pages are here for anyone going down the road feeling bad.

Notes

Introduction

1. Deloria, *Behind the Trail of Broken Treaties,* 86.
2. Fink, *Major Problems in the Gilded Age and the Progressive Era,* 2–3.
3. "Steel King Schwab Talks of 'the Land of Opportunity,'" *Idaho Statesman,* September 2, 1907, 1, and *New York Times,* August 31, 1907, 2.
4. Fogleman, "From Slaves, Convicts, and Servants to Free Passengers," 45–47, emphasis added.
5. Horn, *Adapting to a New World,* 65, 69.
6. Goldsby, *A Spectacular Secret,* 6.
7. See "Registers of Servants Sent to Foreign Plantations," *Virtual Jamestown,* http://www.virtualjamestown.org/indentures/about_indentures.html. Original manuscript volumes of registers, *The Lord Mayor's Waiting Books* and *Agreements to Serve in America,* are held by the Record Office of the City of London and the London Guildhall. These have been modernized and reprinted in Ghirelli, *A List of Emigrants from England to America* and Kaminkow and Kaminkow, *A List of Emigrants from England to America.*
8. Frethorne, "Letters to His Parents."
9. John Baldwin, "A Letter from Virginia," in Jehlen and Warner, *English Literatures of America,* 126.
10. Elizabeth Sprigs, "Letter to Mr. John Sprigs in White Cross Street near Cripple Gate, London, September 22, 1756," in Calder, *Colonial Captivities, Marches, and Journeys,* 151–52.
11. Francis Bacon, "Of Plantations," in Jehlen and Warner, *English Literatures of America,* 97.
12. Aphra Behn, *The Widow Ranter,* in Jehlen and Warner, *English Literatures of America,* 237.

13. Ibid., 245.
14. Ibid., 254.
15. William Strachey, "A True Reportory of the Wrack and Redemption of Sir Thomas Gates, Knight," in Jehlen and Warner, *English Literatures of America,* 107.
16. Robert Beverley, "History and Present State of Virginia," in Jehlen and Warner, *English Literatures of America,* 229; Nathaniel Bacon, "Manifesto Concerning the Present Troubles in Virginia," in ibid., 227.
17. Abrahams and Foss, *Anglo-American Folksong Style,* 12–36, 78–81; Coffin, *British Traditional Ballad in North America,* 8; Hart, *Ballad and Epic,* 31, 34; Gummere, *The Popular Ballad,* 73, 114.
18. Lloyd, *Folk Song in England,* 31. As early as 1932, ballad scholars like Gordon Hall Gerould were discussing ballads as "documents of social history" (*The Ballad of Tradition,* 263). During the middle decades of the twentieth century, folklorists influenced by the structuralist movement in anthropology started to organize their understanding of ballads around stable taxonomies of ballad types. Recent scholarship has returned to an understanding of ballads as commentary on the epistemic worlds of their singers and audiences and the immediate contexts in which they are sung; see Atkinson, *The English Traditional Ballad,* 1–17. On the ballad as archive of folk knowledge, see Wimberly, *Folklore in the English and Scottish Ballads;* Gerould, *The Ballad of Tradition,* 135, 152.
19. Fumerton, "'Not Home,'" 479.
20. Ibid., 501.
21. Ibid., 504.
22. On the travel of the ballad, see Davis, *Traditional Ballads of Virginia,* 10, 15, 22; Entwistle, *European Balladry,* 240–41; Gerould, *The Ballad of Tradition,* 255–73.
23. Kulikoff, *From British Peasants to Colonial American Farmers,* 47–48.
24. Wilentz and Marcus, *The Rose & The Briar,* 1.
25. Bendix, *In Search of Authenticity,* 123.
26. See also Walkowitz, *City Folk.*
27. Whisnant, *All That Is Native & Fine,* 13.
28. See Sobel, *The World They Made Together.*
29. Cohen, *Rainbow Quest,* 5.
30. On the rise of bluegrass as a genre, see Cantwell, *Bluegrass Breakdown* and Rosenberg, *Bluegrass.*
31. Roach, *Cities of the Dead,* 2, 3.
32. Landberg, "Prosthetic Memory," 148–49.
33. Trouillot, *Silencing the Past,* 26–27.

1. No Land of Opportunity

1. Kulikoff, *From British Peasants to Colonial American Farmers,* 11.
2. Sharp, *In Contempt of All Authority,* 85.
3. Kulikoff, *From British Peasants to Colonial American Farmers,* 17; Sharp, *In Contempt of All Authority,* 90.
4. Hill, *Change and Continuity,* 41.
5. Phillips, "The Medieval Background," 1; Wrightson, *English Society,* 133; Wallerstein, *The Modern World System,* 42. See also Bartlett, *Making of Europe.*
6. Hindle, "'Not by Bread Only'?" 46–47; Hindle, *On the Parish,* 33.
7. Kulikoff, *From British Peasants to Colonial American Farmers,* 26.
8. Ibid., 18.
9. Sharp, *In Contempt of All Authority,* 127–44, 157; A. E. Smith, *Colonists in Bondage,* 186; Hill, *Change and Continuity,* 182; Kulikoff, *From British Peasants to Colonial American Farmers,* 17–18.
10. Sharp, *In Contempt of All Authority,* 177; P. Clark, "Popular Protest and Disturbance in Kent," 378.
11. Kulikoff, *From British Peasants to Colonial American Farmers,* 16.
12. Hindle "'Not by Bread Only'?" 39.
13. Wrightson, *English Society,* 122; Games, *Migration and the Origins of the English Atlantic World,* 17; Slack, *Poverty and Policy,* 44–48; A. E. Smith, *Colonists in Bondage,* 166–67.
14. Kulikoff, *From British Peasants to Colonial American Farmers,* 22.
15. Hill, *Change and Continuity,* 220.
16. Ibid., 223.
17. Hindle, *On the Parish,* 79–81; King and Tomkins, "Introduction," 1–31.
18. Wrightson, *English Society,* 141.
19. Hindle, *On the Parish,* 22, 169; Beier, *Masterless Men,* 21, 26.
20. Wrightson, *English Society,* 42; Salerno, "Social Background of Seventeenth-Century Emigration," 45; Beier, *Masterless Men,* 23–24.
21. Beier, *Masterless Men,* 23.
22. Bailyn, *Voyagers to the West,* 23; Games, *Migration and the Origins of the English Atlantic World,* 17; P. Clark, "Migrant in Kentish Towns," 138–39; Wrightson, *English Society,* 43; Beier, *Masterless Men,* 71.
23. P. Clark, "Migrant in Kentish Towns," 139–40; see also Fumerton, "'Not Home.'"
24. Fumerton, *Unsettled,* 13; Bailyn, *Voyagers to the West,* 21; Laslett, *The World We Have Lost,* 156.
25. Hill, *Reformation to Industrial Revolution,* 44.
26. P. Clark, "Migrant in Kentish Towns," 117.

27. Ibid., 138–39.
28. Ibid., 144. See also Kent, "Population Mobility and Alms"; Rollison, "Exploding England"; Slack, "Vagrants and Vagrancy in England."
29. Beier, *Masterless Men,* 38; Wrightson, *English Society,* 126, 127.
30. Slack, *Poverty and Policy,* 23.
31. Salerno, "Social Background of Seventeenth-Century Emigration," 48; Hindle, "'Not by Bread Only'?" 49–50.
32. Sharp, *In Contempt of All Authority,* 173, 181; Hill, *Change and Continuity,* 182.
33. Hindle, "'Not by Bread Only'?" 45.
34. Slack, *Poverty and Policy,* 43.
35. Wrightson, *English Society,* 127–28; Finlay and Shearer, "Population Growth and Suburban Expansion," 38.
36. Games, *Migration and the Origins of the English Atlantic World,* 17.
37. Fumerton, *Unsettled,* 12; Finlay and Shearer, "Population Growth and Suburban Expansion," 50–51.
38. Kulikoff, *From British Peasants to Colonial American Farmers,* 27.
39. Wrightson, *English Society,* 122.
40. Hill, *Change and Continuity,* 48; Wrightson, *English Society,* 132.
41. Hill, *Change and Continuity,* 51; A. E. Smith, *Colonists in Bondage,* 165.
42. Wrightson, *English Society,* 125.
43. Horn, *Adapting to a New World,* 261.
44. A. G. R. Smith, *Emergence of a Nation State,* 169.
45. Horn, *Adapting to a New World,* 92–93.
46. Sharp, *In Contempt of All Authority,* 34.
47. Ibid., 15.
48. Wrightson, *English Society,* 177; Sharp, *In Contempt of All Authority;* Slack, *Poverty and Policy,* 146.
49. On customary poor-relief practices and ethics of hospitality, see I. Ben-Amos, "Gifts and Favors"; Heal, *Hospitality in Early Modern England;* Hindle, "Dearth, Fasting, and Alms"; McIntosh, "Poverty, Charity and Coercion in Elizabethan England." Steve Hindle interrogates the facticity of the imagined resource of community in "Exclusion Crises."
50. Beier, *Masterless Men,* 159.
51. Hindle, "'Not by Bread Only'?" 55–57.
52. Hindle, *On the Parish,* 4, 11–12. See also Slack, *Poverty and Policy,* 17–32; Slack, *From Reformation to Improvement,* 53–76; and Slack, "Poverty and Politics in Salisbury," 176.
53. Hill, *Society and Puritanism,* 125.

54. Slack, "Poverty and Politics in Salisbury," 174.
55. Wrightson, *English Society,* 164.
56. Hindle, *On the Parish,* 35–42.
57. Sharp, *In Contempt of All Authority,* 47.
58. Hill, *Change and Continuity,* 188.
59. Hindle, "'Not by Bread Only'?" 52.
60. Ibid., 62.
61. A. E. Smith, *Colonists in Bondage,* 137.
62. On the evolution of bureaucratic approaches to poor relief, see Slack, *Poverty and Policy,* 113–37, 194–95; see also Slack, "Poverty and Politics in Salisbury," 164–203; Beier, *Problem of the Poor;* Hindle, *On the Parish,* 171–455.
63. Slack, *Poverty and Policy,* 30; see also Slack, "Poverty and Politics in Salisbury," 180–83; Slack, *From Reformation to Improvement,* 77–101.
64. Beier, *Masterless Men,* 150.
65. Ibid.
66. Hakluyt, *Principal Navigations,* 266, 268.
67. Ibid., 270.
68. Edward Williams, *Virginia: More Especially the South Part Thereof, Richly and Truly Valued* [1650], *Virtual Jamestown,* 2002, http://etext.lib.virginia.edu/etcbin/jamestown-browse?id=J1076, 4–5.
69. Hindle, *On the Parish,* 135.
70. Bailyn, *Voyagers to the West,* 20; Fogleman, "From Slaves, Convicts, and Servants to Free Passengers," 44–45.
71. Bailyn, *Voyagers to the West,* 61; Canny, *Europeans on the Move,* 54; Fogleman, "From Slaves, Convicts, and Servants to Free Passengers," 45; Shammas, "Origins of Transatlantic Colonization," 30.
72. Horn, *Adapting to a New World,* 2, 5.
73. Canny, *Europeans on the Move,* 63.
74. Kulikoff, *From British Peasants to Colonial American Farmers,* 62; Wrigley and Schofield, *Population History of England,* 220.
75. Games, *Migration and the Origins of the English Atlantic World,* 1.
76. Canny, *Europeans on the Move,* 61.
77. Fogleman, "From Slaves, Convicts, and Servants to Free Passengers," 67–68. See also Altman and Horn, *"To Make America,"* esp. 1–29.
78. Horn, *Adapting to a New World,* 33.
79. Kulikoff, *From British Peasants to Colonial American Farmers,* 55–56.
80. Beier, *Masterless Men,* 162–63; A. E. Smith, *Colonists in Bondage,* 90–117. Convict transportation was forbidden by Virginia after 1670 and resumed in 1716.
81. Beier, *Masterless Men,* 163; A. E. Smith, *Colonists in Bondage,* 12.

82. Games, *Migration and the Origins of the English Atlantic World,* 77.
83. A. E. Smith, *Colonists in Bondage,* 68–69. See also Thompson, "William Bullock's 'Strange Adventure.'"
84. A. E. Smith, *Colonists in Bondage,* 69–70.
85. Games, *Migration and the Origins of the English Atlantic World,* 77.
86. Galenson, "'Middling People' or 'Common Sort'?" 505.
87. Beier, *Masterless Men,* 163.
88. Cressy, *Coming Over,* 119, 122; A. E. Smith, *Colonists in Bondage,* 35, 39.
89. A. E. Smith, *Colonists in Bondage,* 26.
90. Cressy, *Coming Over,* 135.
91. A. E. Smith, *Colonists in Bondage,* 125.
92. Ibid., 215.
93. Frethorne, "Letters to His Parents," 167.
94. Games, *Migration and the Origins of the English Atlantic World,* 101; Kulikoff, *From British Peasants to Colonial American Farmers,* 84.
95. Horn, *Adapting to a New World,* 333.
96. A. E. Smith, *Colonists in Bondage,* 299.
97. Horn, *Adapting to a New World,* 269.
98. Breen and Innes, *"Myne Owne Ground,"* 73.
99. A. E. Smith, *Colonists in Bondage,* 13.
100. Carr, "Emigration and the Standard of Living," 272; Kulikoff, *From British Peasants to Colonial American Farmers,* 84.
101. Horn, *Adapting to a New World,* 155.
102. Frethorne, "Letters to His Parents," 166.
103. Kulikoff, *From British Peasants to Colonial American Farmers,* 75–76.
104. Breen and Innes, *"Myne Owne Ground,"* 60; Games, *Migration and the Origins of the English Atlantic World,* 82.
105. Games, *Migration and the Origins of the English Atlantic World,* 89.
106. Breen and Innes, *"Myne Owne Ground,"* 67.
107. Hobsbawm, "Crisis of the Seventeenth Century," 5.
108. Beier, *Masterless Men,* 3.
109. Wallerstein, *The Modern World System,* 117.
110. Polanyi, *Great Transformation,* 37. Polanyi here explicitly refers to agricultural-mercantile transformations in late eighteenth-century and early nineteenth-century Europe, but he outlines a pattern that we can see at work at this earlier moment in British history as well.
111. Hobbes, *Leviathan,* 140.
112. Horn, *Adapting to a New World,* 14–15.
113. Games, *Migration and the Origins of the English Atlantic World,* 9; Games also challenges Fischer, *Albion's Seed;* see ibid., 245, n. 15.

114. Fumerton, *Unsettled,* xiv.
115. Hill, *Change and Continuity,* 189.
116. Walter and Wrightson, "Dearth and the Social Order in Early Modern England," 34.
117. Hill, *Change and Continuity,* 133, 234.
118. Wrightson, *English Society,* 172; Galenson, "'Middling People' or 'Common Sort'?" 521.
119. Laslett, *The World We Have Lost,* 36.
120. Sainsbury et al., *Calendar of State Papers,* No. 331; A. E. Smith, *Colonists in Bondage,* 82.
121. Cressy, *Coming Over,* 135.
122. Bullock, *Virginia Impartially Examined,* 14; J. Child, *A New Discourse of Trade,* 208; Horn, *Adapting to a New World,* 63, n. 60.
123. Scott, *England's Troubles,* 50.
124. Walter and Wrightson, "Dearth and the Social Order in Early Modern England," 23–24.
125. Ibid., 29.
126. Ibid., 36.
127. P. Clark, "Popular Protest and Disturbance in Kent," 370.
128. Hill, *Change and Continuity,* 233.
129. Winstanley, *"The Law of Freedom" and Other Writings,* 85.
130. Hill, *Change and Continuity,* 226–31.

2. Murder the Brother Who Killed the Tree

1. Collins, *America Over the Water,* 80.
2. See Anderson-Green, *Hot-Bed of Musicians;* Lornell, *Virginia's Blues, Country, & Gospel Records,* 205; Huber, *Linthead Stomp,* 300; Tribe, *The Stonemans,* 75.
3. AFS 01365 A01.
4. Bronson, *Child Ballads Traditional in the United States,* 239.
5. AFS 09152 B02.
6. AFS 0876 A01.
7. Best and Marcus, "Surface Reading," 9.
8. As I learned from the American Indian literary critic Paula Gunn Allen, the plants and animals represented in her family's Laguna Pueblo oral tradition—coyotes, deer, hummingbirds, corn pollen—connect the people to the land and convey a deeply located sense of responsibility and identity.
9. Wilentz and Marcus, *The Rose & The Briar,* 1.

10. See Newman, *Ballad Collection, Lyric, and the Canon;* Dugaw, "On the 'Darling Songs.'"
11. See Groom, *Making of Percy's Reliques.*
12. Percy, *Reliques of Ancient English Poetry,* 41–42.
13. Twitchell, "Incest Theme"; Taylor, "Texts of 'Edward,'" 225; Taylor, *Edward and Sven I Rosengard,* 23, 26.
14. W. McCarthy, "William Motherwell as Field Collector"; McDowell, "Manufacture and Lingua-facture of Ballad-Making," 153–54.
15. Motherwell, *Minstrelsy Ancient and Modern,* 340–42.
16. Davis, *More Traditional Ballads of Virginia,* 62.
17. Coffin, "'Mary Hamilton.'"
18. AFS 0876 B03.
19. Taylor, *Edward and Sven I Rosengard,* 27.
20. Ibid., 24.
21. Barry, Review of Taylor.
22. Coffin, "Murder Motive," 316. See also Blum, "'Edward' and the Folk Tradition"; Bronson, "Edward, Edward"; Twitchell, "Incest Theme."
23. Toelken, *Morning Dew and Roses,* 159.
24. Ibid., 31–32.
25. Ibid., 33.
26. Fox, "Remembering the Past in Early Modern England."
27. Atkinson, *The English Traditional Ballad,* 136.
28. Whitlock, *Historic Forests of England,* 13–16. See also Whitelock, *Beginnings of English Society,* and Page, *Life in Anglo-Saxon England.*
29. Swanton, *Anglo-Saxon Chronicle,* 221.
30. Whitlock, *Historic Forests of England,* 22.
31. "Charter of the Forest" (1217), in Rothwell, *English Historical Documents,* 337–40.
32. Jones, "Swanimotes, Woodmotes, and Courts of 'Free Miners.'"
33. Grant, *Royal Forests of England,* 40.
34. Ibid., 167–72, 183; Langton, "Forests in Early-Modern England and Wales," 5.
35. Neilson, "Early English Woodland and Waste." See also C. Young, *Royal Forests of Medieval England.*
36. Grant, *Royal Forests of England,* 184–86; Whitlock, *Historic Forests of England,* 26–27; Langton, "Forests in Early-Modern England and Wales," 4.
37. Cantor, *Civilization of the Middle Ages,* 564.
38. Marcus, *Naval History of England,* 32.
39. Chew, *World Ecological Degradation,* 122.
40. Whitlock, *Historic Forests of England,* 27.

41. Langton, "Forests in Early-Modern England and Wales," 4. On forests and imperialism, see also Albion, *Forests and Sea Power;* Bunker and Ciccantell, *Globalization and the Race for Resources,* 123–35; Barton, *Empire Forestry;* Pogue Harrison, *Forests.*
42. Grant, *Royal Forests of England,* 185–86.
43. Albion, *Forests and Sea Power,* 123.
44. Ibid.
45. Holinshed, *Chronicles of England, Scotland, and Ireland,* 358–59.
46. Kulikoff, *From British Peasants to Colonial American Farmers,* 18.
47. Grant, *Royal Forests of England,* 188–89.
48. Albion, *Forests and Sea Power,* 126.
49. Chew, *World Ecological Degradation,* 117–29.
50. Marcus, *Naval History of England,* 34.
51. Sharp, *In Contempt of All Authority,* 191.
52. Griffin, "Resistance, Crime, and Popular Cultures," 50.
53. Horn, *Adapting to a New World,* 82; Sharp, *In Contempt of All Authority,* 173, 181; Hill, *Change and Continuity,* 182. On rural anti-enclosure uprisings, see also Allan, "The Rising in the West."
54. Slack, *Poverty and Policy,* 43.
55. Albion, *Forests and Sea Power,* 91.
56. Bunker and Ciccantell, *Globalization and the Race for Resources,* 132.
57. Ibid.
58. Marcus, *Naval History of England,* 182.
59. Chew, *World Ecological Degradation,* 122–23.
60. Albion, *Forests and Sea Power,* 231–80.
61. Warde, "Woodland Fuel, Demand, and Supply," 81.
62. An ambitious project to map and chart longitudinal historical changes to the English woodlands was proposed in 2005 by John Langton of St. John's College, University of Oxford, and a cohort of researchers. For more information, see "Forests and Chases of England and Wales, c. 1000 to c. 1850," http://info.sjc.ox.ac.uk/forests/ or Langton and Jones, *Forests and Chases of England and Wales.*
63. Albion, *Forests and Sea Power,* 136.
64. Griffin, "Resistance, Crime, and Popular Cultures," 50.
65. Whitlock, *Historic Forests of England,* 36, 69.
66. Ibid., 24–25, 120.
67. Ibid., 38.
68. Cheeseman, "Ownership and Ecological Change," 68.
69. Horn, *Adapting to a New World,* 418. See also Butler, *Awash in a Sea of Faith.*
70. Wimberly, *Folklore in the English and Scottish Ballads,* 38, 122–27.

71. On the environment and early modern literature, see Hiltner, *Renaissance Ecology;* Hiltner, "Early Modern Ecology."
72. Kulikoff, *From British Peasants to Colonial American Farmers,* 76.
73. Horn, *Adapting to a New World,* 130.

3. Two Sisters and a Beaver Hat

1. Paton, Review of *Horton Barker.* See also Lawless, *Folksingers and Folksongs in America,* 35; Whisnant, *All That Is Native & Fine,* 233–35; Coltman, *Paul Clayton and the Folksong Revival,* 46; Barker, *Traditional Singers.*
2. Davis, *More Traditional Ballads of Virginia,* 35–50.
3. Child ballad 10; see versions A–U in F. Child, *English and Scottish Popular Ballads,* 1:118–41.
4. See version A in Davis, *Traditional Ballads of Virginia,* 93–95, and version AA in Davis, *More Traditional Ballads of Virginia,* 33–40.
5. See versions B–J in Davis, *Traditional Ballads of Virginia,* 95–103, and versions BB–JJ in Davis, *More Traditional Ballads of Virginia,* 40–50.
6. Davis, *Traditional Ballads of Virginia,* 97–100; Davis, *More Traditional Ballads of Virginia,* 48.
7. Bronson, *Child Ballads Traditional in the United States,* album typescript, 3; see also Davis, *Traditional Ballads of Virginia,* 100–2. In a fascinating version sung by Clarsy Deeton Laws of Burnsville, North Carolina, in 1950, the suitor gives the older sister a "beaver hat," and the "youngest one thought hard of that." The suitor then gives the younger "a gay gold ring." In a fit of mutual jealousy, the oldest pushes the youngest in, but both sisters end up in the water. The youngest drowns, while the eldest is rescued by the miller and then hung for her crime (AFS 10005 A17; AFS 10006 A01). For commentary on the versions, see Coffin and Renwick, *British Traditional Ballad,* 32–36, 213–15.
8. Davis alone documents eleven versions of "The Two Sisters" featuring the beaver hat sung in Virginia alone in the 1910s and 1920s *(Traditional Ballads of Virginia, More Traditional Ballads of Virginia).* See also Mildred Creighton's 1962 version of "The Two Sisters," transcribed by George Goss and reprinted in W. K. McNeil, *Southern Folk Ballads,* 150–53.
9. Davis, *Traditional Ballads of Virginia,* 95.
10. Toelken, *Morning Dew and Roses,* 33.
11. Emberley, *Cultural Politics of Fur,* 46–47.

12. Bunker, *Making Haste from Babylon,* 236; Crean, "Hats and the Fur Trade."
13. Chaucer, "Prologue," line 272.
14. Stubbes, *Anatomie of Abuses,* 50–51.
15. Bunker, *Making Haste from Babylon,* 232.
16. Ibid., 233. See also Allaire, *Pelleteries, manchons, et chapeaux de castor.*
17. Müller-Schwarze and Sun, *The Beaver,* 139.
18. Bunker, *Making Haste from Babylon,* 241.
19. Ibid., 233.
20. Crean, "Hats and the Fur Trade," 379; Emberley, *Cultural Politics of Fur,* 67.
21. Ibid., 66.
22. Müller-Schwarze and Sun, *The Beaver,* 144.
23. See Wolf, *Europe and the People Without History,* 158–94, Cronon, *Changes in the Land,* 82–107. See also Merchant, *Ecological Revolutions,* 50–57, and passim.
24. Wolf, *Europe and the People Without History,* 161.
25. Ibid., 194.
26. EBBA 30314.
27. EBBA 21127.
28. EBBA 21263.
29. EBBA 21080.
30. EBBA 20782.
31. EBBA 21269.
32. EBBA 30557.
33. EBBA 22351.
34. EBBA 30882.
35. Sharp, *In Contempt of All Authority,* 35; see also Tilly, "Food Entitlement, Famine, and Conflict."
36. On the theme of beaver hats as signs of overextension and ruin, see also "The Humours of Rag-Fair" (published 1756–90), in which we find among the secondhand goods offered at the fair a "beaver fine, / brought from a broken draper" (EBBA 31251). Even in the eighteenth century, the purchase of a beaver hat would have represented several weeks' wages for a draper, a dangerous financial overextension in the name of fashion.
37. EBBA 30980.
38. Child ballad 10, *English and Scottish Popular Ballads,* 1:118–19.
39. Taylor, "English, Scottish, and American Versions of the 'Twa Sisters,'" 243–44.
40. Davis, *Traditional Ballads of Virginia,* 100–2.

41. Abrahams and Foss, *Anglo-American Folksong Style,* 23; Foss, "More on a Unique and Anomalous Version of the Two Sisters."
42. Bunker, *Making Haste from Babylon,* 233.
43. Weatherill, *Consumer Behaviour and Material Culture,* 95–102.
44. Ibid., 133.
45. Spufford, "Cost of Apparel," 688.
46. On clothing, see also Harte, "Fabrics and Fashions"; Lemire, *Dress, Culture, and Commerce.*
47. Hakluyt, *Principal Navigations,* 267–68.
48. Shammas, *Pre-Industrial Consumer,* 78–79.
49. De Vries, "Peasant Demand Patterns and Economic Development."
50. Thirsk, *Economic Policy and Projects,* 125.
51. Ibid., 175.
52. Ibid., 2–3.
53. Ibid., 1–23.
54. Wrightson, *Earthly Necessities,* 200. See also Wrigley, "Divergence of England."
55. Braudel, *Capitalism and Material Life,* 235.
56. Weatherill, *Consumer Behaviour and Material Culture,* 194–96; Wrightson, *Earthly Necessities,* 299–300.
57. W. Smith, *Consumption and the Making of Respectability,* 73.
58. Wrightson, *Earthly Necessities,* 300.
59. The seventeenth century represents only the leading edge of what many have described as the English "consumer revolution" of the eighteenth century. See Berg, *Luxury and Pleasure in Eighteenth Century Britain;* Berg, *Age of Manufactures;* Berg and Eger, *Luxury in the Eighteenth Century;* Haggerty, *British Atlantic Trading Community;* McKendrick, Brewer, and Plumb, *Birth of a Consumer Society;* Perking, "Social Causes of the British Industrial Revolution."
60. On the fur trade as a source of surplus and inequality, see O'Brien, *Dispossession by Degrees,* 81.
61. Weatherill, *Consumer Behaviour and Material Culture,* 76.
62. See ibid., 70–90.
63. Brenner, *Merchants and Revolution.*
64. Festa, "Personal Effects," 49.
65. Shammas, *Pre-Industrial Consumer,* 42.
66. Ibid., 93.
67. Walter and Wrightson, "Dearth and the Social Order in Early Modern England," 23–24.
68. Ibid., 29.
69. Hobbes, *Leviathan,* 140.

70. On "red cloth" narratives, see Bailey, *African Voices of the Atlantic Slave Trade,* 108–13; Pearson, *Black Legacy,* 35–42; Gomez, *Exchanging Our Country Marks,* 200–8.
71. Mack Sturgill, "First Lady Visits Whitetop," *New River Notes,* http://www.newrivernotes.com/va/whitetop1lady.htm.
72. Merchant, *Ecological Revolutions,* 55.

4. To Sink It in the Lonesome Sea

1. AFS 09477 B02.
2. Coffin, *British Traditional Ballad in North America,* 155; Davis, *More Traditional Ballads of Virginia,* 340.
3. Davis, *Traditional Ballads of Virginia,* 516.
4. Bronson, *Child Ballads Traditional in the United States,* 19, 85, 86.
5. AFS 09155 B03; AFS 10007 A11.
6. Rediker, *Between the Devil and the Deep Blue Sea,* 47.
7. Games, *Migration and the Origins of the English Atlantic World,* 101; Kulikoff, *From British Peasants to Colonial American Farmers,* 84.
8. A. E. Smith, *Colonists in Bondage,* 299.
9. Carr, "Emigration and the Standard of Living," 272; Kulikoff, *From British Peasants to Colonial American Farmers,* 84.
10. Horn, *Adapting to a New World,* 155.
11. Trevelyan, *Sir Walter Raleigh,* 1–26.
12. Lacey, *Sir Walter Ralegh,* 34.
13. Trevelyan, *Sir Walter Raleigh,* 33.
14. Ibid., 40.
15. Ibid., 91.
16. See W. H. McNeil, "Introduction of the Potato into Ireland."
17. Spenser, *A View of the Present State of Ireland,* 158–59.
18. Lacey, *Sir Walter Ralegh,* 108.
19. On Raleigh in Ireland, see Trevelyan, *Sir Walter Raleigh,* 32–45; Lacey, *Sir Walter Ralegh,* 34–39; Hennessey, *Walter Raleigh in Ireland.*
20. Beier, *Masterless Men,* 150.
21. On the culture of patronage and the interpenetrated literary-scientific-promotional achievements of Raleigh's cohort, see Miller, *Invested with Meaning.*
22. Trevelyan, *Sir Walter Raleigh,* 77.
23. Ibid., 70–71.
24. Ibid., 105–27.

25. On Raleigh's literary endeavors, see May, *Sir Walter Ralegh,* 25–52; Greenblatt, *Sir Walter Ralegh,* 57–98.
26. Raleigh, *Selected Writings,* 38.
27. In Kolodny, *Lay of the Land,* 11; see also May, *Sir Walter Ralegh,* 55–58.
28. Frohock, *Heroes of Empire,* 27.
29. May, *Sir Walter Ralegh,* 18.
30. Bradbook, *School of Night,* 31.
31. Dolle, "Captain John Smith's Satire," 73.
32. Fuller, *History of the Worthies of England,* 419.
33. F. Child, *English and Scottish Popular Ballads,* 139.
34. See May, *Sir Walter Ralegh,* 9; see also Raleigh, *Discourse Touching a War with Spain.*
35. Raleigh, *Works,* 8:687.
36. Rediker, *Between the Devil and the Deep Blue Sea,* 84.
37. Davis, *More Traditional Ballads of Virginia,* 339.
38. Marx, *The Eighteenth Brumaire,* 124.
39. Harrison, *Description of England,* 194.
40. P. Clark, "Popular Protest and Disturbance in Kent," 369.
41. Hakluyt, *Principal Navigations,* 270; Beier, *Masterless Men,* 93–95.
42. Brunsman, "Subjects vs. Citizens," 564.
43. Beier, *Masterless Men,* 93; Ennis, *Enter the Press-Gang,* 30–32.
44. Brunsman, "Subjects vs. Citizens," 565; Rediker, *Between the Devil and the Deep Blue Sea,* 295. See also Usher, "Royal Navy Impressment During the American Revolution."
45. Defoe, *Some Considerations,* 13.
46. Rediker, *Between the Devil and the Deep Blue Sea,* 33.
47. Ibid., 301.
48. Ibid., 93.
49. Ibid., 217–18.
50. Ibid., 226.
51. Ibid., 5.
52. Pepys 1.418–419; EBBA 20196.
53. Pepys 4.197; EBBA 21859.
54. EBBA 21730.
55. Barlow, *Vision of Columbus,* 140–41.
56. Thoreau, *Sir Walter Raleigh,* 18, 83.
57. Rediker, *Between the Devil and the Deep Blue Sea,* 221.
58. Ellis, *Holinshed's Chronicles,* 749.

5. Seduction of the House Carpenter's Wife

1. AFS 10010 A01.
2. Bronson, *Child Ballads Traditional in the United States,* 7–8. See also Davis, *Traditional Ballads of Virginia,* 442. Sung by Pearl Jacobs Borusky at Antigo, Wisconsin, in 1940 (AFS 4984 A2), and George Hart, in Konnarock, Washington County, Virginia, on November 8, 1921 (Davis, *Traditional Ballads of Virginia,* 442).
3. Davis, *Traditional Ballads of Virginia,* 441.
4. AFS 10004 A16.
5. Bronson, *Child Ballads Traditional in the United States,* 2.
6. As sung by Adolphus Small (Dol Small), Nellysford, Nelson County, Virginia, recorded 1950 (AFS 10004 A02). In the version sung by Rushia Richardson in Vinton, Virginia on September 11, 1922, it ends with lament from the unfaithful wife: "I wish to the Lord I had never been born / And died when I was young; / I never would wet my rosy cheeks, / With no man's lying tongue" (Davis, *Traditional Ballads of Virginia,* 592).
7. Abandonment has been a consistent theme in the scholarship of Ruth Gilmore. See Gilmore, "Tossed Overboard"; Gilmore, "Abandonment"; Gilmore, *Golden Gulag.*
8. EBBA 21765.
9. Ibid.
10. Wrightson, *English Society,* 67.
11. See P. Young, "Mother of Us All"; Green, "Pocahontas Perplex."
12. Entwistle, *European Balladry,* 237–38.
13. On the revenant lover, see also Shields, "Dead Lover's Return"; Reed, *Demon-Lovers and Their Victims;* Barry, "Ballad of the Demon Lover," 238; Atkinson, "Marriage and Retribution," 602.
14. T. McCarthy, "A Note on Past and Present."
15. Gummere, *The Popular Ballad,* 216; Wimberly, *Folklore in the English and Scottish Ballads,* 230.
16. Atkinson, *The English Traditional Ballad,* 40.
17. Bullock, *Virginia Impartially Examined,* 14.
18. Tycko, "Spiriting," 17.
19. Cooke, *Sot-Weed Factor,* 5.
20. Gardner-Medwin, "Ancestry of 'The House-Carpenter'"; Burrison, "'James Harris' in Britain Since Child."
21. A copy of the DeMarsan imprint survives at the American Antiquarian Society. An identical broadside was reprinted in Philadelphia by

A. W. Auner in 1871. (See Davis, *Traditional Ballads of Virginia,* 271–72.)

22. Coffin, *British Traditional Ballad in North America,* 138.
23. Gardner-Medwin, "Ancestry of 'The House-Carpenter,'" 420. See also Atkinson, "Marriage and Retribution," 596.
24. See Nørjordet, "The Tall Man in the Blue Suit"; Atkinson, "Marriage and Retribution."
25. Drake, *Essay in Defense of the Female Sex,* 14.
26. Kulikoff, *From British Peasants to Colonial American Farmers,* 30.
27. Fumerton, *Unsettled,* 8.
28. Hindle, *On the Parish,* 79–81; King and Tomkins, "Introduction," 1–31.
29. Slack, *Poverty and Policy,* 23; Kulikoff, *From British Peasants to Colonial American Farmers,* 31. On families, see Mendelson and Crawford, *Women in Early Modern England;* Laurence, *Women in England, 1500–1760;* Durston, *The Family in the English Revolution;* Quaife, *Wanton Wenches and Wayward Wives;* Stone, *Family, Sex, and Marriage in England.*
30. Fumerton, *Unsettled,* 65.
31. See Kulikoff, *From British Peasants to Colonial American Farmers,* 36. See also Schochet, "Patriarchalism, Politics, and Mass Attitudes."
32. Kulikoff, *From British Peasants to Colonial American Farmers,* 33–36.
33. Fumerton, "Not Home," 508.
34. See also A. Clark, *Working Life of Women in the Seventeenth Century;* Archer, *Pursuit of Stability,* 196; Rappaport, *Worlds within Worlds,* 36–42.
35. Slack, *Poverty and Policy,* 207.
36. See also Wrightson, "Infanticide in Earlier Seventeenth-Century England"; McDonagh, *Child Murder and British Culture,* 3; Horn, *Adapting to a New World,* 357; Jackson, *New-born Child Murder,* 30–35; Fumerton, *Unsettled,* 10; Slack, *Poverty and Policy,* 198.
37. Fumerton, *Unsettled,* 9.
38. Slack, *Poverty and Policy,* 64.
39. Horn, *Adapting to a New World,* 62; Fumerton, *Unsettled,* 10.
40. Horn, *Adapting to a New World,* 217.
41. Ibid., 248.
42. Ibid., 31.
43. EBBA 30869.
44. Firth, *An American Garland,* 54–58.
45. EBBA 21697.
46. EBBA 22141.

47. EBBA 21947.
48. AFS 04984 A02.
49. EBBA 20752.
50. Dugaw, *Warrior Women and Popular Balladry,* 41.
51. Allen, *Sacred Hoop,* 227.
52. Silko, *Storyteller,* 95.
53. Ibid., 76.
54. Ibid., 65.
55. Allen, *Sacred Hoop,* 227.
56. See also Silko and Graulich, *Yellow Woman.*

Epilogue

1. Lowe, "Intimacies of Four Continents," 208.
2. Reddy, "Modern," 164.
3. Wilentz and Marcus, *The Rose & The Briar,* 349.
4. Gregory, *American Exodus,* 139–52.
5. Dunbar-Ortiz, *Red Dirt,* 221.
6. Melissah Pawlikowski, e-mail message to author, May 23, 2012; Pawlikowski, "'Ravages of a Cruel and Savage Economy.'"

Bibliography

AFS Archive of Folk Song. American Folklife Center. Library of Congress. Washington, D.C.

EBBA English Broadside Ballad Archive. University of California, Santa Barbara. Dir. Patricia Fumerton. http://ebba.english.ucsb.edu/

Abrahams, Roger D. "Patterns of Structure and Role Relationships in the Child Ballad in the United States." *Journal of American Folklore* 79, no. 313 (1966): 448–62.

Abrahams, Roger, and George Foss. *Anglo-American Folksong Style.* Englewood Cliffs, N.J.: Prentice Hall, 1968.

Albion, Robert G. *Forests and Sea Power: The Timber Problem of the Royal Navy, 1652–1862.* Hamden, Conn.: Archon Books, 1965.

Alexander, M. Jacqui. *Pedagogies of Crossing: Meditations on Feminism, Sexual Politics, Memory, and the Sacred.* Durham, N.C.: Duke University Press, 2005.

Allaire, Bernard. *Pelleteries, manchons, et chapeaux de castor: Les Fourrures nord-americaines a Paris, 1500–1632.* Sillery: Septentrion, 1999.

Allan, D. G. C. "The Rising in the West, 1628–1631." *Economic History Review,* n.s., 5, no. 1 (1952): 76–85.

Allen, Paula Gunn. *The Sacred Hoop: Recovering the Feminine in American Indian Traditions.* 1986; repr., Boston: Beacon, 1992.

Altman, Ida, and James Horn, eds. *"To Make America": European Emigration in the Early Modern Period.* Berkeley: University of California Press, 1991.

Anderson-Green, Paula Hathaway. *A Hot-Bed of Musicians: Traditional*

Music in the Upper New River Valley. Knoxville: University of Tennessee Press, 2002.

Aravamudan, Srivinas. *Tropicopolitans: Colonialism and Agency, 1688–1804.* Durham, N.C.: Duke University Press, 1999.

Archer, Ian. *The Pursuit of Stability: Social Relations in Elizabethan London.* Cambridge: Cambridge University Press, 1991.

Atkinson, David. *The English Traditional Ballad: Theory, Method, Practice.* Burlington, Vt.: Ashgate, 2002.

———. "Marriage and Retribution in 'James Harris (The Daemon Lover).'" *Folk Music Journal* 5, no. 5 (1989): 592–607.

Bailey, Anne. *African Voices of the Atlantic Slave Trade.* Boston: Beacon, 2005.

Bailyn, Bernard. *Voyagers to the West: A Passage in the Peopling of America on the Eve of the Revolution.* New York: Alfred Knopf, 1986.

Barker, Horton. *Traditional Singers: Recorded in Beech Creek, North Carolina, by Sandy Paton.* Folkways FA 2362, 1962. Sound recording.

Barlow, Joel. *Vision of Columbus.* Boston, 1787. Early American Imprints, ser. 1, 20221.

Barry, Phillips. "The Ballad of the Demon Lover." *Modern Language Notes* 19, no. 8 (1904): 238.

———. Review of Archer Taylor, *Edward and Sven I Rosengard. Bulletin of the Folk Song Society of the Northeast* 5 (1933): 20.

Bartlett, Robert. *The Making of Europe: Conquest, Colonization and Cultural Change, 950–1350.* London: Allen Lane, 1993.

Barton, Gregory. *Empire Forestry and the Origins of Environmentalism.* Cambridge: Cambridge University Press, 2007.

Beier, A. L. *Masterless Men: The Vagrancy Problem in England, 1560–1640.* London: Methuen, 1985.

———. *The Problem of the Poor in Tudor and Stuart England.* London: Methuen, 1983.

Ben-Amos, Dan. "The Situation Structure of the Non-Humorous English Ballad." *Midwest Folklore* 13, no. 3 (1963): 163–76.

Ben-Amos, Ilana Krausman. "Gifts and Favors: Informal Support in Early Modern England," *Journal of Modern History* 72 (June 2000): 295–338.

Bendix, Regina. *In Search of Authenticity: The Formation of Folklore Studies.* Madison: University of Wisconsin Press, 1997.

Berg, Maxine. *The Age of Manufactures: Industry, Work and Innovation in Britain, 1700–1820.* 2nd ed. London: Routledge, 1994.

———. *Luxury and Pleasure in Eighteenth-Century Britain.* Oxford: Oxford University Press, 2005.

Berg, Maxine, and Elizabeth Eger, eds. *Luxury in the Eighteenth Century: Debates, Desires and Delectable Goods.* London: Palgrave Macmillan, 2003.

Best, Stephen, and Sharon Marcus. "Surface Reading: An Introduction." *Representations* 108, no. 1 (Fall 2009): 1–21.

Black, Jeremy. *A History of the British Isles.* London: Macmillan, 1996.

Blum, Margaret M. "'Edward' and the Folk Tradition." *Southern Folklore Quarterly* 21 (1957): 131.

Bradbook, Muriel Clara. *The School of Night: A Study in the Literary Relationships of Walter Raleigh.* Cambridge: Cambridge University Press, 1936.

Braudel, Fernand. *Capitalism and Material Life, 1400–1800* [1967]. Translated by Miriam Kochan. New York: Harper and Row, 1973.

Breen, T. H., and Stephen Innes. *"Myne Owne Ground": Race and Freedom on Virginia's Eastern Shore, 1640–1676.* New York: Oxford University Press, 1980.

Brenner, Robert. *Merchants and Revolution: Commercial Change, Political Conflict, and London's Overseas Traders, 1550–1653.* Princeton, N.J.: Princeton University Press, 1993.

Bronson, Bertrand Harris, ed. *The Ballad as Song.* Berkeley: University of California Press, 1969.

———. *Child Ballads Traditional in the United States.* 2 Vols. Washington, D.C.: Library of Congress, Division of Music, Recording Laboratory, 1960. Sound recording.

———. "Edward, Edward: A Scottish Ballad." *Southern Folklore Quarterly* 4 (1940): 1–13.

———. *The Singing Tradition of Child's Popular Ballads.* Princeton, N.J.: Princeton University Press, 1976.

Brunsman, Denver. "Subjects vs. Citizens: Impressment and Identity in the Anglo-American Atlantic." *Journal of the Early Republic* 30, no. 4 (Winter 2010), 557–85.

Bullock, William. *Virginia Impartially Examined.* London: J. Hammond, 1649.

Bunker, Nicholas. *Making Haste from Babylon: The Mayflower Pilgrims and Their World. A New History.* New York: Alfred Knopf, 2010.

Bunker, Stephen, and Paul Ciccantell. *Globalization and the Race for Resources.* Baltimore: Johns Hopkins University Press, 2005.

Burrison, John. "'James Harris' in Britain Since Child." *Journal of American Folklore* 80, no. 317 (1967): 271–84.

Butler, Jonathan. *Awash in a Sea of Faith: Christianizing the American People.* Cambridge, Mass.: Harvard University Press, 1992.

Calder, Isabel, ed. *Colonial Captivities, Marches, and Journeys.* New York: Macmillan, 1935.

Campbell, Mildred. "Social Origins of Some Early Americans." In *Seventeenth-Century America: Essays in Colonial History,* edited by James Morton Smith. Chapel Hill: University of North Carolina Press, 1959.

Canny, Nicholas. *Europeans on the Move: Studies in European Migration, 1500–1800.* Oxford: Clarendon Press, 1994.

Canny, Nicholas, and Anthony Pagden, eds. *Colonial Identity in the Atlantic World, 1500–1800.* Princeton, N.J.: Princeton University Press, 1987.

Cantor, Norman. *The Civilization of the Middle Ages: The Life and Death of a Civilization.* New York: Harper Collins, 1993.

Cantwell, Robert. *Bluegrass Breakdown: The Making of the Old Southern Sound.* Urbana: University of Illinois Press, 1984.

Carr, Lois Green. "Emigration and the Standard of Living: The Seventeenth Century Chesapeake," *Journal of Economic History* 52, no. 2 (1992): 271–91.

Cheeseman, Caroline. "Ownership and Ecological Change." In Langton and Jones, *Forests and Chases of England and Wales,* 65–77.

Chew, Sing. *World Ecological Degradation: Accumulation, Urbanization, and Deforestation, 3000 BC to 2000 AD.* Lanham, Md.: AltaMira, 2001.

Child, Francis James, ed. *The English and Scottish Popular Ballads: 1882–1898.* 5 vols. Repr. New York: Cooper Square, 1965.

Child, Josiah. *A New Discourse of Trade.* London: T. Sowle, 1698.

Clark, Alice. *Working Life of Women in the Seventeenth Century.* London: Routledge, 1919.

Clark, Peter. "The Migrant in Kentish Towns, 1580–1640." In Clark and Slack, *Crisis and Order in English Towns,* 117–63.

———. "Popular Protest and Disturbance in Kent, 1558–1640," *Economic History Review,* n.s., 29, no. 3 (1976): 365–82.

Clark, Peter, and Paul Slack, eds. *Crisis and Order in English Towns, 1500–1700.* Toronto: University of Toronto Press, 1972.

Coffin, Tristram Potter. "'Mary Hamilton' and the Anglo-American Ballad as an Art Form." *Journal of American Folklore* 70, no. 277 (1957): 208–14.

———. "The Murder Motive in 'Edward.'" *Western Folklore* 8, no. 4 (1949): 314–19.

Coffin, Tristram Potter, and Roger Renwick. *The British Traditional Ballad in North America.* Rev. ed. Austin: University of Texas Press, 1977.

Cohen, Ronald. *Rainbow Quest: The Folk Music Revival & American Society, 1940–1970.* Amherst: University of Massachusetts Press, 2002.

Coldham, Peter. "The Spiriting of London Children to Virginia, 1648–1685." *Virginia Magazine of History and Biography* 83 (1975): 283.

Collins, Shirley. *America over the Water: A Musical Journey with Alan Lomax.* London: SAF Publishing, 2004.

Coltman, Bob. *Paul Clayton and the Folksong Revival.* Methuen: Scarecrow Press, 2008.

Cooke, Ebenezer. *The Sot-Weed Factor: or, A Voyage to Maryland.* London, 1708.

Crean, J. F. "Hats and the Fur Trade." *Canadian Journal of Economics and Political Science* 28, no. 3 (1962): 373–86.

Cressy, David. *Coming Over: Migration and Communication between England and New England in the Seventeenth Century.* Cambridge: Cambridge University Press, 1987.

Cronon, William. *Changes in the Land: Indians, Colonists, and the Ecology of New England.* 1983; repr. New York: Hill and Wang, 2003.

Cvetkovich, Ann. *An Archive of Feelings: Trauma, Sexuality, and Lesbian Public Cultures.* Durham, N.C.: Duke University Press, 2003.

Davis, Arthur Kyle, Jr. *More Traditional Ballads of Virginia.* Chapel Hill: University of North Carolina Press, 1960.

———. *Traditional Ballads of Virginia.* 1929; repr. Charlottesville: University Press of Virginia, 1957.

Defoe, Daniel. *Some Considerations on the Reasonableness and Necessity of Encreasing and Encouraging the Seamen.* London, 1728.

Deloria, Vine, Jr. *Behind the Trail of Broken Treaties: An Indian Declaration of Independence.* 1975; repr. Austin: University of Texas Press, 1985.

Dolle, Raymond. "Captain John Smith's Satire of Sir Walter Raleigh." In *Early American Literature and Culture: Essays Honoring Harrison T. Meserole,* edited by Kathryn Derounian-Stodola. Dover: University of Delaware Press, 1992.

Drake, Judith. *An Essay in Defense of the Female Sex.* 1696; repr. London: S. Butler, 1721.

Dugaw, Dianne. "On the 'Darling Songs' of Poets, Scholars, and Singers: An Introduction." *The Eighteenth Century* 47, nos. 2–3 (summer 2006): 97–113.

———. *Warrior Women and Popular Balladry, 1650–1850.* Cambridge: Cambridge University Press, 1989.

Dunbar-Ortiz, Roxanne. *Red Dirt: Growing Up Okie.* New York: Verso, 1997.

Durston, Christopher. *The Family in the English Revolution.* Oxford: Basil Blackwell, 1989.

Ellis, Sir Henry. *Holinshed's Chronicles.* Vol. 2. London: J. Johnson, 1807.

Emberley, Julia V. *The Cultural Politics of Fur.* Ithaca: Cornell University Press, 1997.

Ennis, Daniel James. *Enter the Press-Gang: Naval Impressment in Eighteenth-Century British Literature.* Newark: University of Delaware Press, 2002.

Entwistle, William. *European Balladry.* 1939; repr. London: Clarendon Press, 1951.

Festa, Lynn. "Personal Effects: Wigs and Possessive Individualism in the Long Eighteenth Century." *Eighteenth-Century Life* 29, no. 2 (Spring 2005): 47–90.

Fink, Leon, ed. *Major Problems in the Gilded Age and the Progressive Era.* Boston: Houghton Mifflin, 2000.

Finlay, Roger, and Beatrice Shearer. "Population Growth and Suburban Expansion." In *London, 1500–1700,* edited by A. L. Beier and Roger Finlay. London: Longman, 1986.

Firth, C. H. *An American Garland: Being a Collection of Ballads Relating to America, 1563–1759.* Oxford: Blackwell, 1915.

Fischer, David Hackett. *Albion's Seed: Four British Folkways in America.* Oxford: Oxford University Press, 1989.

Fogleman, Aaron S. "From Slaves, Convicts, and Servants to Free Passengers: The Transformation of Immigration in the Era of the Revolution." *Journal of American History* 85, no. 1 (June 1998): 43–76.

Foss, George. "More on a Unique and Anomalous Version of the Two Sisters." *Southern Folklife Quarterly* 28, no. 2 (June 1964): 123.

Fowler, David C. *A Literary History of the Popular Ballad.* Durham, N.C.: Duke University Press, 1968.

Fox, Adam. "Remembering the Past in Early Modern England: Oral and Written Tradition." *Transactions of the Royal Historical Society,* 6th ser., 9 (1999): 233–56.

Frethorne, Richard. "Letters to His Parents, March 20, 1623, April 2–3, 1623." In *The Records of the Virginia Company of London,* vol. 4, edited by Susan Kingsbury. Washington, D.C.: Government Printing Office, 1935.

Friedman, Albert. *The Ballad Revival: Studies in the Influence of Popular on Sophisticated Poetry.* Chicago: University of Chicago Press, 1961.

Frohock, Richard. *Heroes of Empire: The British Imperial Protagonist in America, 1596–1764.* Newark: University of Delaware Press, 2004.

Fuller, Thomas. *History of the Worthies of England.* Edited by John Nichols. London: F. C. and J. Rivington, 1811.

Fumerton, Patricia. "'Not Home': Alehouses, Ballads, and the Vagrant Husband in Early Modern England." *Journal of Medieval and Renaissance Studies* 32, no. 3 (Fall 2002): 493–518.

———. *Unsettled: The Culture of Mobility and the Working Poor in Early Modern England.* Chicago: University of Chicago Press, 2006.

Galenson, David. "'Middling People' or 'Common Sort'? The Social Origins of Some Early Americans Re-examined." *William and Mary Quarterly,* 3rd ser., 35 (1978): 499–524.

———. *White Servitude in Colonial America: An Economic Analysis.* Cambridge: Cambridge University Press, 1984.

Games, Alison. *Migration and the Origins of the English Atlantic World.* Cambridge, Mass.: Harvard University Press, 1999.

Gardner-Medwin, Alisoun. "The Ancestry of 'The House-Carpenter': A Study of the Family History of the American Forms of Child 243." *Journal of American Folklore* 84, no. 334 (1971): 414–27.

Gerould, Gordon Hall. *The Ballad of Tradition.* Oxford: Clarendon Press, 1932.

Ghirelli, Michael. *A List of Emigrants from England to America, 1682–1692.* Baltimore: Magna Charta Book Company, 1968.

Gilmore, Ruth. "Abandonment." Paper presented at the American Studies Association Conference, Washington, D.C., May 24, 2009.

———. *Golden Gulag: Prisons, Surplus, Crisis, and Opposition in Globalizing California.* Berkeley: University of California Press, 2007.

———. "Tossed Overboard: Katrina, Incarceration, and the Politics of Abandonment." Paper presented at the American Studies Association Conference, Washington, D.C., November 6, 2005.

Goffman, Erving. *Stigma: Notes on the Management of Spoiled Identity.* 1963; repr., New York: Touchstone, 1986.

Goldsby, Jacqueline. *A Spectacular Secret: Lynching in American Life and Literature.* Chicago: University of Chicago Press, 2006.

Gomez, Michael Angelo. *Exchanging Our Country Marks: The Transformation of African Identities in the Colonial and Antebellum South.* Chapel Hill: University of North Carolina Press, 1998.

Gowing, Laura. *Common Bodies: Women, Touch, and Power in Seventeenth-Century England.* New Haven: Yale University Press, 2003.

Grant, Raymond. *The Royal Forests of England.* Wolfeboro Falls, N.H.: Alan Sutton, 1991.

Green, Rayna. "The Pocahontas Perplex: The Image of Indian Women in

American Culture." *Massachusetts Review* 16, no. 4 (Autumn 1975): 698–714.

Greenblatt, Stephen. *Sir Walter Ralegh: The Renaissance Man and His Roles.* New Haven: Yale University Press, 1973.

Greene, Jack. *Pursuits of Happiness: The Social Development of Early Modern British Colonies and the Formation of American Culture.* Chapel Hill: University of North Carolina Press, 1988.

Gregory, James. *American Exodus: The Dust Bowl Migration and Okie Culture in California.* New York: Oxford University Press, 1989.

———. *The Southern Diaspora: How the Great Migrations of Black and White Southerners Transformed America.* Chapel Hill: University of North Carolina Press, 2005.

Griffin, Carl. "Resistance, Crime, and Popular Cultures." In Langton and Jones, *Forests and Chases of England and Wales,* 50–62.

Groom, Nick. *The Making of Percy's Reliques.* Oxford: Oxford University Press, 1999.

Gummere, Francis. *The Popular Ballad.* 1907; repr. New York: Dover, 1959.

Haggard, Merle. *Mama Tried.* Capitol Records, 1968. Sound recording.

Haggerty, Sheryllynne. *The British Atlantic Trading Community, 1760–1810: Men, Women, and the Distribution of Goods.* London: Brill, 2000.

Hakluyt, Richard. *The Principal Navigations, Voyages, Traffiques, and Discoveries of The English Nation.* Vol. 13. London: E & G. Goldsmid, 1889.

Hand, Wayland D. "Two Child Ballads in the West." *Western Folklore* 18, no. 1 (1959): 42–45.

Harrison, William. *The Description of England.* Edited by Georges Edelen. Ithaca, N.Y.: Published for the Folger Library by Cornell University Press, 1968.

Hart, Walter Morris. *Ballad and Epic: A Study in the Development of the Narrative Art.* 1907; repr. New York: Russell & Russell, 1967.

Harte, N. B., ed. "Fabrics and Fashions: Studies in the Economic and Social History of Dress." Special issue, *Textile History* 22, no. 2 (1991).

Hartman, Saidiya. *Lose Your Mother: A Journey along the Atlantic Slave Route.* New York: Farrar, Straus, and Giroux, 2007.

Heal, Felicity. *Hospitality in Early Modern England.* New York: Oxford, 1990.

Hennessey, John Pope. *Walter Raleigh in Ireland.* London: Kegan Paul, Trench, 1883.

Hill, Christopher. *Change and Continuity in Seventeenth Century England.* Cambridge, Mass.: Harvard University Press, 1975.

———. *Reformation to Industrial Revolution: The Making of Modern English Society, 1530–1780*. New York: Pantheon, 1967.

———. *Society and Puritanism in Pre-Revolutionary England.* New York: Schocken Books, 1964.

Hiltner, Ken. "Early Modern Ecology." In *A New Companion to English Renaissance Literature and Culture,* vol. 1, edited by Michael Hattaway, 555–68. London: Blackwell, 2010.

———, ed. *Renaissance Ecology: Imagining Eden in Milton's England.* Pittsburgh: Duquesne University Press, 2008.

Hindle, Steve. "Dearth, Fasting, and Alms: The Campaign for General Hospitality in Late Elizabethan England." *Past and Present* 172, no. 1 (August 2001): 44–86.

———. "Exclusion Crises: Poverty, Migration and Parochial Responsibility in English Rural Communities, 1560–1660." *Rural History* 7 (1996): 125–49.

———. "'Not by Bread Only'? Common Right, Parish Relief and Endowed Charity in a Forest Economy, c. 1600–1800." In *The Poor in England, 1700–1850: An Economy of Makeshifts,* edited by Steven King and Alannah Tomkins, 39–75. Manchester: Manchester University Press, 2003.

———. *On the Parish: The Micro-Politics of Poor Relief in Rural England, 1550–1750*. Oxford: Clarendon Press, 2004.

Hobbes, Thomas. *Leviathan: with Selected Variants from the Latin Edition of 1668.* Edited by Edwin Curley. Indianapolis: Hackett, 1994.

Hobsbawm, Eric. "The Crisis of the Seventeenth Century." In *Crisis in Europe, 1560–1660: Essays from Past and Present,* edited by Trevor Aston. London: Routledge, Kegan, and Paul, 1965.

Holinshed, Raphael. *Chronicles of England, Scotland, and Ireland.* Vol. 1. London: Johnson, Rivington, Payne, et al., 1807.

Horn, James. *Adapting to a New World: English Society in the Seventeenth-Century Chesapeake.* Chapel Hill: University of North Carolina Press, 1994.

Hostettler, Agnes. "Symbolic Tokens in a Ballad of the Returned Lover." *Western Folklore* 32, no. 1 (1973): 33–38.

Houlbrooke, Ralph, ed. *English Family Life, 1576–1716: An Anthology from Diaries.* Oxford: Basil Blackwell, 1989.

Huber, Patrick. *Linthead Stomp: The Creation of Country Music in the Piedmont South.* Chapel Hill: University of North Carolina Press, 2008.

Hyman, Stanley Edgar. "The Child Ballad in America: Some Aesthetic Criteria." *Journal of American Folklore* 70, no. 277 (1957): 235–39.

Jackson, Mark. *New-born Child Murder: Women, Illegitimacy, and the Courts in Eighteenth-Century England.* Manchester: Manchester University Press, 1996.

Jehlen, Myra, and Michael Warner. *The English Literatures of America, 1500–1800.* New York: Routledge, 1997.

Jones, Graham. "Swanimotes, Woodmotes, and Courts of 'Free Miners.'" In Langton and Jones, *Forests and Chases of England and Wales,* 41–48.

Kaminkow, Jack, and Marion Kaminkow, eds. *A List of Emigrants from England to America, 1718–1759.* Baltimore: Magna Charta Book Company, 1964.

Kent, Joan. "Population Mobility and Alms: Poor Migrants in the Midland During the Early Seventeenth Century," *Local Population Studies* 27 (1981), 35–51.

King, Steven, and Alannah Tomkins. "Introduction." In *The Poor in England, 1700–1850: An Economy of Makeshifts,* edited by Steven King and Alannah Tomkins, 1–38. Manchester: Manchester University Press, 2003.

Kolodny, Annette. *The Lay of the Land: Metaphor as Experience and History in American Life and Letters.* Chapel Hill: University of North Carolina Press, 1975.

Kulikoff, Allan. *From British Peasants to Colonial American Farmers.* Chapel Hill: University of North Carolina Press, 2000.

Lacey, Robert. *Sir Walter Ralegh.* New York: Atheneum, 1973.

Landberg, Allison. "Prosthetic Memory: The Ethics and Politics of Memory in an Age of Mass Culture." In *Memory and Popular Film,* edited by Paul Grainge, 144–61. Manchester: Manchester University Press, 2003.

Langton, John. "Forests in Early-Modern England and Wales: History and Historiography." In Langton and Jones, *Forests and Chases of England and Wales,* 3–11.

Langton, John, and Graham Jones, eds. *Forests and Chases of England and Wales, c. 1500–c. 1850.* Oxford: St. John's College Research Center, 2008.

Laslett, Peter. *The World We Have Lost: England Before the Industrial Age.* 2nd ed. New York: Scribners, 1973.

Laurence, Anne. *Women in England 1500–1760: A Social History.* New York: St. Martin's Press, 1994.

Lawless, Ray McKinley. *Folksingers and Folksongs in America: A Handbook of Biography, Bibliography, and Discography.* Westport, Conn.: Greenwood, 1981.

Lemire, Beverly. *Dress, Culture, and Commerce: The English Clothing Trade Before the Factory, 1660–1800*. London: Palgrave, 1997.

Lloyd, A. L. *Folk Song in England.* New York: International Publishers, 1967.

Lornell, Kip. *Virginia's Blues, Country, & Gospel Records, 1902–1943*. Lexington: University Press of Kentucky, 1989.

Lowe, Lisa. "Intimacies of Four Continents." In *Haunted by Empire: Geographies of Intimacy in North American History,* edited by Laura Stoler, 191–212. Durham, N.C.: Duke University Press, 2006.

MacFarlane, Alan. *Marriage and Love in England: Modes of Reproduction, 1300–1840*. Oxford: Basil Blackwell, 1986.

Marcus, G. J. *A Naval History of England.* Vol. 1: *The Formative Centuries.* London: Longmans, 1961.

Marx, Karl. *The Eighteenth Brumaire of Louis Bonaparte.* New York: International Publishers, 1969.

May, Stephen. *Sir Walter Ralegh.* Boston: Twayne, 1989.

McCarthy, Terence. "A Note on Past and Present in 'The Demon Lover.'" *Tennessee Folklore Society Bulletin* 47, no. 4 (1981): 173–75.

McCarthy, William B. "William Motherwell as Field Collector." *Folk Music Journal* 5, no. 3 (1987): 295–316.

McCusker, John, and Russell Menard. *The Economy of British America, 1607–1789*. Chapel Hill: University of North Carolina Press, 1985.

McDonagh, Josephine. *Child Murder and British Culture, 1720–1900*. Cambridge: Cambridge University Press, 2003.

McDowell, Paula. "The Manufacture and Lingua-facture of Ballad-Making: Broadside Ballads in Long Eighteenth-Century Ballad Discourse." *The Eighteenth Century* 47, nos. 2–3 (summer 2006): 151–78.

McIntosh, Marjorie. "Poverty, Charity and Coercion in Elizabethan England." *Journal of Interdisciplinary History* 35, no. 3 (Winter 2005): 457–79.

McKendrick, Neil, John Brewer, and J. H. Plumb, *The Birth of a Consumer Society: The Commercialization of Eighteenth Century England.* London: Europa, 1982.

McNeil, W. K. *Southern Folk Ballads.* Vol. 2. Little Rock: House, 1988.

McNeil, William H. "The Introduction of the Potato into Ireland." *Journal of Modern History* 21 (September 1949): 218–22.

Mendelson, Sara, and Patricia Crawford. *Women in Early Modern England, 1550–1720*. Oxford: Clarendon Press, 1998.

Merchant, Carolyn. *Ecological Revolutions: Nature, Gender, and Science in New England.* Chapel Hill: University of North Carolina Press, 1989.

Miller, Shannon. *Invested with Meaning: The Raleigh Circle in the New World.* Philadelphia: University of Pennsylvania Press, 1998.
Mills, Jerry Leath. *Sir Walter Ralegh: A Reference Guide.* Boston: G. K. Hall, 1986.
Motherwell, Robert. *Minstrelsy Ancient and Modern.* Glasgow: J. Wylie, 1827.
Müller-Schwarze, Dietland, and Lixing Sun. *The Beaver: Natural History of a Wetlands Engineer.* Ithaca: Comstock, 2003.
Neilson, H. "Early English Woodland and Waste." *Journal of Economic History* 2, no. 1 (1942): 54–62.
Newman, Steve. *Ballad Collection, Lyric, and the Canon: The Call of the Popular from the Restoration to New Criticism.* Philadelphia: University of Pennsylvania Press, 2007.
Niles, John D., and Eleanor R. Long. "Context and Loss in Scottish Ballad Tradition." *Western Folklore* 45, no. 2 (1986): 83–109.
Nørjordet, Håvard. "The Tall Man in the Blue Suit: Witchcraft, Folklore, and Reality in Shirley Jackson's *The Lottery, or the Adventures of James Harris.*" MA Thesis, University of Oslo, 2005.
O'Brien, Jean. *Dispossession by Degrees: Indian Land and Identity in Natick, Massachusetts, 1650–1790.* Lincoln: University of Nebraska Press, 1997.
Page, R. I. *Life in Anglo-Saxon England.* New York: Putnam, 2008.
Paredes, Americo. *With His Pistol in His Hand: A Border Ballad and Its Hero.* 1958; repr. Austin: University of Texas Press, 2004.
Paton, Sandy. Review of *Horton Barker—Traditional Singer, Journal of the International Folk Music Council* 16 (1964): 165.
Patterson, Orlando. *Slavery and Social Death: A Comparative Study.* Cambridge, Mass.: Harvard University Press, 1982.
Pawlikowski, Melissah. "'The Ravages of a Cruel and Savage Economy': Ohio River Valley Squatters and the Formation of a Communitarian Political Economy, 1768–1782." Paper delivered at the conference of the Society for the History of Early American Republic, 2011.
Pearson, William. *Black Legacy: America's Hidden Heritage.* Amherst: University of Massachusetts Press, 1993.
Percy, Thomas. *Reliques of Ancient English Poetry.* Edited by J. V. Prichard. London: Bell, 1876.
Perking, Harold. "The Social Causes of the British Industrial Revolution." *Royal Historical Society Transactions,* 5th ser., 18 (1968): 123–43.
Phillips, Seymour. "The Medieval Background." In *Europeans on the Move,* edited by Nicholas Canny. Oxford: Clarendon Press, 1994.

Pogue Harrison, Robert. *Forests: Shadow of Civilization.* Chicago: University of Chicago Press, 1993.

Polanyi, Karl. *The Great Transformation: The Political and Economic Transformation of Our Time.* 2nd ed. Boston: Beacon, 2001.

Prior, Mary, ed. *Women in English Society 1500–1800.* London: Methuen, 1985.

Quaife, G. R. *Wanton Wenches and Wayward Wives: Peasants and Illicit Sex in Early Seventeenth Century England.* New Brunswick: Rutgers University Press, 1979.

Raleigh, Walter. *A Discourse Touching a War with Spain, and of the Protecting of the Netherlands* [1603]. In *Works,* 8:299–316.

———. *Selected Writings.* Edited by Gerald Hammond. Manchester: Fyfield Books, 1984.

———. *The Works of Sir Walter Ralegh, KT.* Vol. 8. New York: Burt Franklin, 1964.

Rappaport, Steve. *Worlds within Worlds: Structures of Life in Sixteenth-Century London.* Cambridge: Cambridge University Press, 1989.

Reddy, Chandan. "Modern." In *Keywords for American Cultural Studies,* edited by Bruce Burgett and Glenn Hendler, 160–64. New York: New York University Press, 2007.

Rediker, Marcus. *Between the Devil and the Deep Blue Sea: Merchant Seaman, Pirates, and the Anglo-American Mercantile World, 1700–1750.* Cambridge: Cambridge University Press, 1987.

Reed, Toni. *Demon-Lovers and Their Victims in British Fiction.* Lexington: University Press of Kentucky, 1988.

Renwick, Roger. *English Folk Poetry: Structure and Meaning.* Philadelphia: University of Pennsylvania Press, 1980.

Roach, Joseph. *Cities of the Dead: Circum-Atlantic Performance.* New York: Columbia University Press, 1996.

Rollison, David. "Exploding England: The Dialectics of Mobility and Settlement in Early Modern England," *Social History* 24 (1999): 1–16.

Rosenberg, Neil. *Bluegrass: A History.* Urbana: University of Illinois Press, 1985.

Rothwell, Harry, ed. *English Historical Documents.* Vol. 3: *1189–1327.* London: Eyre & Spottiswoode, 1975.

Sainsbury, W. Noel, et al. *Calendar of State Papers, Colonial Series, 1661–1668.* London, 1860–.

Salerno, Anthony. "The Social Background of Seventeenth-Century Emigration to America." *Journal of British Studies* 19, no. 1 (Autumn 1979): 31–52.

Schochet, Gordon. "Patriarchalism, Politics, and Mass Attitudes in Stuart England." *Historical Journal* 12, no. 3 (1961): 413–41.

Scott, Jonathan. *England's Troubles: Seventeenth-Century English Political Instability in European Context.* Cambridge: Cambridge University Press, 2000.

Shammas, Carole. "Origins of Transatlantic Colonization." In *A Companion to Colonial America,* edited by Daniel Vickers, 25–43. London: Blackwell, 2003.

———. *The Pre-Industrial Consumer in England and America.* Oxford: Clarendon Press, 1990.

Sharp, Buchanan. *In Contempt of All Authority: Rural Artisans and Riot in the West of England, 1586–1660.* Berkeley: University of California Press, 1980.

Shields, Hugh. "The Dead Lover's Return in Modern English Ballad Tradition." *Jahrbuch für Volksliedforschung* 17 (1972): 98–114.

Silko, Leslie Marmon. *Storyteller.* New York: Arcade Books, 1981.

Sinclair, Andrew. *Sir Walter Raleigh and the Age of Discovery.* London: Penguin, 1984.

Slack, Paul. *From Reformation to Improvement: Public Welfare in Early Modern England.* Oxford: Oxford University Press, 1998.

———. *Poverty and Policy in Tudor England.* London: Longman, 1988.

———. "Poverty and Politics in Salisbury, 1597–1666." In Clark and Slack, *Crisis and Order in English Towns,* 164–203.

———. "Vagrants and Vagrancy in England, 1558–1664." *Economic History Review,* n.s., 27, no. 3 (1974): 360–80.

Smallwood, Stephanie. *Saltwater Slavery: A Middle Passage from Africa to American Diaspora.* Cambridge, Mass.: Harvard University Press, 2007.

Smith, Abbott Emerson. *Colonists in Bondage: White Servitude and Convict Labor in America, 1607–1776.* Boston: Peter Smith, 1965.

Smith, Alan G. R. *The Emergence of a Nation State: The Commonwealth of England, 1529–1660.* London: Longman, 1997.

Smith, Reed. "The Traditional Ballad in America, 1933." *Journal of American Folklore* 47, no. 183 (1934): 64–75.

———. "The Traditional Ballad in the South." *Journal of American Folklore* 27, no. 103 (1914): 55–66.

Smith, Woodruff D., *Consumption and the Making of Respectability, 1600–1800.* New York: Routledge, 2002.

Sobel, Mechal. *The World They Made Together: Black and White Values in Eighteenth-Century Virginia.* Princeton, N.J.: Princeton University Press, 1989.

Souden, David. "'Rogues, Whores and Vagabonds': Indentured Servant Emigrants to North America." *Social History* 3 (1978): 23–41.

Spenser, Edmund. *A View of the Present State of Ireland.* London: Laurence Flin and Ann Watts, 1763.

Spufford, Margaret. "The Cost of Apparel in Seventeenth-Century England, and the Accuracy of Gregory King." *Economic History Review* 53, no. 4 (2000): 677–705.

Stenton, Doris Mary. *The English Woman in History.* New York: Macmillan, 1957.

Stone, Lawrence. *The Family, Sex, and Marriage in England 1500–1800.* London: Weidenfeld & Nicholson, 1977.

———. "Social Mobility in England, 1500–1700." *Past and Present* 33, no. 1 (April 1966): 16–55.

Stubbes, Phillip. *The Anatomie of Abuses.* 3rd ed. London, 1585.

Swanton, Michael, ed. *The Anglo-Saxon Chronicle.* New York: Routledge, 1998.

Tawney, Richard. *The Agrarian Problem in the Sixteenth Century.* London: Longmans, Green, 1912.

Taylor, Archer. *Edward and Sven I Rosengard.* Chicago: University of Chicago Press, 1931.

———. "The English, Scottish, and American Versions of the 'Twa Sisters.'" *Journal of American Folklore* 42, no. 165 (1929): 238–46.

———. "The Texts of 'Edward' in Percy's Reliques and Motherwell's Minstrelsy." *Modern Language Notes* 45, no. 4 (1930): 225–27.

Thirsk, Joan. *Economic Policy and Projects: The Development of a Consumer Society in Early Modern England.* Oxford: Clarendon Press, 1978.

Thompson, Peter. "William Bullock's 'Strange Adventure': A Plan to Transform Seventeenth-Century Virginia." *William and Mary Quarterly,* 3rd ser., 61 (2004): 107–28.

Thoreau, Henry David. *Sir Walter Raleigh.* Edited by Henry Aiken Metcalf. Boston: Bibliophile, 1905.

Tilly, Louise. "Food Entitlement, Famine, and Conflict." *Journal of Interdisciplinary History* 14, no. 2 (Autumn 1983): 333–49.

Toelken, Barre. *Morning Dew and Roses: Nuance, Metaphor, and Meaning in Folksongs.* Urbana: University of Illinois Press, 1995.

Trevelyan, Raleigh. *Sir Walter Raleigh.* London: Penguin, 2002.

Tribe, Ivan. *The Stonemans: An Appalachian Family and the Music that Shaped Their Lives.* Champaign-Urbana: University of Illinois Press, 1993.

Trouillot, Michel-Rolph. *Silencing the Past: Power and the Production of History.* Boston: Beacon, 1995.

Twitchell, James. "The Incest Theme and the Authenticity of the Percy Version of 'Edward.'" *Western Folklore* 34, no. 1 (1975): 32–35.

Tycko, Sonia. "Spiriting: Experiences, Reactions, and Representations in London, 1640–1718." Master's Thesis, Columbia University, 2009. http://www.columbia.edu/cu/history/resource-library/Tycko_thesis.pdf.

Usher, Roland. "Royal Navy Impressment During the American Revolution." *Mississippi Valley Historical Review* 37, no. 4 (March 1951): 673–88.

Vries, J. de. *The Industrious Revolution: Consumer Behavior and the Household Economy, 1650 to the Present.* Cambridge: Cambridge University Press, 2008.

———. "Peasant Demand Patterns and Economic Development: Friesland, 1550–1750." In *European Peasants and Their Markets: Essay in Agrarian Economic History,* edited by Jan de Vries, 205–65. Princeton, N.J.: Princeton University Press, 1975.

Waldman, Milton. *Sir Walter Raleigh.* 1928; repr. London: St. James Library, 1950.

Walkowitz, Daniel. *City Folk: English Country Dance and the Politics of the Folk in Modern America.* New York: New York University Press, 2010.

Wallerstein, Immanuel. *The Modern World System: Capitalist Agriculture and the Origins of the European World-Economy in the Sixteenth Century.* New York: Academic Press, 1974.

Walter, John, and Keith Wrightson. "Dearth and the Social Order in Early Modern England." *Past and Present* 71, no. 1 (May 1976): 22–42.

Warde, Paul. "Woodland Fuel, Demand, and Supply." In Langton and Jones, *Forests and Chases of England and Wales,* 78–85.

Weatherill, Lorna. *Consumer Behaviour and Material Culture in Britain, 1660–1760.* London: Routledge, 1988.

Whisnant, David. *All That Is Native & Fine: The Politics of Culture in an American Region.* Chapel Hill: University of North Carolina Press, 1983.

Whitelock, Dorothy. *The Beginnings of English Society.* New York: Penguin, 1968.

Whitlock, Ralph. *Historic Forests of England.* New York: A. S. Barnes, 1979.

Wilentz, Sean, and Greil Marcus, eds. *The Rose & The Briar: Death, Love, and Liberty in the American Ballad.* New York: W. W. Norton, 2005.

Wilgus, D. K. "Shooting Fish in a Barrel: The Child Ballad in America." *Journal of American Folklore* 71, no. 280 (1958): 161–64.

Wimberly, Lowry. *Folklore in the English and Scottish Ballads.* 1928; repr. New York: Frederick Ungar, 1959.

Winstanley, Gerrard. *"The Law of Freedom" and Other Writings.* Edited by Christopher Hill. Cambridge: Cambridge University Press, 2006.
Wolf, Eric. *Europe and the People Without History.* Berkeley: University of California Press, 1982.
Wrightson, Keith. *Earthly Necessities: Economic Lives in Early Modern Britain.* New Haven: Yale University Press, 2000.
———. *English Society, 1580–1680.* New Brunswick: Rutgers University Press, 1982.
———. "Infanticide in Earlier Seventeenth-Century England." *Local Population Studies* 15 (1975): 10–22.
Wrigley, E. A. "The Divergence of England: The Growth of the English Economy in the Seventeenth and Eighteenth Centuries." *Transactions of the Royal Historical Society,* 6th ser., 10 (2000): 117–41.
Wrigley, E. A., and R. S. Schofield. *The Population History of England, 1541–1871.* London: Edward Arnold, 1981.
Young, Charles. *The Royal Forests of Medieval England.* Philadelphia: University of Pennsylvania Press, 1979.
Young, Philip. "The Mother of Us All." *Kenyon Review* 24 (summer 1962): 391–441.

Index

Joanna Brooks is professor and chair of the Department of English and Comparative Literature at San Diego State University. She has authored or edited five books on early American literature, history, and culture, including *American Lazarus: Religion and the Rise of African-American and Native American Literatures* and *Transatlantic Feminisms in the Age of Revolutions.* She is also the author of *The Book of Mormon Girl: A Memoir of an American Faith.*